ORCHESTRA

Edited by André Previn

Interviews by
MICHAEL FOSS

Photographs by
RICHARD ADENEY

Doubleday & Company, Inc.
Garden City, New York
1979

This book was designed and produced by
George Rainbird Limited
36 Park Street, London W1Y 4DE for
Doubleday & Company, Inc.,
245 Park Avenue,
New York, NY 10017

First edition in the United States of America

ISBN: 0–385 15808–4

Library of Congress Catalog Card Number:
79–7944

House Editor: Elizabeth Blair
Picture researcher: Linda Proud
Indexer: Jean Gay

Printed and bound by Jarrold & Sons Ltd, Norwich
Colour plates originated by Gilchrist Bros Ltd, Leeds
Text filmset by SX Composing Ltd, Rayleigh, Essex

This edition printed in Great Britain

Frontispiece: André Previn

ORCHESTRA

Contents

List of Colour Plates

A CONDUCTOR'S VIEW

by André Previn

Do you know what my favourite musical sound in the world is? It's the sound of an orchestra tuning up. The purposeful chaos that begins after the oboe plays an A hasn't failed to thrill me in a lifetime of concern about music. It's a promise of things to come, the miracles of Mozart, the wit of Haydn, the grandeur of Beethoven, the colours of Debussy, the opulence of Strauss — all of it, the cornucopia of the orchestral repertoire is waiting to be revealed, lying dormant within the greatest instrument ever invented: the Symphony Orchestra. I suppose I hear the tuning up process a thousand times a year, but it never fails to have its effect on me. The first time I heard it was when I was five years old and my father took me to an all-Brahms programme of the Berlin Philharmonic, with Furtwangler conducting. It thrilled me then and it thrills me still. I suppose I never went through the maze of various childhood ambitions: to be a fireman, a mountain climber, a decathlon champion, or a magician. All it took was one downbeat and I knew I was going to spend the rest of my life chasing after music.

My father was a successful lawyer in Germany. He was also a very good amateur pianist, amateur in the French sense of the word. He played constantly and with enthusiasm, an enthusiasm untroubled by fistfuls of wrong notes. We had chamber music in the house regularly, and evenings of his accompanying friends who could sing Lieder, and he took me to concerts regularly. I started piano lessons when I was five and made rapid progress. My father was dead keen on sight-reading. After dinner, he and I would sit down and bang through the four-hand versions of all the standard Symphonies, at the correct speed and damn the mistakes. I learned the symphonies of Beethoven, Schubert, Mozart, Haydn and Brahms that way, and to this day I can remember what colours the bindings were, where the tricky page turns came, and that the Primo part of the second movement of the 'Pastoral' had four bars torn off which I would have to fake. It was all inexact and exciting and sloppy and wonderful, and I wish that the custom of four-handed music at home were still as much in vogue as it was then. It's a hell of an education. Shortly after the Furtwangler concert I mentioned, my father thought it was time for me to hear an Opera. Quite correctly, he reasoned that a child's first exposure to that particular art form should not be too long, so he ruled out the evening-filling works. Quite incorrectly, however, he opted for the nearest one-act Opera available, which happened to be *Salome*. Neither the steaming story nor the erotic score were exactly perfect fare for a six-year-old, but to top it off, the German opera houses in those days did not believe in short-changing their customers with just a short work. Therefore, after the interval, *Salome* was followed, inexplicably, with the ballet *Coppelia*. I was, understandably, confused, and for years afterwards was under the impression that Herod ruled a toy shop. Never mind; I loved it all with happy lack of discrimination. I was given my very own small portable record player (the kind you wound up) and my first records at Christmas time were of Stokowski and the Philadelphia playing the Debussy Nocturnes. The far-off trumpets in 'Fetes' drove me nearly mad with excitement, and I blunted several packages of needles repeating the moment of their entrance. My father's taste in music was conservative and Germanic, and whenever he was confronted by a new work, he would say condescendingly 'Well, it's not the *Eroica*!' Much later in my life, I tried convincing him that new pieces were not meant to be another *Eroica*, nor was it the composer's intention to replace the *Eroica*, but I'm afraid I made no dent in his opinion. As recently as 1978, when confronted by a rather hostile audience in the middle of an all-Messiaen programme I was conducting, I told them this story about my father, and I like to think it actually helped a bit.

In 1939 we went to the United States, by way of a year in Paris, and my music studies continued there. I have always had great good fortune in teachers. Professor Breithaupt at the Berlin Conservatory had laid down a good Teutonic foundation, and in the States I became the pupil of Joseph Achron, Mario Castelnuovo-Tedesco, and much later, Pierre Monteux. I was taught not only the piano, but Theory, Counterpoint, Orchestration, and Conducting. Only in my public school life did I loathe the music instruction; at the time, it was an American conceit to teach a course called 'Music Appreciation', during which we were told exactly what the composer wanted us to think during every bar, with programmatic schemes attached to the most abstract pieces. I so resented this straitjacket that I would deliberately hand in papers outlining the wildest content for the tamest works, and was given failing marks. I quite enjoyed the class, however, since a lot of it consisted of listening to phonograph records. When I was thirteen years old, I did odd musical jobs after school, in order to make enough money to buy records. I demonstrated electric organs at a Department Store, I played the piano at a Dancing Academy, and I improvised scores for a cinema house which specialized in running old silent films. That was great fun, but unfortunately short-lived. One afternoon I was pounding away the appropriate music for a '20's 'Flaming Youth' movie, did not watch the screen, and was blithely unaware that the main attraction, a revival of D. W. Griffith's biblical masterpiece *Intolerance* had begun. I was enthusiastically playing a Charleston during the scene depicting the Last Supper when the manager of the theatre came storming down the aisle, and I was unemployed two minutes later. On the more serious side, I entered two Piano Competitions, and came in Second in both. Now, in my opinion, First is, of course, wonderful, and Fiftieth easily excusable, but Second was ignominious, and I have never really liked the aura of Competitions since.

Sometimes, when I reminisce, it seems to me that I have already had the luxury of several lives, at least musically. I have spent time pursuing almost every kind of job possible within the music profession before finally settling down during the past twenty years to conducting. I've been a rehearsal pianist, a film composer, a dabbler in jazz, an arranger and orchestrator, an orchestral pianist, and a pit conductor. Although I am often plagued with regrets that I did not have the strength of character to consolidate my efforts into becoming an acceptable conductor earlier in life, I cannot help but admit that I do not truly think any of my chameleon existance was a waste of time. I learned something everywhere and have tried valiantly to put it to use. The longest period of time I spent on a treadmill was a ten-year stretch of working in the film business. This came about in a rather strange way. In 1948 I was living and studying in California and eking out extra money by making arrangements for local radio shows. MGM Studios was then the undisputed champion of the film makers, and part of their annual product consisted of musical films in which Jose Iturbi played on white pianos at the edge of Esther Williams' swimming pools. He was required, at one time, to play something which bordered on a quasi-jazz improvisation, and although he was an excellent pianist, this particular area was no-man's-land for him. Someone at the studio had heard of me and figured, with remarkable acumen, that I would do the writing required both quickly and cheaply. So I was contacted and contracted. I wrote the necessary piano part and then suggested with diffidence that I would also like to write the necessary orchestral accompaniment. They suggested a fee which enabled me to buy lunch at the canteen, but I accepted happily since it was yet again a new venture for me. The experiment was a success, at least by the standards involved, and I was assigned more work. I spent the next ten years toiling in Hollywood and gathering invaluable experience. Of course I was involved with fifth-rate music, but the practical aspects of the work were wonderful. To begin with, each of the major studios had a contract orchestra of its own. These orchestras consisted of, approximately, sixty musicians who were veterans of the most prestigious symphony orchestras of the country. Their playing capabilities were beyond criticism, and their sight-reading prowess was legendary. Even the current London Orchestras, with their uncanny sight-reading, were not quite as amazing. My work enabled me to stand in front of the MGM orchestra on the average of twice a week, rehearsing new music and getting it recorded as quickly as possible.

I am still of the opinion that no conservatory, no great teacher, is as sure a pedagogue as practical experience. I learned to orchestrate quickly, learned what can be expected of orchestral players, both musically and psychologically, and found a rehearsal technique which still comes in handy to this day. I formed a Trio, with Israel Baker, the violinist, and Edgar Lustgarten, the cellist, and we played innumerable concerts on the West Coast of America. I met musicians of the highest calibre, Bernard Herrman, Miklos Rozsa, John Williams, Alex North, and early on in my life there, made a lasting alliance with professional orchestrators such as Conrad Salinger, Herbert Spencer, Alex Courage, and Al Woodbury, who were all able to fill reams of manuscript paper with phenomenally expert orchestral sounds overnight. The days I spent in the company of these men were, of course, the most amusing, and the anecdotes regarding our work would fill a separate book. One time I was assigned to write the title music to a blistering melodrama. The official composer of the score was a kindly, elderly gentleman who had made his mark in New York writing Operetta melodies. He was an imposing figure with a leonine head of white hair and the ability to make the producers think that he was the resurrection of Beethoven. He handed me a single line melody of some ten bars, along with the instructions that he wanted it to sound 'really BIG'. I took the tune home and proceded to work out a five-minute orchestral piece that sounded like all the excesses of 'Pines of Rome' put together. Came time for the recording, and the composer was on the podium, conducting with sweeping gestures. The producers were standing in back of him in attitudes of awe. I was sitting on a chair near the rostrum as unobtrusively as possible, following my partitur. At the noisiest and most fraudulently grandiloquent moment, the composer leaned down towards me, never slackening his beat, and stage-whispered to me, 'Did I write this?'

Another time it became necessary, for story reasons too tedious to recount, for the hero and heroine of a film to attend a chamber music concert. I was told to find a piece within the Public Domain (no copyright fees necessary) and record it. I picked the first movement of the Schumann Piano Quintet, and spent a couple of happy hours recording it with the string principals of the studio orchestra. The finished disc was sent up to the Producer. He called me in a state of elation. 'That's a terrific piece, kid', he allowed. 'I really love it. In fact I like it so much that I want you to record it again, but this time, use the whole orchestra along with the piano.' After a pause during which I examined the phone to see whether it was really working, I pointed out that the word Quintet had certain semantic priorities and that I really couldn't change Schumann after all this time. The producer grew impatient. 'Don't be silly, kid,' he said. 'It sounds like hell with just those couple of fellers scraping away. Now do it again, and nice.' In retrospect, I suppose it would have been philosophically more adult of me, considering the circumstances, to go along with his plan, but I didn't. I refused and was fired off the film. By the way, the sequence never appeared at all in the final product.

But these stories are too numerous and too similar for me to recount now. I interrupted my work at MGM by having to do my National Service for two years. During the last year of it, I was assigned to the Sixth Army Band in San Francisco, where I tried to play the flute (unsuccessfully) and made hundreds of arrangements (more successfully). In addition to the endless required marches, I did some really weird things, such as writing Concert Band arrangements of Chabrier's 'Espana' and of the Shostakovich First Symphony. I also met Norman Carol, now the leader of the Philadelphia Orchestra, and we would sneak off whenever possible and play Sonatas. The most important moment of those years was when I met Pierre Monteux, then the conductor of the San Francisco Symphony, and began to study with him. He was the kindest, wisest man I can remember, and there was nothing about conducting he didn't know. He was also wonderfully insular in his interests. One day I showed up for my lesson, in army uniform, and told him that I had been put on overseas duty and would probably be sent to Tokyo. Monteux gave it only a second's thought. 'That is not a good idea,' he said. 'I also heard about the Tokyo Orchestra and went there, but, believe me, it is not worth that long trip.' What a lovely man. One time he heard me conduct a last movement of a Haydn symphony, one of the rollicking prestos. Afterwards, he beckoned me over to him. 'Tell me,' he asked, 'did you think the orchestra was playing well?' Fearing a trap, I hesitated. Finally I said Yes, I thought they had played very well. 'So did I,' said Maitre. 'Next time don't interfere with them.' What absolutely perfect advice. I have never forgotten it.

After I finished my National Service, I stayed on in San Francisco to study with Monteux for a further year, and then returned to my work in Hollywood. I composed and scored a lot of films, some pretty good ones, some totally reprehensible ones, and most of them innocuously forgettable. But I grew more and more discontented. It had never been my ambition to remain a film composer, and the prospect of a lifetime in that strange community filled me with apprehension. The studio orchestra musicians, also driven by discontent, had formed various rehearsal orchestras, which met whenever possible, to play through some symphonic repertoire, just for the sheer relief. They were conducted often by Miklos Rozsa and Bernard Herrman, and sometimes by me. At one of these evening get-togethers, my friend Schuyler Chapin was in the audience. He was then the head of the classical department of CBS records. He took me for a drink afterwards and told me quite solemnly that he thought I might make a good conductor, given a lot of very hard work. He saw to it that I met Ronald Wilford, of Columbia Artists, a management firm of enormous prestige. Ronald made me an offer. He said that he would hound me around the country's provincial orchestras for a year. At the end of that year he would come to another concert. If I had overshot my ambitions, he would tell me so in no uncertain terms, and I could still go back to my stultifying but lucrative film work. If, on the other hand, he then thought I should pursue it for a lifetime career, I would have to give up everything else. I agreed instantly, and found myself, shortly after, in cities I had never heard of, conducting orchestras of every size and description, professional, semi-professional and amateur. The fees didn't always equal my expenses but I didn't care. I was happy. I was also working like a dog, learning scores, widening my repertoire, and in general learning the profession. The year passed, and Ronald and Schuyler gave me the green light. I returned to California, sold my house, quit my film work, and left, both physically and spiritually. I am, as I said before, grateful to the years I spent in Los Angeles. I met some brilliantly talented people, made good friends, and garnered valuable experience. But I have never looked back with fond nostalgia. The film business, for a musician, is a quicksand. The comforts are too easily acquired, the work, although long in hours, is short of challenge, and the atmosphere deadly. The Los

Angeles climate is seductive and the orange juice the best in the world, but as for the rest – no thanks.

So here I was, in 1961, trying to be a conductor. The first orchestra in America to take me seriously was the one in St Louis. Their manager was a witty and generous man named William Zalken, and it was he who allowed me to conduct programmes of Brahms, Britten, Mozart, Copland, Beethoven and Shostakovich, without ever inferring that my recent background was not of the right sort. I had some success there and other orchestras of comparative size and acclaim followed suit and engaged me to guest conduct. I was very lucky, I worked very hard, and I lived in airports. I learned what touring was about. Romanticized novels and imbecilic films have given the public a strangely contorted view of the travelling classical artist. Limosines, fawning managers, exotic ladies, and standing ovations are science fiction, certainly for a great many years. Lost luggage, freezing coaches, mounting laundry, and incredible hotel rooms are more to the point. However, I was doing what I had always wanted to do, and was in a glow of ambition. I didn't mind any of the tribulations, and I revelled in every moderate success. In 1967, my luck was amazing. Sir John Barbirolli had been the conductor-in-chief of the Houston Symphony in Texas for some years, and now wanted to move on and spend more time with his beloved Hallé Orchestra. Houston was looking for a replacement, and after quite a few guest conducting engagements, offered me the post. I was happy beyond description. My own orchestra, every conductor's dream! I remember with minute recall the day I signed my contract. After the pens were put away, I wandered through the Concert Hall, which was empty, but set up for the evening's concert. I looked at the stage, with chairs and stands in place, and had a feeling of almost total elation.

It would be nice if I could now tell you that life in Houston was a series of triumphs. Nice, but not true. The orchestra, as a body of players, was excellent. They were enthusiastic and cooperative and worked very hard. I took part in lots of chamber music, introduced quite a bit of new repertoire, and enjoyed the work thoroughly. But the management and the Board were not terribly taken with me. I was volubly ambitious in my plans for more extensive touring, I advocated lots of new music, and I was socially reclusive, not for reasons of misplaced snobbism, but for reasons of endless studying. My conducting during the Houston years naturally took me to a great many other orchestras. In 1965 I had begun to do the occasional concert with the LSO and had loved making music with them. But when, in 1968, they came to me, offering me the post of Principal Conductor, I had not been able, in my most private dreams of glory, to imagine such a thing. I was overwhelmed. I worked out a schedule which permitted me to accept their amazing offer without disregarding my commitments in Houston, and for a year, I commuted. London to Texas is quite a commute, not only in miles but in culture shock. I took a flat in London, the size of an overnight compartment on a train, and had a slightly grander version of the same in Houston. Things there grew worse. My inability to cope with the artistic thinking of the

Board, or possibly their inability to meet with mine, led to an impasse, and after my second year it was with mutual sighs of relief that we called it a day. I was sorry to leave my friends in the orchestra, with many of whom I am still in contact, but I was off to realize an ambition that had beset me since the first day I had alighted at Heathrow Airport: I was going to live and work in England.

I had been an anglophile of long standing. Mine is a peripatetic life style and I have been in most of the parts of the so-called civilized world. I have been momentarily seduced by the vigour of New York, by the femininity of Paris, by the unearthly beauty of Norway, as well as by countless other places, but from the first moment I set foot in England, many years ago, I had it firmly in mind that someday I would live there. It wasn't just the fact that London was indisputably the musical capital of the world; it was the countryside, the villages that look as if the calendar had been firmly stopped a century ago, and the second-nature politeness of everyone I met. And there was something else as well. In the past decade it has been mentioned often that I have a strong proclivity to English music. But the fact is that this predilection does not stem from my life in England; it was one of my earliest student enthusiasms. The first piece of twentieth-century music to captivate me totally was the Viola Concerto of Walton's and when I was about fourteen, I made a trek to a record shop in Los Angeles which specialized in imports, and bought the 78s of the work. This first enthusiasm led to my discovery of endless other English music, and one must remember that in those days it was not the international export item it has fortunately become since then. Scores and records had to be specially ordered and sent from London, or from Blackwell's in Oxford, and I had to wait months sometimes before the prize was delivered into my hands. Therefore, when I became the Principal Conductor of the LSO and could give free reign to this admiration, I felt extremely fortunate. One of my first recording ventures with the orchestra was to put the Nine Symphonies of Vaughan Williams on disc, and my programmes were soon filled with Elgar, Walton, Britten and Tippett. It gives me great joy to contemplate that I have played English music all over the world by now, not just of the composers already mentioned, but works by Nicholas Maw, John McCabe, Lennox Berkley, Richard Rodney Bennett, Malcolm Arnold, Wilfred Josephs, Max Davies, Gordon Crosse, Benjamin Frankel, Oliver Knussen, Butterworth, and Ireland. It is curious to me that this wonderful music took so long in becoming an international commodity. It has been proposed that much of it is so nationalistic in flavour that it does not communicate well in other countries, but surely that is a spurious argument. After all, what is more nationalistic than Tchaikovsky, and wouldn't it be bizarre if it were only played in Moscow? In fact, it is the more apparently nationalistic part of English music that has proven to be the biggest success in, for instance, the United States. The Fifth and Third Symphonies of Vaughan Williams, with their gentle country walks, have provoked standing ovations in New York and Chicago, thus once again proving that theories about music can be disproven by the simple act of making the music accessible to a new audience. I have become close friends with many of the English composers, most particularly with William Walton, and their encouragement and advice has been unstinting and unfailing.

There are two distinct and separate facets of orchestral life. One is the life at home, in other words in the home city of that orchestra, and the other is on tour. Let me examine them one at a time. 'Home' means not only the normal concert season, but also recording sessions, television, other peripheral work, and the administration and planning of the orchestra's artistic and business future. While the management, the conductor, and the involved soloists are conscious of plans at least two years in advance, the playing members of an orchestra must be content, most times, to be handed a schedule which takes them through a couple of months. In England, the orchestral player has a very arduous time of it. The pay is far from munificent, and the London players, since they are salaried by the session, are probably the hardest working lot in the world. It is not in the least unusual for a major London orchestra to have three working sessions a day, in other words, nine hours of playing. This might include a rehearsal, a recording, and a concert, all within twenty-four hours. Sandwiched into a day during which the orchestra, as a body, only has two sessions, might be an independent film session, a jingle for an advert, or a pop session for records, during which the virtuoso instrumentalists are reduced to playing the most simplistic drivel imaginable. It is a high tribute to them that their concert work does not reflect this sometimes hysterical existence, and that their playing standards are so unfailingly high. The orchestras of America, Germany and Austria, for example, lead a much more sanguine life. Their financial security is far higher, and therefore it is possible for the players to concentrate almost 100 percent of their time in simply being members of a great orchestra, to take pride in that fact, and to have the luxury of plenty of rehearsal time for each concert. Certainly, some of the players teach, or play for the commercial media, but they do so for individual personal reasons, and not out of sheer necessity. In eleven years with the LSO, I have grown quite used to the facts of life surrounding the London musical scene, and the result is that I am now often amused in America when the orchestras rebel at having an extra work session scheduled. One obvious example is the fact that it is not permitted to rehearse an American orchestra on tour, while an English orchestra not only is used to daily practice, but insists on it. Rehearsals in London, until a few years ago, had an extra deadly liability attached. The Royal Festival Hall, being the home of all the London orchestras, was always booked solid, and so rehearsals had to take place in any one of a dozen possible venues. These rehearsal halls were often at opposite ends of the city, and when we had two sessions in two different places, separated only by the lunch break, the intervening, necessary move, with traffic at its infamous worst, did not assuage the already frayed nerves of the players. Now, with the acquisition of a permanent rehearsal hall, Sir Henry Wood Hall, life is at least free from that particular horror.

14

I mentioned before that the sight-reading abilities of the English orchestras are phenomenal. This is due, to a large extent, to the fact that their musical life is made so frenetic. Rehearsals are by necessity not leisurely, and the English player has had to learn to cope with the most fiendish playing problems in the shortest possible time. Most American orchestras like to rehearse every detail, every nuance, carefully and repeatedly, until the requirements are fixed and safe. London orchestras often have to rehearse without stopping, rather like marathon runners drinking a cup of water while running. I have often requested certain changes in the playing and gone right on conducting. These changes are then either marked, or simply remembered, but rarely rehearsed to the fullest. Then comes the concert, and almost without exception, everything is in its place and beautifully played. Even after all these years I am still amazed and full of admiration for this peculiar talent of the musicians.

One of the questions inevitably asked of conductors is 'Isn't it very difficult to face so many different orchestras within each season?' Well, the answer is yes, but, on reflection, surely it isn't as difficult for a conductor to face a new orchestra as it is for the orchestral player to deal with a different conductor so often. Remember that the standard repertoire has been played by any experienced player hundreds of times, and yet each conductor has his own peculiarities, his own wishes, his own demands. New phrasings, new bowings, new dynamics have to be put into the parts, old ones laboriously rubbed out, only to have the same exercise repeated a few weeks or months later. No wonder that there is a healthy state of cynicism within the ranks of any orchestra, no wonder that the favourite target of jokes is so often the conductor. After all, the argument goes, if the conductor makes a mistake, gives a wrong cue, miscounts, or forgets, who is really going to be aware of it? The baton is silent, but if the mistake of the wielder of that baton results in a clarinet player's wrong entrance, why, surely, it will be the clarinet player who is faulted by the listeners. Many years ago, when I first started with the LSO, Barry Tuckwell was still the principal horn. He was a friend and he gave me some hilariously true advice. 'When you get lost,' he said, 'and you will, everybody does at one time or another, just make some elegant vague motions and we'll put it all to rights quickly enough. But for God's sake don't lose your nerve and start flogging away at us, then we'll get lost too and everybody's in trouble.' I have always been glad that I kept up my piano playing. I conduct concertos from the piano quite often, and I play chamber music obsessively. I think it is a great mistake for conductors to give up their original instrument. It is a dangerous trap to stand on a rostrum week after week, year after year, demanding certain methods of playing from an orchestra, without actively reminding oneself of how damned difficult it is to play and to physically produce a musical sound. I am quite convinced of this and have told young conductors so, many times.

Players have their own ways of dealing with conductors they do not admire. The day of the despot seems to be pretty well over, and the fear that struck the hearts of the players when Toscanini or Szell or Reiner was on the podium is a thing of the past. A reproof from a player, gentle or otherwise, is now much more prevalent. Two examples: I had invited a young conductor to do a concert with the LSO. He began the first rehearsal with the Beethoven Seventh, a symphony which the orchestra had played with every conductor listed in Grove's Dictionary. He spent twenty minutes on the first four bars, always dissatisfied and growing more and more abusive. Finally, he shouted at Roger Lord, the distinguished principal oboe, and sang the offending phrase to him from the podium. 'That's how I want it played,' he yelled, 'not the way you've been doing it!' Roger Lord is not only a superb player with the most innately musical instincts imaginable, but he is also a polite, soft-spoken gentleman of the old school. He was not fazed by the youngster's rage. 'I'm so sorry,' he said in dulcet tones. 'Would you care to hear it your way, just once?' Another time, a guest conductor whipped his way through part of the Enigma Variations at an unplayable tempo. One of the players spoke up. 'Excuse me,' he said, 'but that's simply too fast.' The conductor turned sarcastic. 'Too fast for whom?' he demanded. 'Since you ask,' said the musician, 'too fast for Elgar.'

Soloists provoke reactions as well, but not verbal ones. Admiration, disregard, or stoicism are mirrored on the players' faces, and anyone with experience can read these reactions easily. A few months ago, Itzhak Perlman recorded the Sibelius Concerto with the Pittsburgh Orchestra and me. He played the fiendish cadenza with an easy virtuosity that bordered on disdain for all its difficulties. I looked around at the faces of the string players. They were leaning forward, quite riveted, and I was touched that what I saw was pure admiration, untinged by envy or perhaps lost dreams. It was unselfish approval of the highest order.

Now let me examine the problems of touring with an orchestra for a bit. To the layman, the presence of an orchestra on a stage is a matter which is taken for granted. The mountainous problems of actually getting that orchestra to that stage must be kept from an audience. Think about it: one hundred or more players to transport around the world, together with all the instruments, the music library, the administrative staff, accompanying members of the Press, wives and friends. Planes to charter, train tickets to book, coaches to hire, adequate hotel accommodations to see to, travel time not to exceed a certain amount of hours a day, restaurants to find while on the road, local managements to sort out, foreign currency to reckon with, *per diem* payments to the players, acoustical problems in the various concert halls, adequate seating arrangements in these auditoriums, local receptions to cope with – the list goes on and on. It is a miracle that tours happen at all. The financial problems are truly staggering, and with the rising costs of everything it has become an almost unsolvable muddle. I have toured with quite a few orchestras during my career: the LSO, the Pittsburg, the Vienna, the Chicago, and the Royal Philharmonic. There is nothing in life quite comparable to life on tour. On the average, six concerts a week are played, and with few exceptions, each one is in a different city. The LSO used to be the most touring orchestra in the world, and in my time I have taken them on sixteen major tours. We've been all around the world and we've played to every possible kind of audience. We've played in elegant concert halls, school gymnasiums, outdoor arenas, and local conference halls. We've had no time to get our tails pressed or our nerves quietened. I've seen the orchestra so worn out that they were asleep standing up backstage, but I've never seen them at less than peak effort during a performance. The final reserves of adrenalin seem bottomless. We've been on stages where it has been impossible to see or hear, but somehow the music has always come across. I can think of no professionals, with the possible exception of the Astronauts, who show more courage in the face of adversity. Once, we were on tour in Czechoslovakia. We arrived on a Sunday night, in a resort town out of season, after a gruelling trip from Romania. We staggered into the designated Hotel and found a sleepy desk clerk, who looked up from his girlie magazine with undisguised surprise. 'We're the London Symphony Orchestra,' we announced, 'and we're dead tired. Could we get the rooms sorted out quickly, please?' The man regarded us with a total lack of comprehension. He had never heard of us, he announced. He had not been told we were coming, and he had a total of thirteen rooms available to us. There was a silence which was comparable to the last minutes preceding the mutiny on the Bounty. We asked whether there were other hotels in town. He shrugged philosophically. 'You can try,' he said. 'But, on a Sunday night . . . ,' and left the sentence unfinished. We dispatched runners to the other hotels, decided to burn the tour manager's effigy later, and returned to more pressing matters. 'Well, we'll eat while we wait,' I said; 'where is the dining room?' Another eloquent shrug, 'The kitchen is closed, gentlemen.' The situation grew more ominous. I had to think quickly. 'But you have a wine cellar?' 'Yes, that we have.' I rallied. 'Fine,' I said, 'start bringing up bottles to the dining room.' We tottered into the restaurant and began to drink. The natural ebullience of musicians began to take over; stories were told, and we began to find the whole mess hilarious. After two hours, one of the players nudged me, pointed to the dining room entrance, and said in an awestruck voice, 'Look!' There, in the doorway, was one of our bachelor musicians. He had gone out into this deserted resort town, without knowing a single word of the language, and here he was, with not one, but *two* pretty girls hanging on to him. The orchestra knew a virtuoso when they saw one. They gave him a standing ovation.

Since becoming the Music Director of the Pittsburgh Symphony in 1977, I am often asked to compare American orchestras with those in England. I have already mentioned the differences in financial matters, and in administrative periphery, but actually, when it gets right down to it, when it comes to the playing, the making of music, the coping with the life, then I cannot say that I find any great differences. Talent is universal. The practice and perfection of an instrumentalist is the same the world over. The curious mixture of cynical boredom and deep love of music manifests itself in every orchestra everywhere. There is a great deal of pride involved in being a member of a symphony orchestra. Now that there are audition committees, rather than as in the old days when the conductor did his auditioning privately and with total and sole authority, it is, if anything, more difficult for a new player to find a place in an established orchestra. The auditions are becoming tougher and tougher, because the players themselves want to make sure that the reputation of the orchestra is upheld, and its achievements unthreatened. Certainly it is possible to see open boredom during particular rehearsals, with surreptitious crossword puzzles and paperback books being scanned during fifty-bar rests, but the overall love of music is never far beneath the surface. Some years ago, someone in the London press accused the LSO of a whole catalogue of misdemeanours: slovenliness, tardiness, drinking, womanizing, the lot. The orchestra took this litany quite calmly. But then, the man quoted in the article went too far. He accused them of not caring about the music, and of playing only because it was a way for them to earn a salary. That tore it, and the indignation was towering. Our principal bassoon, Bob Bourton, probably spoke for all of them when he said to me, 'Let the fellow accuse me of anything and everything, I've possibly been guilty of some of those things at one time or another, but by God, no one can say I don't love music!!!' And he meant it, every word. He was genuinely shocked and hurt, and for good reason. The life of an orchestral musician is a truly difficult one, and the one thing that makes it all possible is the fact that there is a solid gold love of music behind the troubles of every working day. Why else would they put up with it? Why else, on their all-too-few nights off can you find musicians at other people's concerts, listening and evaluating and arguing? Why else do chamber music splinter groups appear during difficult tours and manage to play through that kind of repertoire during an afternoon's breather? Even if given a choice of another profession, if it were offered by some magic wand, replete with security and less impossible conditions, I doubt if any of us would trade in our professional lives. A Symphony Orchestra is the greatest instrument in the world, with the greatest repertoire available. It is an honourable, thrilling and fine organization to belong to. Musicians are stubborn, argumentative, opinionated, unpredictable, and quixotic, but most of all, they are proud.

As I write this, I have been without a holiday for many years. That statement has no self-pity in it, it is just a statement of fact. In the past month I have conducted in Philadelphia, New York, Vienna, London and Chicago. In two weeks I will return to my Pittsburgh Orchestra, and a month later, to the LSO. It's quite a schedule. I share that kind of schedule with all my colleagues, mine is not unique. But at the end of every tiring day, of every gruelling trip, there is the reward of the music. Great music, greater than any interpretation of it can ever be. It keeps the word 'boredom' away from our vocabulary, and it makes future efforts sound inviting. What other profession can make such a claim?

I'm a very fortunate man.

PROLOGUE: VETERAN

RAYMOND CLARK

I seem to remember being mixed up with music all my life, from a tiny boy. Oh well, it goes back so many years I find it difficult to recall. My father was a great enthusiast, a violinist in his way, no professional but very keen, very amateurishly keen. I come from Yorkshire, from Leeds. Why, I never left Leeds until 1926 when I came down to London, so I had plenty of time to learn.

In a way it was my own decision to take up the cello. I never went to a music school, I was always privately coached. My tutor was a very keen, sensitive man, an excellent teacher who thought I should take a real interest in music. My father saw I did my daily practice and hovered over me like . . . well, like a father. Of course it was years before I got near professional standard. But my teacher was a diligent man, a remarkable man.

My musical life just developed somehow or other, through the efforts of my teacher and others. I seemed to have a musical bent, you know, and so they encouraged me and I kept going. I'm trying to think, when did I enter the profession? I can't remember exactly. I'm getting to be an old man now. Well, I've got to be, I'm seventy-eight. I would say I started in the cinema in Leeds, when every big cinema had its orchestra. Oh, I played in several of those. The standard of playing was just about competent, and you were supposed to put your hand to different instruments. I played the cello and doubled on banjo and guitar. I also played with the Leeds Symphony Orchestra, for what it was worth. It was only a kind of semi-amateur affair, but at all events it gave me plenty of experience of orchestral playing. I was considered by my tutors to be rather an outstanding musician, even as a kid. I think I impressed with my quickness and my good sight-reading, and having a good ear I could always be expected to play in tune. So I just went ahead taking whatever came until about 1926. Then I decided to come to London.

I didn't think the orchestral life was for me until I got into it. I came to London at the behest of a fellow who was the big cheese in the musical life of Leeds. He was a good violinist who became the chief fixer, you might say, and he had me running about with him all over the shop in the north, and eventually he brought me to London, to play in a big cinema — what was it called? My memory is bad . . . yes, the New Gallery Cinema in Regent Street. For a while I was more or less absorbed in that business, but it was not difficult to go from cinema to orchestral work. There were chances to deputize. Oh, I was in some demand after a time

19

because the number of good orchestral players in those days was rather meagre. There were plenty of scrapers. I was a freelance, playing casual-like, just pleasing myself. Third desk today, fifth desk tomorrow, just bring the cello and play. That's how it was. A very loose-knit profession. All I had to do really was to sit down and play the cello. I'm not boasting, but it just happened that if people heard me I was immediately on their list, you see. I was considered to be particularly good, so I never had any difficulty getting along in London. The BBC Symphony was formed in 1930 and I was with them from the beginning as sub-principal cello. I stayed with that orchestra until 1945, right through the War years, first in Bristol under the bombing – Oh, a bad time – and then in Bedford.

In the old days pay was rather poor and we didn't have much to run about with. The general rule in London was pay by the session, no real contract, you were just there if you could play well and keep a nice clean front. No security, no pension. Once a chap was in, provided he was a reasonable player, he stuck it. Some fly-by-nights came and went, but if they did they weren't missed. All the good players in London were known by name and had a certain reputation on their own account. But in an orchestra or not, we still did whatever came along. Someone would offer a date, you'd look in your diary and away you would go. Before the War there wasn't that much regular work for the orchestras, and the orchestral musician took whatever he could get.

But my facility was good on the cello, and I didn't find it hard. I left the BBC after the War and joined Beecham's new Royal Philharmonic as principal. I played the first notes of the first public concert of that orchestra – the William Tell Overture. At the same time Walter Legge was forming the Philharmonia and asked me to play in that. I sat as sub-principal until, after a short time, the principal left, and I fell into that position. I gave up the Royal Philharmonic and remained with the Philharmonia for about 21 years. That orchestra was a bit superior. Legge saw to it that he had only the best players, and the best conductors. He had a good ear for a player, a fine judgment of conductors, and a keen sense of business. I wouldn't say he was difficult – at least not with me – but you had to be on your guard. He was a bit of a dictator, though a clever man at running an orchestra. Of course, he got the best conductors, and we got to know them well. We had von Karajan for years and Klemperer for about as long. Yes, I remember poor old Klemperer well. By jove, he was a hard task-master. Everything had to be right on the spot. Well, I think I found him an inspiring conductor, I think most of us did. He was getting old, and a bit of a wreck, but he still had his faculties, and he did know how to conduct. His beat wasn't good, but it was usually within half a beat of the right place. Well, I never took any notice of the beat, I just followed the music. And of course those conductors had fine players to work with. Dennis Brain was first horn. I recall when he died, what a shock to the orchestra. We lost the finest musician of the lot when Dennis went. He was a bit of a fly-about, you know. Oh, not half. He used to drive that sports car like a demon. I don't wonder he smashed himself up.

20

We started, in the Philharmonia, as a recording orchestra mainly. I never minded the recording studio, and I don't think the difference between public concert and recording was all that noticeable. If the chaps were playing well, the music went well, and if they weren't, it was up to the section leaders, like myself, to put them right. I think perhaps, in some respects, continental and American string players have the edge on us. In most things, tone, technique, discipline. They have a more rigid structure, less freelance playing. But I don't know. I used to enjoy a change, for the sake of variety. We had a little quartet from the Philharmonia, for our own amusement chiefly. Then it got round that we were a pretty good ensemble and we started getting dates. And in the orchestra we saw so many conductors. With a new name, we'd put him through his paces. We showed him first how we played, and if he wasn't up to much, sometimes the leader, or perhaps one of the principals would quietly take him aside: 'We've always played it this way, and we shall go on playing it this way.' But usually conductors didn't give us much trouble. English orchestras have too little rehearsal. I think that applies to all our orchestras, and sometimes a keen ear can detect it. But in my recollection I think we had a good section of cellos in the Philharmonia. Somehow, I don't know quite how it came about, it was one of the best sections in the orchestra, partly because I was a bit of a tyrant. I think I can be said to have polished up that section, and got them round to my way of thinking, and my way of playing too. It was a happy orchestra. But I've never been a member of any other kind of orchestra. Musicians down here are a happy lot really.

Raymond Clark

Beginning

Real talent takes a long time to mature, to learn how to bring what character you have into sound, into your playing . . . And that takes a whole life.

BUD FREEMAN, in Studs Terkel, *Working*

FROM the beginning I heard my father playing the piano, and music was always going on in the house. I started on the piano but didn't like it, because I couldn't come to terms with practising. Everybody else was having fun. I'd be about seven or eight. My piano teacher was rather perceptive and let me drop it. He said, 'The boy's bound to come back because there's a modicum of talent in him.' I don't know about the modicum of talent, but round about thirteen I suddenly realized that I was totally useless at everything, so if I was to do anything it would *have* to be music. Then I started practising, and everything else got in the way.

Music became a part of life, a way of life, very early, and I never rebelled against it. My father is a composer, a teacher, and plays clarinet, sax and piano. My mother's a violinist with the Seattle Symphony Orchestra. I had instruments in my hands at a very early age. I'm told I started playing trumpet when I was four. I don't know if I believe that. My folks never pushed me to practise, and I always enjoyed it. It was very natural for me to take up music. I played trumpet and I took some piano. I was terrible at that. I used to practise hours and hours, and I just couldn't get the hang of it. I was so bored with it. I began the trumpet seriously about six or seven, and that can be hard on the mouth, before the teeth are formed. I remember playing without my front teeth, upper and lower. I distinctly remember having a heck of a time. But my embouchure and mouth seem all right now, they work well for me, so I hope starting early hasn't caused any hidden trouble in the mouth. I did have braces on my teeth, though, when I was about fourteen. And playing was very difficult then, next to impossible. With the braces, I had to put wax on them. Oh, I had a heck of a time.

My mum played the piano, Winifred Attwell style, and my dad had a drum kit. He'd always wanted to be a drummer, so he played with a band, a little dance band. But he never really got good at it. I remember the first playing I ever did was when I was three, at some parties round the corner. It was novel for a bloke down our way to have a drum kit,

Anthony Camden
(second right)

so my dad used to take it along and set it up. He made me a little drum out of an old tom-tom and I'd sit next to him having a bash with sticks cut from a mop-handle. I'd sit next to him and copy him, swigging lemonade when he had his beer. That's how I got interested in drums, because there was one around, in our house in North Lambeth.

I was a violinist first. But I had very bad asthma, and I took up the oboe to help the asthma. After about six months I gave up the fiddle, the asthma was cured. I was then about sixteen. The oboe came quite easily. Certain people seem to have a bent for certain instruments, and however hard you try to become a string player, if you're a wind player, that's what you become. But it's a very good thing for a wind player also to play a string instrument, learning to do the long line, the long phrases with the bow. It was in my mind that I would become a musician. But I think my father — the bassoon player Archie Camden — rather fancied business for me — at least, if I failed the music scholarship then I should go for business. But I got the scholarship, playing oboe, within two years of starting. My first teacher got me going very well. The oboe has a reputation for difficulty, but I settled quickly on it.

There were some gas-pipes in the cellar which I made into primitive flutes and started playing. At nine or ten I graduated to bamboo pipes, and then to the recorder. That was the fashion then, to play the re-

23

corder in school. I had awful piano lessons and couldn't read music until I was about fifteen. But I must have had a good ear. My piano teacher plonked at the top of the piano and I picked it up by ear, and never did any practice but got by. I began the clarinet at Dulwich College. I really wanted to play the oboe, but my granny told me that would give me consumption, so my father suggested I learn the clarinet first and then go on to the oboe. I think I picked the oboe because we had some old records of Leon Goossens playing a Handel *Concerto Grosso*, and there's something special about his playing, as there is with Casals or Kreisler — it's that quality. Perhaps if I'd first come upon Kreisler playing the Beethoven fiddle concerto, I might have wanted to be a violinist. It's hard to know how basic an instrument is to you. Anyway, when I left school I was settled on the clarinet.

My father was a bassoon player, very good one, and his elder brother played too, and uncle Frank who lived next door but one, very fine trumpet player, and my mother was a good amateur singer and pianist. So I'm afraid I was destined. Well, I used to declare that I was going to be a musician, and I was a *very* bad pianist, then one day my father trapped me into playing the bassoon. He said I could have a brand new instrument if I would practise. So that's what happened, I started to practise hard. My father taught me bassoon. People say it's not possible to teach one's own children, and it isn't normally, it leads to rows, doesn't it? But in general I got on pretty well with my father. I remember when I went to Trinity — my father was professor there. He said, 'Forget I'm your father.' He was the professor, I was the student. About the second lesson, we'd only been going ten minutes, I began to argue. 'Right,' he said, 'that's it. Go home. Tell your mother why you're home early.' Needless to say I didn't go, I lurked about . . .

We all played, all had our instruments. Father chose the harp for my sister Marie and me because in his day women only entered the orchestra as harpists. Father was mainly a conductor, but he was a violinist first — leader of the Carl Rosa Opera when his father conducted. And my eldest brother was violinist and conductor too. All Eugene Goossens. Mother was in the opera company. She was born in America where her parents, both operatic singers, were travelling. I've got a poster at home: The Boston Opera Company, 1868, Mr and Mrs Aynsley Cook — my maternal grandparents. Grandfather Goossens came from Bruges about 150 years ago. So both sides of the family were travelling all their lives, and I suppose I'm still a bit of a gypsy. I was born almost in the train, on tour. We settled in Liverpool and started our lessons there. I played the violin as well as the harp, and of course we all played the piano. I had no qualms about following the musical profession. Well, father's word was law really. I adored the opera, which we always visited when father and his company came to Liverpool. At seven I wanted to be an operatic singer. I sang and acted the stories of all the operas, got dressed up, just singing everything, all the parts. Father thought about it, but decided

A young musician plays a small harp in a school orchestra

that singing wasn't as safe as an instrument. The voice goes early. But I just wanted to be on the stage, that called me. Anything to do with the stage. And I'm still the same. When I was first with the BBC, at Savoy Hill and later at Broadcasting House, I did all their revues and amateur dramatics. I was their leading lady for about five years. Oh, they were the best fun of my life.

All the males in my family played a brass instrument. It was pretty obvious that I had to take up a brass instrument, or one wasn't a member of the Civil family. In musical dynasties it's expected that the children will follow on, and the children are in it before they can think. You see, I have six children and they all play, mainly strings. Now, one boy who's sixteen just doesn't bother at all – comes home from school, slings the instrument under the piano and there it stays. The other lad, who plays the cello, is as keen as mustard. I think it wrong to insist on kids prac-tising. Well, old man Borsdorf had several sons playing the horn. Francis told me that he and his brother Emile would have to play horn duets for the old man, and they never finished a lesson until Francis had an awful blue ring on his lips, and Emile invariably used to faint. Sometimes if the old man didn't like their playing he'd hit them on the back of the neck. That tough old Saxon way. I can see both sides of it. There's no doubt that parents can help make a real musician by getting the kids to practise. In some cases it does seem to pay dividends.

25

I think my father intended me for music before I was born. You see, he was a Dublin van driver, and we lived in two rooms. The fiddle was a passport to a better life. I think this went for a lot of fiddle players from poor families, specially the Jewish players from the East End of London. The outlay for a cheap fiddle was small, and lessons needn't be expensive. My father, an amateur player, was more interested in the fiddle than in music. He liked the violin as a sound, but he didn't know much of the literature, perhaps because he started late. I began when I was four, on a little tin fiddle fromWoolworth's. I heard him practising and started, you see. After a while I got fed up and refused to do any more. In about a year, I'm told I asked to begin again, though I can't imagine why. I had a proper baby-size fiddle, lessons, and my father supervised my practice. His help, which was rather basic, was nonetheless important, a kind of foretaste of Suzuki method. I didn't fight my father's plans. Well, the alternatives were so awful. Perhaps it's not the best way to go into music, but a lot of my older colleagues began like that. In my youth the big job for youngsters in Dublin was Guinness's Brewery — not for the drink but for the wonderful welfare schemes. For me, it would have been Guinness or the Civil Service.

Marie Wilson

In our family nobody was musical, but everybody was artistic. My father was a very talented painter, and my mother had many gifts, in painting, in writing. My father died when I was four, but before I was born, or even conceived, he wrote a poem to my mother saying: 'He will be Csaba, and he will be a musician.' Apparently there was a pressure on me! My mother, a teacher of languages who had to take up Russian just after the War in Hungary, tells me I was already singing Russian songs at two-and-a-half, before I sang in Hungarian. It was agreed and obvious that I had to study music. At six years old I was taken to the violin class. I was very stiff, physically, and though I had a good voice and good musical imagination, most teachers gave me up as a bad job. I enjoyed life and had many, many interests in history, and languages. I spoke English well before I was taught it. I learnt from books, films, radio. The films of Laurence Olivier were the strongest influence, and made me absolutely mad about English. But this impediment, this lack of physical flexibility, lasted until my early twenties. I did very hard work on the violin, in my adolescent years, but it wasn't obvious for a long time that I would become a professional musician.

My parents took me dancing when I was about four, because they thought that would be good for deportment and movement. Then the War came, and my father stopped me going to the dancing academy on account of the air-raids. On my tenth birthday, as a special treat, I asked to go to the cinema, a rare event in our house. Anyway, the film I saw in Warrington had an orchestra in it — Olivia de Haviland, I think, was playing the violin — and that caught my fancy. At home I stood in front of the mirror and rubbed two knitting-needles together. At last, I asked for a violin. My parents were horrified, but bought me a half-size fiddle and I started lessons. One day I asked to be taken to the Liverpool Philharmonic. I remember the concert. Myra Hess played the piano, and Jelly d'Aranyi and her sister played the Bach Double. I came home with my mind made up to be a violinist. My parents thought it was just a childish whim.

My parents were both painters, and my sister's also a painter. The family was only vaguely interested in music, but I come from a home were the arts were respected, so my taking up music wasn't a shock. Some families think music is terribly dangerous. When it was seen that I couldn't paint, music was the next best thing. I learnt the piano and didn't get on with it. Then at school, when I was about eleven, the class made bamboo pipes. I got obsessed with this, made more and more, and spent *all* my time playing them, so the natural thing was to go on to the flute. I wasn't much interested in music, it was just flute-playing, a kind of monomania. A lot of orchestral players have no great passion for their profession, they don't put their emotions into it. It's a way to make a living, or have a nice life. Practical considerations weigh high. But for me, I was just swept off my feet for some strange reason. It was the flute or nothing. Absolutely.

Maybe it was unusual, the way I came to music. The family is from West Pennsylvania, Somerset County, farmers, a variety of occupations, but no musicians at all. Large families, too. Ask my dad what instrument he plays and he says 'radio'. We went to South Carolina with the military. In school, for no very good reason, I wanted to play trumpet in the music class, but dad thought trombone looked kind of nicer, so we rented one. I was eleven, mad about baseball, running about. But now the school was offering the band. I guess that's what it was – I hadn't been offered that before. A fellow of my own age moved from Texas, and he was more advanced than I was. I began to make comparisons. Our family moved to Fort Worth and by that time I was more and more interested. There was a lot of activity in the schools in the South West – a marching band, a school orchestra, a concert band, a lot of musicians.

During the War I was sent away to an aunt in the country. The only school still left was a private girls school, which took boys for kindergarten only. But the War came and I was stranded there, only boy in a class of twenty or thirty girls. I'd be about nine. Apparently I was a bit of a nuisance and they wondered what to do with me. So they gave me a fiddle, just to keep me occupied. And here I am, still at it. I found I had a certain aptitude. Not, I think, so much an aptitude for music, but I'm good with my hands, and I was fairly facile. I'm not a fanatical musician who'd die if I didn't play. I've got too many irons in the fire, always other things to do. But I got round the instrument well, and my aunt, who had played a bit, made me practise. I don't think any young kid wants to practise, specially a string instrument. But I did, and was facile, so I won prizes here and there. I had a keen teacher. She gave me impossible things to play and I struggled through them. I played the solos at the school concerts. One just went on. By that time it was too late to resist, I was already in the rut. My education, a good grammar school education, hadn't actually taught me to do anything. I was good at music and it seemed natural to keep going. I won these damn competitions and the next thing I knew I was at the Guildhall.

I'm the oddball, no other musicians in my family. We had a little record-player and a large number of records, mostly hand-me-downs – a lot of Tony Martin, some ancient Caruso, Galli-Curci, Gigli, a few instrumental pieces like the Ritual Fire Dance. I'd expected to be a rock singer, maybe going into the Met chorus as second best. My aunt had a subscription to play and I struggled through them. I played the solos at the school from that. My mother said, 'You'll never make a living as a singer. With your allergies? How can you think about singing when you're sneezing all the time? Take up a string instrument – something reliable.'

I had a grandfather who was a champion player on the Northumbrian pipes. My father was a miner and worked in the pits as a boy. He was mad keen on the violin, the 'little fiddler' they called him in the village. I don't know where he got a violin – they were poor people – but I'm told he would come home and practise until he was exhausted, then fall asleep with the fiddle in his hand. He had taught himself, but he later went to Newcastle, took a few lessons, got a job in a theatre and eventually came to London, to play in the old Gaiety Theatre. By the time I was four my father started teaching me the violin. He himself had a beautiful tone and loved the instrument, but he had started late, and without good teaching. He was determined to realize in me all that he had been unable to achieve. He worked me very hard, and I seemed to have a natural talent. But being so young, I hated those long lessons and the interminable practice that he demanded. We had awful rows — we were very much alike.

I was brought up in central New York State, in the Finger Lake region, where the Iroquois Indians lived. Ours was a little farming town, scattered dairy farms. My father was a clergyman, my mother a teacher, both sang, my father played the violin, my mother the piano. There were records in the house, chiefly piano — Rubinstein playing Beethoven. My mother started me on the piano when I was about five. We started again the next year, and the next. The usual case — learning from a parent rarely works. By the age of twelve I'd wanted to be a boxer, then a forester, never a musician. Then my friend next door — we were great mates — produced a trumpet from the school band-room, and I wanted one too. But there were too many trumpet players, so the bandmaster said, 'Perhaps you'd like one of these.' What was it? 'Oh, that's a trombone,' he replied. My introduction to the instrument. I started lessons, at about twelve, and immediately things went very well.

I have a psychological theory. My uncle was a very good amateur cellist who remained amateur only because his father wouldn't let him go on with it. He was a cynical and embittered man, a great tease, and I was very frightened of him. I don't think there was any malice in him, but he scared a small lad. I often wonder if I took up his instrument to beat him at his own game. When I was quite small my mother died and I went to live with grandparents. My grandfather was a very keen, very bad amateur fiddler. He'd learnt by correspondence course, on the Scottish border, miles from anywhere. My first recollections are of music floating upstairs after I'd been shoved off to bed. But perhaps I was more influenced by old trio recordings — Cortot, Thibaud, Casals — and being taken to Birmingham Town Hall, just once as a small boy, to hear Casals play. And I heard also, in a broadcast sometime during the War, Leon Goossens play. I've no idea what he played. All I can *vividly* remember is the sound of the oboe, which I'd never identified before. That sound jumped out and left its mark for all time. I suppose music will eventually come out regardless. But I had no formal tuition until I was sixteen-and-a-half or seventeen. I'd driven the family mad trying to teach myself the piano. The War was on. No one in the house was interested in music. I battered away until they could bear it no longer and decided to get me organized. Then I announced I didn't want to learn the piano anyway, I wanted cello lessons.

Michael Nutt

Nobody in my family was what you'd call a musician, but there was a lot of emphasis on music, maybe not playing, but listening. From my earliest memory, we always went down for the Philadelphia Orchestra at the May Festival in Michigan. So I grew up with 'serious' music. I remember when I was about ten my parents went square-dancing and I saw a five-piece dance band. I couldn't believe it, I didn't believe you could make music with less than 100 people. It was a revelation – I didn't think you could do it. At school, I got a saxophone from the local music store, then that broke, so I got a clarinet and just stayed with that. And from the age of twelve I wanted to be a musician playing in an orchestra, but it was like wanting to be a baseball player. What was involved? I had no idea. I had no idea even if I had any talent. It just seemed a neat thing to do. Well, I was lucky. The guy I studied with pushed me real hard, gave me tons of music, and I practised like mad. My mother read somewhere that Jascha Heifetz said you must practise two hours a day. I'd get up about 6.30, start blowing the damn thing, furious, tired, hating it, but I did it. I remember when I was in high school every minute was music. I was playing records even when doing homework. I worked in my parent's store, which had a record department, and I'd take all my pay in records. I had about 1000 by the time I got to college. I knew every one of them, you know, and I've still got them. Out of print now, and not all good, but all classical, all very middle-class. Just ham and potato type music. I wanted to compose too. I'd get these big things – *Heldenleben*, things by Strauss and Mahler – and try to write like that. Kind of silly, very naive. But I was very intensely caught up in music. I didn't do anything else.

30

Training

Decide now for yourself whether a good orchestral violinist be not of far higher value than one who is purely a solo player. The latter can play everything according to his whim and arrange the style of performance as he wishes, or even for the convenience of his hand; while the former must possess the dexterity to understand and at once interpret rightly the taste of various composers, their thoughts and expressions.

LEOPOLD MOZART, *Fundamental Principles of Violin Playing* (1756)

A Bad Case

RODNEY FRIEND

FOR the last fifteen years, since I've been leader of two great orchestras, I have been on the receiving end of very sad phone-calls — 'Why didn't I get through my audition?' I've been asked that on both sides of the Atlantic. Sometimes I would have to say, 'You failed because you really don't know how to play the orchestral repertoire.' It's not good enough to play a concerto fairly well, very many can do it. Training in music colleges, at least on string instruments, is too much aimed just at solo command of the instrument. Of course, parents think they have the next Heifetz, the next Piatigorsky, and I think it's up to the music schools to point out this isn't the case. There are maybe twenty-five master string players — great soloists — in a *decade*. What percentage is that of all the string players going through the schools? Thousands of players, very, very few soloists. But I do feel that a great many highly gifted string players, quite as gifted in their way as some who are doing the solo circuit, are falling by the wayside because they are not being prepared for what they will have to do, which is play in an orchestra. To play in the great orchestras of the world should be looked on as a privilege, an honour. And that attitude should be fostered in the schools of music.

I remember when I was approached to be associate concertmaster of the London Symphony Orchestra, when I was twenty, and I also had a solo debut with Barbirolli and the Hallé in the Festival Hall, I thought it was some kind of insult — to be asked to play *in* an orchestra rather than *with* an orchestra. Looking back, I think that was a dreadful opinion to have.

I'm not trying to dissuade anyone from a solo or chamber music career. The choice is open. But young players must be trained to play

Sir John Barbirolli at an
audition at Morley College

correctly with others, to play in ensemble, in sections, and to have that
playing dignified as something worthy. If they are not prepared, both
technically and mentally, for what is after all their likely life, then
talented people will fall away from the orchestra, and perhaps away from
music entirely. You must play in the orchestra because you love it, otherwise there's no way you can face forty years of doing just that.

LYNN HARRELL I went to the Curtis Institute with the idea of being a
soloist, and Curtis had the same ambition for me. I was destined, because
people talked that way, to become the next Casals, Feuermann. Somehow
I would just drop into the solo circuit, and my career would blossom from
there. No other course was entertained at Curtis, certainly not orchestral
playing, for which I was in no way prepared. Never in any cello lesson did
I have instruction on such a basic matter as how to follow a conductor,
even as a soloist. I knew nothing about playing in a section, even less
about leading one. I had no lesson on any of the orchestral parts. And
some of that stuff is darn hard to play, some of it actually harder than
things in the solo literature – Wagner, Mahler, Strauss, some of those
parts are so demanding. Never did I study any of them, and as far as I
could see my fellow students didn't look at them either. It was like
orchestras didn't exist. The school had a student orchestra, but who

32

cared? If you were caught in a practice-room going over an orchestral part, you were reckoned a strange kid — 'What you trying to do? You chicken? Don't want to be a soloist?' You were ostracized, literally. A terrible, terrible situation.

I was at Curtis only one year, and at Julliard one year also. And Julliard was, in that way, exactly the same. I was supposed to be one of the 'lucky' ones, picked out for exceptional talent, and I was 'spared' the orchestra because I didn't have time for it. Now, I'm still bitter about that. I missed so much music because for a cellist outside the orchestra your playing is a little bit limited, and unless you play in an orchestra, which most good music students are going to have to do anyway, you don't really have a full training as a musician.

C E C I L J A M E S In those days — I went to the Royal College of Music in 1930 — we didn't play through the repertoire. Good lord, no, nothing like it. In my four years I may have played three Beethoven symphonies and one Brahms. Things like Beethoven 9 we knew nothing about whatsoever. I believe it's a bit the same now. Students have to queue up, almost, to play in the college orchestra. But I think I was lucky because Malcolm Sargent conducted the first orchestra then, and he was marvellous. He ran it like a professional orchestra, no alibis, it had to be right. If you made an excuse — a reed perhaps — he'd say, 'Can you tell that to the public at the concert?' And because there were only four bassoon players in the whole College, I played in all the orchestras. A terrible indignity to play in third orchestra — the 'Jazz Band', we called it — but it meant I got through more music.

A puzzled violinist watches the conductor in rehearsal

After a couple of years I started doing a few outside jobs. Sargent might need someone for the orchestra he had in Leicester. Money! I think £2 8s. was the top fee then for a symphony concert. I loved playing those concerts. And of course you'd play in every amateur orchestra that would have you. My father dispatched me to the Royal Amateur – very distinguished. It was dreadful. Awful noises. And everybody looked so old, about ninety. I got paid, but I hated it. The funny thing is that I go occasionally to play for them now, and they've become very good, and everybody looks so young!

GARY KETTEL I'd be about twelve, just getting into the classical stuff. That's when I did my first gig at the Festival Hall, when I was twelve, with the London Insurance Orchestra – a semi-professional lot. They needed six percussionists, and I got in with the fellow who was teaching me. I had an old dress suit from across the road and my dad cut it down. I remember everyone else got a guinea expenses but I only got 10s. 6d., being considered half fare.

I was still on both sides of the musical fence. I was playing guitar in a pop group, and I sometimes wish I'd done more of that. But I was really enjoying the classical side, and beginning to think of it as a career. I was playing in a local orchestra out at Walthamstow, the Forest Philharmonic with Frank Shipway. He was a pupil of Barbirolli – always said fagotto instead of bassoon. It was only amateur, but we met every Monday and played proper pieces, like Tchaikovsky symphonies. That was really good. By the time I got to the Royal College at sixteen, I'd done a lot of orchestral pieces, playing timpani. And I was still playing pop guitar.

I auditioned for the Academy and the College. Jimmy Blades and some doctor of music heard me at the Academy. I had to play a piano piece, which I completely messed up – terrible thing by C. P. E. Bach. Then I did the percussion bit which was no problem. The judges went aside and I heard this doctor, an old-fashioned gent, say 'I don't think we can let this chap in. He can't play the piano and he hasn't got his O Level exams.' I was going to study percussion! 'Look,' said Jimmy Blades, 'you can't keep a chap like this out.' So they offered me a place, but I chose to go to the College. Alan Taylor, the timpanist at Covent Garden Opera – a very fine player, one of the best – was there. No offence to Alan, but he was such a nice bloke that when you took him a piece for help, he'd listen and say, 'Yes, that'll sound fine. Let's go and have a cup of tea.' I see him now, and we have a few pints, but he's very straight, tie and suit, short hair. He asked me once to get a hair cut, and offered to pay for it. It came to 5s. 'That's not short enough,' he said, 'here's half a crown.' I learnt a lot from Alan, just watching him on timps. Another fellow taught percussion, but he was only good at military noises on the side-drum. He didn't get on with vibraphone or xylophone, because he didn't read very well himself. I think with percussion, more than most instruments, you learn most from just playing. Any date – 'No money. You'll get a cup of tea. Oh, and bring your own music stand' – that sort of thing. I did a lot of that.

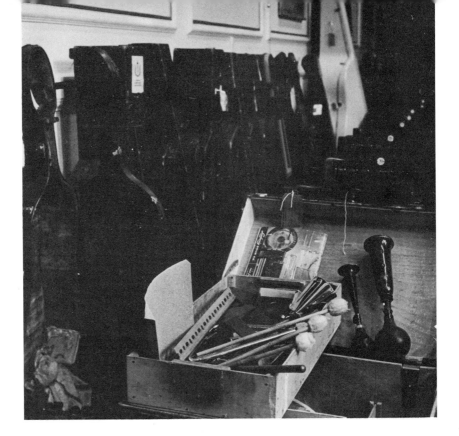

Motor horns have been used to give zest to the percussion

In a way, playing in orchestra in college was a waste of time. An orchestral player, by the time he leaves college, should have played all the Beethoven and Brahms symphonies, some Haydn and Mozart, a bit of Wagner, Mahler, Strauss, *The Rite of Spring*, and a lot more – all standard orchestral stuff. Instead we'd spend six weeks rehearsing one programme, often as not with a duff conductor. And the rest of the instruction wasn't up to much. One hour a week on your principal instrument, half hour on your second study, and two hours of lectures – about what Beethoven had for breakfast. You don't want to know that, do you? You want to bash hell out of *The Rite of Spring*, see if you can get that right. For musical theory, we had twenty minutes a week. That's a joke. The bloke only has time to set the exercises and say, 'You've got parallel fifths, you'll fail the exam.' My teacher was very good. 'Look,' I'd say to him, 'I might have parallel octaves, which are against the rules, but I like them there. It sounds OK to me.' 'Yes,' he'd reply, 'but you must learn to mix the cement before you can build the house.' I asked him to do something else – teach me some orchestration. And I think that pleased him. And I learnt a bit about figured bass, though I'm only a percussion player.

I got banned from playing the piano because I was so often late. Old professors at these places still believe that you can't be a musician if you can't play the piano. My professor at the College, a pleasant old bloke, insisted I do two hours' piano practice a day. But there weren't even enough practice-rooms for pianists, and I wanted to play percussion and timps, not piano. He couldn't understand that. Finally, I was asked to

35

leave the College after a year and a bit, because I was deputizing in a West End musical instead of rehearsing in orchestra. I was earning money and getting experience. The registrar said either stay and give up outside work, or do that and leave. Now, if they had offered a good, tight training, then I think they can insist on no outside work. I thought about it. No question but that I wanted to be a professional musician, and I reckoned I was learning the job better from actual practice than in a school of music. That was the end of my formal training.

Schools of music here in England seem to do very little to prepare players for orchestral life. In a way, I agree that students shouldn't be playing outside and neglecting their studies. But the studies must be worthwhile and have something to do with life after college. Here in London the only way to get your playing known is to do dates and play well. The College is not going to get you a job. You get those letters after your name – A.R.C.M., L.R.A.M., and so on. But you go along for a date – say second oboe with the London Symphony Orchestra. They don't look at those letters, they listen to you. That's what it's about.

ANTHONY CAMDEN I can't think of many good things to say about the musical tuition. As an oboe player you could spend the whole of the week getting your reed ready for the lesson. No one taught reed-making and as you knew little about it, you relied greatly on the oboe teacher. Sometimes it was only in the last few minutes of the lesson that your cutting and sandpapering got a reed to go, then in five minutes the lesson was over. As for orchestral experience, I think I played in the orchestra three times in my four years, and on two occasions by coincidence it was the same piece – Dvorak G major Symphony. I got my playing experience outside the College, among the amateurs and evening students of Morley College – three pieces every Tuesday night. That's where I learnt the repertoire, not in the Royal College. Nor did the theory lessons do me much good. I resented getting to College for a 9 o'clock theory lesson, followed by an oboe lesson at 5 p.m., with no hope of getting a practice-room in between. Just one hour of oboe tuition a week. That was the justification of a full-time music student!

TOM STORER I chose to do National Service because the family was dead against me wasting any more time messing about on the cello. I should say that I was a mathematician at this point, maths and physics, and I had a university scholarship to take up. But I had to get away from home, and provincial lads didn't leave home quite so readily then. Military service gave me a breathing space. I thought a lot about music and did a lot of practice. Then I applied to the Royal College without telling anyone and got a place. I arrived home, demobbed, new suit, and announced I was going to the RCM. That would be 1950. Father cut me off with the proverbial shilling. I could come home for holidays, but that was all.

The College was a disappointment, a hopeless training for an orchestral player. They just weren't interested in orchestras. This was a great surprise for me, because I'd been brainwashed in the National Youth

Orchestra, which did a marvellous job dignifying the orchestral player. But like so many string players, I went to college with no idea of actually becoming an orchestral player. I had some dizzy notion of joining a chamber orchestra. Or better still, forming a string quartet — if I could find three other mugs who'd live in a railway carriage. I was very high-minded. I didn't want to be a soloist, but chamber music was the thing. I was perhaps a difficult student. Starting so late, I needed technical help, and at twenty-one I was too old and independent for a certain kind of teaching. I was awkward and insecure about the cello, but of course, looking back, I see I did learn valuable things from my teacher. I did my stint in the orchestra, a few standard works very much stuck in the late-nineteenth-century repertoire. Nothing modern, unless written by a professor, and definitely nothing baroque. I remember trying to get the harpsichords in the College collection out, get them working. But for the College, those instruments were museum pieces, safer behind glass. I mean, Bach was all right if he was brought up to date, played on the piano, or rescored for hundreds of strings by Stokowski.

In my last year, I thought I should probably aim at joining a symphony orchestra. I'd done my share of amateur orchestral dates outside, pretty poor stuff, 30s. plus the bus fare. But I had no contacts in the profession and no clear plans. I just started writing away for auditions. Then I heard that the London Symphony Orchestra was auditioning, and they accepted me for extra work, to my amazement, for I hadn't finished at the College. Six months later I got a membership of the LSO. I've been there ever since.

I remember the registrar at the College asking me if I was playing with the LSO. 'Yes,' I said, very proud. 'Pity,' he replied, 'I thought we'd make something of you.'

On tour in East Europe in 1974, members of the Royal Philharmonic Orchestra take part in a wedding celebration

Better Ways

JOHN DE LANCIE In 1936 Tabuteau accepted me as a student in the Curtis Institute. I was fifteen. Our hope — we wind players — was to join eventually one of the major American orchestras. But in the case of piano, voice, violin and cello, yes, they all thought, and still think of themselves, without exception, as being potential soloists. The new Heifetz, the new Casals. Now, we know in life that it doesn't work out that way. Very many of the string players will play in orchestras. But it is not a bad idea to start off with the aim of being the best. It requires that kind of mentality to push you to a level of excellence. And the Curtis Institute also paid great attention to orchestral playing. When I was a student Fritz Reiner was the conductor, and we had an orchestra that was, I would say without hesitation, only inferior to the three or four best American orchestras. My class alone provided the solo oboes for about seven major orchestras. And so it was with the other instruments. Today, fifty-five members of the Philadelphia Orchestra are from the Curtis, many in the New York Philharmonic, in the Boston Symphony, and so on in all the good American orchestras.

I don't think orchestral training is that much of a problem in America. Of course, the Curtis Institute, Julliard, and the Eastman School train the bulk of our good orchestral players, and it's not too hard for those few schools to attract teachers of quality. I think the common complaint, that students don't get through the repertoire, is not valid. More important is the lack of very high quality training in the student orchestras. That's the problem. Curtis was successful in the old days very largely because Reiner ran the orchestra. He worked the students the same as a professional orchestra, and it was a brutal, excruciating experience. He accepted nothing less than the best. No music school is going to produce players that really understand the orchestral trade unless it has a top-notch conductor. A third-rater doesn't understand what the orchestral profession is all about. A young violinist, to become a great performer, needs a great teacher. We agree on that. Why, then, do we expect to train great orchestral players under third-rate conductors? How do you get first-class conductors? Money will attract them.

For many years the orchestral programme was seriously neglected at the Curtis Institute, but since I've become the director we're starting a plan similar to the one that produced the great success of forty years ago. We don't go through a large repertoire, but any concert we do is prepared and played to the limit. An intelligent student doesn't need to play all the Beethoven symphonies, or the 100 odd symphonies of Haydn. If a student knows how to prepare a few works from each musical era, then he or she can apply that lesson and way of working elsewhere. It's physically impossible to put students through all the repertoire. But you can successfully train them for four or five concerts in the school year, taken by a really fine conductor, and prepared to the ultimate. We were trained in that way, and when we walked into the major orchestras we seemed to know what to do.

A limited amount of music has been written for the trombone so music for other instruments is often adapted for the trombone as practice pieces

RAYMOND PREMRU I had just the right teachers when I went to the Eastman School in Rochester, aged eighteen. Education in America is very well organized. I have a great admiration for my English colleagues. In the past, opportunities for good tuition have not been as good as today. Consequently many fine players here in England are practically self-taught. But I am grateful for the system in America because it threw in my path the right two people for me – Gladys Leventon for composition, and Remington for trombone.

At Eastman, there was a great concern about security – how times have changed! – and the chances of getting a job in an orchestra in America seemed very slim, a thousand to one perhaps. And the odds against a composer were even worse. So I intended to teach in the public schools, as I suppose most students did – for security. But then I thought that was not what I really wanted to do, so I changed and went all out for composition and performance. So much for security. I think Eastman gave adequate orchestral preparation. The teaching was good, by people who worked from experience, having been principals in various orchestras, so they knew the task in hand. And yet they didn't just teach the repertoire, and that's that. That can be bad, because the real nature of the instrument may be neglected. Remington for instance, his approach to music and the trombone was through breathing and singing, based on *bel canto* style. Certainly we played trombone pieces, but the trombone is short of good literature, so we pinched a lot, like the Bach cello suites, difficult but marvellous, for expression and phrasing. We played a lot, a lot of wind ensemble works, and a lot of orchestral playing. But Remington himself didn't spend much time on orchestral repertoire. That's not so necessary for a brass player, you can always pick it up. But a sense of musicianship, a sense of style, to play a line and interpret the music – that's what is important, and what Remington concentrated on. So many orchestral players, if they are not first chair players, can play the subsidiary orchestral parts, but are lacking in overall musicianship.

(overleaf)
The orchestra rehearses in
the Henry Wood Hall

(opposite)
André Previn

ALFIO MICCI At Eastman, unlike Julliard or Curtis, we had a broad educational base. We studied English and philosophy, languages — academic subjects — as well as orchestral training, theory and counterpoint. Most of us intended to become music teachers. In fact, I too thought I'd be a college teacher, because I didn't know . . . Well, I knew I could never be a soloist, I wasn't that good. While at college I did play in the Rochester symphony, and enjoyed that, and thought about an orchestral career, but the orchestral seasons were then very short, except for the three or four major orchestras. This was 1940–41.

But the Eastman School had prepared me well, stressing the orchestra much more than solo playing. We covered the repertoire pretty well, and I happened to be a very, very good sight-reader, which helped. A lot of the graduates from Curtis and Julliard could play in the orchestra if they practised ahead of time. They had concentrated on solo playing to the detriment of ensemble playing. I don't know that Eastman produced any outstanding soloists, but we sailed into orchestral jobs very well trained.

PETER HADCOCK In my third year at Eastman I had a lucky break. The Buffalo Philharmonic, about sixty miles from Rochester, found themselves a clarinet short for a tour. They were doing *Till Eulenspiegel* and Prokofiev 5, and needed someone to help out on either E flat or bass clarinet. Thank my lucky stars, the job got passed to me, so I played the tour and was later offered the E flat job. There I was playing professionally two years before I'd finished college. I found I could shuttle back and forth between Buffalo and Rochester pretty well.

Being a student bears no comparison with being a professional. All the things I'd been told as a student, which I thought a line of bull and nitpicking, I suddenly realized, they're important. So in my last year, when I was already playing in Buffalo, those lessons at Eastman were a goldmine to me. The guy I studied with was the best teacher I could possibly have had. I loved Eastman, I really did. I had this job and I was committed to orchestral playing, absolutely. After I left I used to think back to what it was like. Within a couple of years at Buffalo I was first clarinet, and when you're young that's the job to have, if you're first you're fantastic.

I didn't find it difficult going in so young, still a student. No, really I didn't. I found the standards lower in Buffalo than at Eastman. I could hardly believe it when some poor horn player just barely squeaked through an orchestral solo. People would shuffle and murmur 'Bravo', but it wasn't that good, it certainly wasn't perfect. Our teachers at Eastman knew orchestral playing, and they were excellent. They got the student orchestra sounding very good. And then going to Buffalo, for a while I found it a shock, because the playing wasn't so good.

RONALD BARRON Cincinnati was something of a cultural centre. A lot of Germans settled in the valleys there, right around the river. Being, you might say, the farthest south of the northern cities, Cincinnati tried to reach kids in the south. In the United States you often have to go a long way for special training. Now, I have students from Oregon, California.

below
Ronald Barron

This summer a fellow from South Carolina is studying with me. He's the trombone teacher at the university in one of the towns where I grew up. That turns me round — to come a thousand miles to see me! I'm not so much impressed as fascinated. In this profession, if people think you're good they'll come to you.

Anyway, in Cincinnati I started at the bottom of the heap. I wasn't good enough for the wind ensemble. The next year I got into the brass choir, playing bass trombone. I was a scrawny little runt and I could feel my chest expanding every couple of weeks, huffing, puffing, working overtime to keep the instrument going. In my third year I got good enough for the orchestra — third trombone, I thought that was just great. I was having a ball, because there are some good parts, a lot of roots in the chords, you just fill up the horn and honk away. I see now I was developing a sound, an orchestral concept in sound, filling the instrument, adding to the elementary technique I learnt as a kid. I don't think that's a bad idea, getting a student going with a nice sound, blowing through the instrument and waiting for physical development to add fullness. Finally, I was principal in the orchestra and in the brass choir. Also, to defray a bit the cost of education, I did some time as copyist for the marching band. All the marching arrangements were originals. The football games, where the band played, were coming right up, so they grabbed me and said 'Get home and copy these parts.' Little lyre parts, about three inches by five inches, that needed meticulous copying. I burnt the midnight oil. But I'm happy I did that, because the marching band is a unique part of the American brass tradition.

I got a music degree. By necessity most of the students there aim at a teaching career. I wanted to play professionally, that's the reason I bothered to go, but the competition is so fierce you must approach that ambition with a lot of reservation. However, since I did make it as a professional, I see the music education at Cincinnati was good for me. It satisfied two criteria. First, there was a teacher, Ernest Glover, whom I respected and with whom I wanted to work. Then there were good players around, and plenty of opportunity to hear all kinds of music. Cincinnati had a good, full-time, big symphony orchestra. I guess I must say now that they had run of the mill artists and conductors, but I heard the standard repertoire for the first time by a good orchestra, which knocked me out. And looking at the orchestra on stage, I could see my teacher there, in the brass section. Ernie had been around for a long time. He had played with Frank Simon in the Armco band as a soloist, then joined the orchestra. He'd produced a real good environment for brass players in the conservatory, and that helped the orchestra. His students kept coming in with a unified approach and the same style of playing. The blend of the trombones I admired, and the trumpets and low brass really played well together. As I look back, I've changed my thinking perhaps, I'm a different player. But at the time it was great, very good for me.

CSABA ERDELYI At fourteen I took the very tough examination for the Bartok School for Music in Budapest. I was accepted on the violin, and from then on our general education served the purpose of becoming a musician. By 11.30 each morning we were free for music. The teachers, both academic and musical, were excellent, really hand-picked. Now I see that my teacher wasn't brilliant in technique, but she was an all-rounder in the Greek sense of education, for body and for mind and for music. Just what I needed, to equip myself for the battles of life. I still have the exercise books with all the comments on my playing, and I read them now with great interest because they dug very deep.

When I was eighteen the professor from the Academy of Music came to look over the entry for next year. And to my great shock he said he wouldn't recommend me for the fiddle faculty. 'Maybe on the viola,' he said. I didn't listen too much, just practised for the examination on the violin. I thought I played well, and a note arrived confirming my entry for the next year. I went away on a happy summer holiday. But when the year began, I didn't find my name in the violin class. I went to the office — surely there was some mistake. 'Oh yes,' they said, 'you are supposed to be in the viola class.' So he had remembered, but it was the most awful shock for me. I didn't play the viola, I didn't even have an instrument. The ground just slipped away. I became ill and was nursed from one sickness to another. Finally I presented myself to the viola professor.

He is a great soloist, the Lionel Tertis of Hungary. His name is Pal Lukacs, and before him the viola was not a proper study in the Academy, it was a sort of by-product of the fiddle, a second study. But he put the viola on the map in central Europe. I told him I could not help myself. 'I don't think I want to play your instrument.' I had to get a viola from the store-room, and all I could find was a *huge* ugly box. It was so large I couldn't reach the notes in the first position. I took that to my first viola lesson. A complete disaster, and I became ill again. So for two terms I didn't have a proper lesson. Ulcers appeared on my body, and I couldn't explain that they were not blood-poisoning, just nervous tension. At the end of the first year the professor said he couldn't give me a mark. 'You are stretching beyond your limit,' he said, 'I suggest you go back on the fiddle and take the teacher training course.' That of course was a terrible degrading thing to say. My pride just went purple, and on that huge viola I practised until I produced something, which was by no means good, but showed my will power, and Lukacs gave me the next year to prove myself. I made sure I got a better, smaller instrument for the next year, and then I made a reasonable showing which secured my place among the average students.

I suppose it is quite difficult for a student to go from violin to viola, but for me it was terribly hard because I just didn't want to. The approach is completely different . . . if one is still groping. Anyway, that was the second year. I knew inside me that this terrible period would pass, because I found I was stronger than most of the successful students. I had a friend with very easy fingers, one of the virtuosi. Today he is sitting at the back of an orchestra, with a big belly and a couple of children. He does

Musicians may have to play in unlikely surroundings. The Royal Philharmonic Orchestra visited Rila Monastary near Blagoevgrad, Bulgaria, on their East Europe Tour, 1974

not look happy. His life has overrun his easy fingers and facility on the violin. So in my third year I won an international competition as a student, on the viola. That made my professor teach me seriously. Then we had arguments about music and technique, because although I was very, very green, I had so much assurance of what was right for me. He saw red and thought I was impertinent. At one point he refused to teach me any more, and when my lesson came he went to the bar for an hour. Our relationship was full of trouble, but I have great respect for him, and when I go back to Hungary now we have a great time.

I see now there is a stronger teaching tradition in Hungary than in England. In the Academy in Budapest there was one very tough training for soloists, chamber musicians, and orchestral players. There were demands that you met or you fell out. You see, Hungary is a small country, with only one Academy. There is a great competition for places. And under the present State system, the Academy takes some responsibility for the careers of its graduates. So whatever goal one might have in mind, everybody goes through the same drill. The instruction is constant and highly intensive, and goes on for five years. We covered a great deal of repertoire, and anyone who couldn't manage the demands of the instrument, or the music, was just dropped.

Alternatives

ANTONY PAY It was not in my mind to become a professional musician. I had this idea to make a career in science, and went to Cambridge to read mathematics. But from the age of thirteen I had been in the National Youth Orchestra, and musically that was probably decisive, because that was an orchestra of very high quality — at best approaching professional standards and surpassing bad professional standards almost all the time. Everybody is keen and enthusiastic even if the technical side is sometimes lacking, and the conductors are always good. So I had several years in the NYO, and it was certainly clear that music was an important part of my life, though I still thought it wasn't essentially a very serious thing to do. It was serious to do something more intellectual — maths. But I was rapidly aware that there were so many better mathematicians than I at Cambridge, yet at that time there were no better clarinet players at the university. So it seemed sensible when I left, to concentrate on the thing I did best, specially since I spent so much time playing the clarinet that I ploughed my exams in the second year.

JOHN FLETCHER For me, as for others I know, the National Youth Orchestra was a wonderful training, a forming point. In the NYO, and at home, I was encouraged to regard music as a hobby which one must pursue seriously and to the very best of one's ability. The thought of going into the profession never really occurred to me at that stage. Then, about my third year of university, I suddenly found something happening to me as — I've been amused to observe — it happened to others who went to university to get proper degrees in proper subjects leading to proper jobs. My degree was in chemistry and natural sciences, followed by a Dip. Ed. I was going to be a teacher, like the rest of the family. Then I had this horrifying thought that the Cambridge University Orchestra would probably be the best orchestra I would ever play in, for the rest of my life. Would I tell my children, with some resentment, that I might have been a very good player? So I decided to have a go at the profession.

I played the horn in Cambridge most of the time, and a little trombone — the tuba was too cumbersome to cart down from Leeds. Cambridge was then the most remarkable centre for amateur music-making. Playing at a very decent level but with great innocence, one could get through an enormous amount of music in a very short time. Always on too little rehearsal, and if anything went wrong we could only smile. But I look round the profession now, at my vintage, and see so many players from Cambridge University, and all people who went there with a vague view of doing a 'proper' job. It's an uncomfortable fact that not many of the *music* undergraduates at Cambridge were much good at playing. But we were separate from official university music, Fred Karno's Army, packing in whatever we could — orchestra, chamber music, playing for pleasure in the privacy of four walls. One heard remarkable playing, good as well as bad.

On the face of it I'm envious of those who had a proper musical training

Rehearsals can be dull when a musician is waiting to play

at music college. All that time doing long notes and arpeggios, tonguing exercises, working on music in practice and theory. I just got up and played things, did what I was good at and ignored — or had to ignore — what I was no good at, which of course is a rather shaky foundation for a professional musician. One lives with that — no proper technical grounding. But having taught for the last twelve years at places like the Royal Academy of Music, I find the time wasted very distressing. In theory there is all the time in the world, yet in fact students may just piddle about. I believe that if you're stretched and interested, you can do more in half an hour, packing practice into a corner of the day, getting at it in a concentrated fever, than you can do in a whole day of official time-tables. Those people reading science at Cambridge, who have walked into posh London orchestral jobs, did they really have time to do all those arpeggios properly? Surely they just worked with more intensity and intelligence.

And I wouldn't be surprised if I didn't get as much orchestral experience at Cambridge as I would at a music college. In the London Symphony Orchestra we still take on board people who've never played Beethoven symphonies, never seen them, and were never encouraged to see them. That's very, very sad. And there are still fiddle players perfecting the Cesar Franck Sonata, which they'll never be asked to play after college. I wonder, does everyone expect to be a soloist? That's hideously unrealistic, so stupid. But there is this tradition, specially among strings, that nobody wants to play in an orchestra. It's awful to think that people are sliding into orchestras because they couldn't play the Franck Sonata or the Beethoven quartets. English orchestral players have certain virtues, like their fantastic sight-reading ability. That comes from necessity, from the way we work. But our training is defective, unbalanced.

ROBIN McGEE I was a pianist at the Royal Academy of Music, but after a year of that I went into the Army for three years, into the cavalry as a pianist. Nice image, isn't it? Playing the piano on a horse. But with the Household Cavalry I played the piano a lot and the trumpet a little — very badly. Later, having finished at the Academy, I taught the piano. I'm naturally gregarious, I like people and like working with them, and already I was feeling dissatisfied with those lonely hours shut up with my piano. I went to Germany with my brother, playing piano and violin stuff, and at Bayreuth I was allowed to sit in the opera-pit with the orchestra. That was a new world — Wagner. I thought 'I'll never get anywhere near this marvellous music on the piano. The only thing is to play an orchestral instrument.' I heard of Stuart Knussen, whom I didn't know, who claimed that he could teach anyone to play the bass to a respectable standard in six months, specially if one had a musical background. I thought that's what I wanted to do, to play in an orchestra. I was tired of the lonely key-bashing of the pianist. So I met Knussen and he got me a bass and gave me free lessons for a year, which I later repaid him. And within six months, obviously with his influence, I *was* playing in an orchestra. The thing was that I could always read what I was sup-

Robin McGee

posed to be doing, even if I couldn't play it. Bit like now! I knew the musical demands, it was just a question of getting them on another instrument. I felt I had a chance on the bass, because it was so neglected. There was no definite school of playing. I don't know if there is one even now.

Knussen was my only teacher. I began to do extra work with the major London orchestras, but I also went to places like Bexhill, deputizing for the princely sum of £2. Just a municipal band on the sea-front, but some good players went there, and I learnt a lot, having to play by myself. Eventually I got on the extra list of the Royal Philharmonic and enjoyed the last days of Beecham. I was very green, and found the work terribly taxing. I was trying to learn the instrument and the repertoire at the same time. Now, when I'm teaching, I try to help people avoid that tight-rope. Knussen helped by making me practise Brahms symphonic bass-parts from the start, marvellous music even in the bass line, and a lot of technique in them too. I had the one advantage of experienced sight-reading, so even if the passage was beyond me I knew when to stop trying, which saved me from wrong entries and mucking up the section. But to be on the Festival Hall platform, sight-reading the Bartok *Concerto for Orchestra* and Berlioz' *Fantastic Symphony*, as I actually did, put me off those pieces for years. It was such a shattering effort trying to stay aboard. Well, with next to no technique and no experience either it was unbelievably hard.

I definitely wanted to get into an orchestra. I auditioned for the BBC Concert Orchestra and played grotesquely – staggered through C major – but was offered the job. I was amazed. Tausky, the conductor, said, 'This boy is a pupil of Knussen. He will be good.' 'OK,' said the principal bass, 'but he won't stay. When he's learnt the job here, he'll be off to a symphony orchestra.' 'No, no,' said Tausky, 'he'll be a good boy. He'll stay.' Luckily, no one asked me if I would stay. Six months later the Royal Philharmonic had a vacancy for no. 4, and I was only no. 4 – and last – with the Concert Orchestra. I auditioned for the RPO without telling Knussen. His name and influence had got me into the Concert Orchestra, I wanted to do this on my own. I was offered the job, did a bit of grovelling at the BBC and asked to be released. They were fairly furious, not unreasonably so, but they did release me, and I was off, a fully-fledged orchestral bass.

ALAN CIVIL For good fiddle playing a kid has to get going early, but lots of brass players don't touch an instrument until their late teens. An early start on brass can be disastrous — too much pressure on growing teeth. It's amazing, the dental X-rays I've seen, of teeth forced right back. Kids start blowing brass instruments the wrong way and by fourteen or fifteen they can play in a certain manner, but it's all wrong, and when the muscles are fully developed they won't be able to play at all. I know horn players like this, and by then it's almost impossible to correct.

I started with Aubrey Brain, but I don't think he was a good teacher. He could play, and if you used your loaf you could listen and copy. But he didn't explain the embouchure, the breathing, the control – just 'You missed a note. Do it again.' Looking back, I think the way people learned in England, specially horns, was entirely due to the players themselves, listening and sorting things out. There's no tradition of musical teaching in England. You fall into it, as second best, if you can't get into an orchestra or don't make it professionally. You *resort* to teaching. Now, in America, many musicians set out to be teachers and are properly trained, and their players benefit.

Fortunately for my playing, I joined the Army. I would have been called up anyway, towards the end of the War, so I thought I'd better get into something musical. I volunteered – about the only time ever – for the Royal Artillery band in Woolwich, a huge establishment of over a hundred, with an extremely good orchestra, lots of talented musicians drawn in by the War. Quite an eye-opener. I signed on and did nearly nine years, leaving in '52. From Woolwich, I could continue lessons and also start working in London — West End shows, that kind of thing. I practised a lot, in those Army days, sometimes at six in the morning, to get peace and quiet in the band-room. Tuition was a bit of a problem. I had some private lessons, and tried to get to the Royal College, but then we were off to North Africa and I had to drop out. I had a little spell at the Guildhall, and a short time at the Academy, but I never completed any course. My plan was to leave the Army and possibly go to a music college. But I was establishing a slight reputation and was getting so much work that I by-passed the colleges. I came out of the Army on a Tuesday and was working with the Royal Philharmonic that same day.

I don't think I missed anything. I flitted around, gleaning what I could, playing anywhere. The great experience was in this huge Artillery orchestra at Woolwich. It was a military band, but was also capable of symphony concerts. We dabbled with all sorts of music, playing all day long, morning to night. There was possibly as much string playing as band playing, so I saw the proper repertoire, but we also went the rounds of the seaside piers and bandstands. Operatic selections from *Tosca, Bohème*, etc, with band instruments playing the singing parts. Amazing how different the real *Tosca* is from the version on Eastbourne bandstand. But we kept our wits about us, saw a bit of life, and a lot of music. No, I don't regret the lack of formal musical education.

John Ronayne

JOHN RONAYNE Very often musical training bears no relation at all to what is going to happen later. But then, the expectation of students is not always to become orchestral players. I don't honestly know what I thought. When I look back all that seems to have happened to a different person. Somewhere there's a break between what I was and what I've become since. But I do know I wanted to learn to play the fiddle as well as I possibly could.

I found the life at the Guildhall very nice, because I'd been isolated in Dublin. In my time, to be a fiddle player was a bit sissy. I was the only person in my whole school who did a thing like that, and I was rather self-conscious dragging my fiddle-case about. I remember I was excused games on a Thursday, to have my lesson. At the Guildhall, there were hundreds of musicians about my own age, and I used to spend all day in the place. I played a lot of chamber music, and poker in the brass room. I enjoyed it very much. It was a way of life.

Life

*With this, as the beer began to find its mark, there arose among the
musicians all sorts of discourse touching their art, just as sailors,
when they meet, are wont to talk of their winds, peasants of their cattle,
hunters of their dogs, and every man of what he can do and understand.*

F. E. NIEDT, *Musikalische Handleitung* (1700)

BILL LANG

MY father died when I was about eleven. My family came from
Mayo, but I was brought up in Yorkshire, on a small-holding in
the Pennines. We had a gramophone, one of the wind-up kind
with a big horn. And my dad played the flute, only as an amateur because
he'd been a ship's engineer who had a stroke when I was quite young,
but he still played a bit with a nice sound. That's all the music we had . . .
Oh, and my granddad, he could play the tin whistle like mad. He was an
Irishman. They played duets and I thought it was fantastic.

At the bottom of the fields there'd been a quarry and the company had
built a band-room there, nicely sheltered. I'd hear the band rehearsing,

Brass band day in London.
Some players of brass
instruments first played in
a village band

only a village band, but they sounded wonderful to me, and so I started. Before that, when I was nine, I'd take the rubber hose from my mother's wash-tub and play all the bugle calls on that, which made it terribly easy when I finally got a bugle. And then when I got to the cornet that seemed easier still. My father taught me to read music, but he didn't know the fingering, so a young man in the band wrote them down. I got an instruction book which showed me the scale and the chromatic scale, and then I was away. The bandmaster was a quarryman, living on the edge of the moors, but he was a good musician and did all the band arrangements. He got me this cornet. 'I want you up the house in six months,' he said, 'to hear what you can do.' Well, he sent for me rather early, after three months, and I could see he was pleased, though he was terribly strict. 'Can you go further?' he said. I got as far as a dotted rhythm, which I know beginners find difficult, then I must have made a wrong note. He said, 'No, no, do it again,' but he didn't tell me my mistake, so like a lad I made the same error — three times. 'Now what's this?' he said, a bit impatient, striking the kitchen table. He was giving me a hint and wanted me to say 'flat', but I said, 'It's wood.' 'And so is your bloody head,' he replied.

After that we got on well. I had no more lessons, but if I wanted to know something I'd ask him and he'd give me a little talk. And all the men in the band were very helpful, *everyone* in that brass band. By the time I was twelve I was in a dance band too. I had a Czech trumpet — all the cheap brass instruments came from there — which was quite good. I think it cost £4 5s. and I paid for it at 2s. 6d. a week, taken from what I could earn with it. I was only twelve. You see, my father died and any bit was useful. We only got 10s., but that was a lot of money in the thirties. I was helped along all the time, learning from colleagues, though I didn't go to anyone for lessons. As a kiddy, you imitate anyway, like a monkey, and you don't start analysing it until after. At fourteen I was living with my auntie and had just started working in the building trade. Sometimes I'd get home on a Saturday to find a telegram from a Leeds studio — a solo cornet had fallen ill, could I get up there? Away I'd go and sight-read, working in the dance-band had taught me that. I was only a lad, but I was expected to get the work done, and that made me get going very quickly.

When I was sixteen I was solo cornet with the Black Dyke Mills Band. There were four top cornets, going down soprano, E flat, ripieno and flugel. The principal played all the important stuff and the other three played the loud parts, all playing from the same music but leaving certain things out. After the War, I came back from the forces and won the cornet championship of Great Britain. And I had a quartet from the band which won the Lord Nuffield Prize six times in succession. So we really did quite well with the band while I was in it. And the repertoire — fantastic. Fellows like Elgar and John Ireland wrote for brass band, lots of beautiful works. And transcriptions, Wagner, Tchaikovsky, the lot. In something like Mendelssohn's Italian Symphony I think we could do those string passages better than the fiddles, because we could triple-tongue, you see.

I was brought up a stone-mason and bricklayer, that's my trade. And

I was quite happy working, building during the day and playing whenever I could, evenings and weekends. In fact, this last month was a bad one for us in the London Symphony Orchestra. We did *Star Wars* for John Williams and then we had scheduled several sessions on *Superman*, but those had to be postponed. So I took a couple of building jobs again, and very much enjoyed it. I built an open fireplace in bricks, the small hand-made rustics, and I paved the hearth a little bit fancy. I liked that. I've always loved the building trade. Well, my introduction to orchestral playing was really with the West Riding Education Orchestra, round the schools with only twenty-one players. That was three days a week and two short concerts a day. Then I was back on the buildings. The firm I worked for gave me time off, didn't seem to mind at all. And I used to do Messiahs of course. There's a lot of that in the north of England, and I was in great demand, perhaps thirty in a season, Newcastle, Huddersfield, the whole North East, and right down to Lincoln. Then, in 1953, I got a letter from Barbirolli asking if I'd go and play for the Hallé Orchestra. The fellows I worked with said I didn't want to be a builder all my life, so I should go along, though I've always loved the building trade.

In the early days the Hallé was only a seasonal orchestra. It was Barbirolli who made it full-time. A lot of the players used to go to the seaside in the summer — Scarborough, Isle of Man — in the seaside bands, then back to Manchester for the winter season. Many of the old principals had been in the cinema-pit, and they were fine musicians, fantastic sight-readers. They told me that in Hamilton Harty's day they would put on a Mahler symphony with only one rehearsal. They had a lot of experience, playing all kinds of music. Well, I used to play a bit of jazz, swing and that stuff too. About 1947 I was in Ted Heath's band one summer, in Blackpool. Dennis Brain had just finished as guest artist. There was Stan Roderick, Kenny Baker had just finished, Jack Parnell was the drummer and sang too.

When I got to the Hallé in '53 everything was new, repertoire, everything. It was peculiar. Barbirolli was very nice to me, an extremely nice man to play with, and he offered me a job — 3rd trumpet, 1st cornet, and assistant 1st. I took it, and I was terribly disappointed in the beginning. In the brass band you play more or less all the time, but in the orchestra you rest and come in, but it has to be spot on. A different business altogether. Just a few notes, but important. I found myself hanging around the orchestral band-room a lot, and I was getting awful depressed. I had a lot of time to kill in Manchester, because I lived in Yorkshire and it wasn't worth going home between rehearsal and concert. I started going to a fine music library near the Free Trade Hall, just to kill time. And I got to reading, things like the letters from Bernard Shaw to Elgar on brass bands. Then I read Berlioz writing about Arban, the famous cornet player, and how Arban played a certain clarinet solo in *The Trojans* so much better than the clarinet player. I realized that's why trumpet parts in Berlioz are so duff, if not tonic and dominant just simple intervals, because the cornet has all the interesting parts. I learnt that in the Hallé. Before I would not have dreamt of going to a music library, because I haven't even been to a music school. But I was getting interested in my new life. Then first trumpet had trouble with his teeth and they decided to push me up to first. I told Barbirolli that I hadn't enough experience. 'I'm the one to judge that,' he said, getting on his high horse. 'Yes,' I replied, 'but you're not playing the bloody trumpet. You'll have to keep off my back for a while.' He did that, and I settled down and enjoyed playing for him. Then in 1961 I came down to London to join the LSO as principal trumpet. I've been with them ever since.

LYNN HARRELL When I was eighteen I tried out for the Tchaikovsky cello competition. I got to the finals but didn't win a prize. Then my mother died in a car-crash — my father had been dead a few years — and suddenly being orphaned I didn't know what to do. Leonard Rose, who was as much adviser and friend as cello teacher, said he thought there were two ways to build a solo career. Go through the ranks of an orchestra, save money, then leave, get a manager and start playing some solo concerts. Or win a big, international competition. I wasn't too keen on more competitions, and I thought, 'Well, Piatigorsky played in an orchestra, Casals did, Feuermann, Rostropovich, Rose, Starker. If it was good enough for them, it's good enough for me.'

Shortly after my mother was killed, I went to Cleveland to visit Robert Shaw, the choral director and an old family friend. I wasn't thinking of orchestras, or orchestral playing. I'd been doing some solo work. In the previous year I'd played sixty recitals in Canada, for Jeunesse Musicale. And in Cleveland, when I went along to play for George Szell I took a Beethoven sonata and the Dvorak concerto. But Szell heard me, offered me a place in the orchestra, and I accepted, though I had never played any of the orchestral literature. He hired me because I played well, that's what he said. He told me that I was there for my ability and not for my experience. I would make lots of mistakes, he said, but not to worry or get nervous, just play and try to relax, enjoy the music, listen and learn. That was a great relief, because before the first rehearsals I was struggling hours a day, trying to prepare myself. For I'd never played in an orchestra, not even a conservatory orchestra. But it was certainly a great thrill when I began in Cleveland, to hear a violin section like that, and solo winds play that way and so in tune. And I think, in a way, Szell was right to hire young, inexperienced players of ability, because then he could mould them into the kind of chamber musicians he wanted.

I had it at the back of my mind that I'd stay a short time in the Cleveland Orchestra — a year or two. But once I got to Cleveland I lost contact with my past, with Rose, with all my young colleagues from Meadowmount where Ivan Galamian taught the string virtuosos of America. I didn't see Pinky Zuckerman or Itzhak Perlman, and I felt isolated and lonely. Then, not having my soulmates to gripe to, I began to enjoy myself in Cleveland, a bit to my surprise. The key was music, and music in those Cleveland days was played so beautifully, and it was such great music. All new to me. I didn't know the orchestral repertoire, I hardly knew any Mozart even, not the symphonies, nothing. Rose told me, 'You

Coffee break during
rehearsal

go to Cleveland, study, practise the solos, I'll keep you there just a couple of years . . .' Well, after two years I was just starting to have fun.

I played in the section two years, then the principal cello chair became vacant. I asked Szell about auditioning. We discussed it and he decided to put me straight into the position – I didn't have to audition. I stayed with the orchestra another six years. Sometimes, then, I got frustrated, thinking I couldn't really express myself in a section. So I stopped for a moment and tried to analyze what had been so exciting at the beginning. That excitement came from a kind of innocence which led to discoveries. I hadn't known how to follow a beat. I hadn't known the repertoire. I hadn't known where to place my attention – sometimes watch the beat, sometimes keep half an eye on the beat but follow another section, sometimes lead with the cellos. Psych things out, you just can't be passive. The conductor has only a few big beats in a bar, and we've got a lot of notes to play. All that had been new and exciting. Then I realized, well, I was getting a little dissatisfied because I'd learnt those things. So I thought, let's try to explore the business further.

It came to mind first that very often I was going into the rehearsal not knowing the part, sight-reading it. I don't like the conductor having to tell me what to do, it takes away some of my creativity in the job. But unless I learnt the part, and even the piece, I'd be stuck in that position. OK, so I'll go over the piece. And getting the orchestral score, the full score that I'd never seen before, I found a whole new thing to do – to learn to read a score. That took a lot of time and effort. Then I started buying records – 'Oh, that fellow takes it at quite a different tempo.' And that got me trying to decide what I preferred, and why. And when a conductor came with a new piece, I'd try to put myself in his shoes. He would be nervous, with the Cleveland Orchestra for the first time. What would he say? how much rehearsal would he need? what parts would he work on, and in what order? how much time will he spend on this or that? And noting what he actually did, and comparing it with my expectation, suddenly I found the job once again so busy and interesting that I was really involved.

The fact is in the meantime I'd read a lot of musical writings and come across the book on violin playing by Mozart's father, Leopold, written in 1756, the year of Mozart's birth. And here is Mozart's father saying that an orchestral musician is more valuable than a soloist because he has so much music to play and so many different styles to play in. And I thought that was so true today as well. I loved being part of a huge Mahler symphony. I liked being rooted in one place with one orchestra. I liked the sense of communal responsibility in the section rather than the soloist's individual burden. That's where I was when I left. I was enjoying playing, enjoying the repertoire so much that I was in considerable doubt whether to leave. But I thought I'd better break the bond then, because in fifteen or twenty years I might not be able to. Family, or just too long in the orchestra, might prevent me trying the jump into other musical worlds. If I could not hack it then, financially or emotionally, I felt I would have missed out. For I thought I should be a soloist at some time, and I was curious what the musical worlds outside the orchestra were like. I thought I could always go back. So I left Cleveland, certainly a little prematurely to the way I was feeling, but in other ways it was an ideal time. Szell had just died and my contract came to an end. The management would hardly permit another yearly contract. Yet if I signed for three years, the new music director, whoever it might be, would have new plans and different ideas, and I'd get all involved with him, trying to work with conviction while he forged the orchestra in his image. So I thought I'd better get out before that all starts.

HUGH MAGUIRE My father was a schoolteacher, my mother a country-girl from the middle of Ireland. My father married twice. His first wife had six children, none of whom were musical. His second wife had another six, all of whom became professional musicians. Yet it was my father who was the musical one, a singer in the church choir. He made me practise before I went to school, playing my little pieces while he ate his breakfast. I was four when I began on the fiddle, very young, astonishingly young for a backward place like Dublin fifty years ago. I had a good teacher for whom I have an immense regard, not because he was a good fiddle player, or a very good instructor – I'm not sure he was either – but because he was such a stimulating man. He encouraged me to listen, to buy records, which were expensive for me. I listened to Kreisler, Heifetz and so on, and I learned as much from them as from my teacher. But he had a great ability, a great flair for encouragement. A very funny man. Great drinker, great gambler, and still is. When I go to Dublin I often meet him at the races. It's easy in Dublin, you get on a bus and in ten minutes you're there. You go into the bar, and there is my old teacher with his cronies. 'Sure, I've got a great tip for yer . . .'

In 1945 I came to London, where things were still fairly grim. I went to the Academy to study with a man called Spencer Dyke, who had heard me play in Dublin and got me to come over. He was very kind to me when I arrived in London at the tail-end of the War, city of black-outs, fog and rationing. We'd suffered shortages in Ireland, but coming here was a great shock. It was the first time I'd been away from home. Then my father died, bless his soul, and I didn't know whether to go back, to support my mother, or to turn away from home and continue studying. In fact, I managed to do both, though it meant absenting myself from time to time during the academic term, to go off on a ballet tour, or something like that.

My first professional dates were with the band of the *Ballet de Champs Elysées*, a French company run by Roland Petit. I think it was a nine week tour – would you believe the audacity of going off like that in the middle of term? But I needed the money. A marvellous German refugee family in Dublin had raised a small fund to keep me at the Academy, but I had to earn more to help my mother. So there I was, sitting at the first desk of this small orchestra, and after three weeks the leader left. I found myself leading, aged eighteen and still a student. Curiously, I didn't find that too tough, though I'd had very little experience. And I had all the big orchestral solos to play – *Swan Lake*, etc. I remember we also did a Stravinsky ballet called *Jeu des Cartes*, which I found *incredibly* difficult, just to keep in the right place. Some ten years later I met it again, playing as an extra with the Philharmonia, and when I sat down to it I was amazed at how simple I now found it. On that first ballet tour, I did not know the problems of a leader. It was a small pit orchestra, possibly not very good, and I just played, that's all.

The London Philharmonic had fixed this ballet orchestra, so I now found I had a connection with the LPO. I was asked to go along to play in the Albert Hall with a man called Bruno Walter, whose name I had only seen on records. That was most astonishing, because suddenly one was in the presence of a great historical figure, whose reading of the music was so illuminating, so stimulating. A wonderful experience. At that time, just after the War, the LPO was very much *the* orchestra. It fired the public imagination by reviving all those great conductors who'd been lost to

England during the War. Men like Walter, Furtwangler, Koussevitsky, Victor de Sabata, who was possibly the greatest, though he is forgotten because his career was overshadowed by Toscanini. De Sabata was the greatest, most musical conductor I ever came across, absolutely overwhelming, his knowledge of the repertoire, his control, his command. The thought, the study, the preparation . . . Well, I didn't know people like that existed.

But then there were the other conductors! Despairing of the general standard of conducting, and trying to avoid an orchestral fate, I went off to Paris in 1950, to take some lessons with George Enesco. I had no money, so I earned a living busking on the streets, and a very good living it was. It was quite easy to earn £5 a day – no, I could earn that in 15 minutes, and that would be like £20 now, or more. The whole secret of playing in the street is to choose your pitch well, then it doesn't matter how badly you play, as out of tune and scratchy as you please. Get a place where people have time to stop and listen. Piccadilly Circus at rush hour is no good. You want the quiet of the evening. I played outside the Sacré Coeur and had no competition at all. I had the whole place to myself and I never played for longer than 15–20 minutes at a time, simply because my repertory didn't last any longer. Tourists kindly advised me to take up the fiddle professionally. I played there most days, and when the summer came I had enough money for a holiday in the South of France. But I got arrested there. There was a big robbery and the police rounded up all the bandits and vagrants, including me. I was accused of disturbing the peace. I developed a great dislike for the south and hurried back to Paris.

Back in London, I was again with a ballet company as leader, touring, usually for 6 to 12 weeks. I met my wife there – she was a ballerina. Responsibility, the need to earn money – subtly I was being drawn into the orchestra life I had tried to avoid! We did a season at the new Festival Hall, 1951 I think, and I was demoted from leading because you couldn't have a kid leading a London orchestra. The man who took over from me told me there was a leader's job open in Bournemouth. I only knew ballet music, and I didn't want to go to Bournemouth. 'Go on,' he said, 'apply. Don't be stupid.' So I auditioned for Charles Groves and was appointed leader of the Bournemouth Symphony Orchestra. I was to do my first concert with them on a Thursday, in September '52. On the Monday and Wednesday of that week I was with the Philharmonia, sitting as an extra in the suburbs of the orchestra, with Toscanini conducting the four Brahms symphonies. Next morning, I was in Bournemouth, rehearsing for my first appearance that night. I'll never forget the programme: the Academic Festival Overture, which has a lot of notes, then Moiseiwitsch playing the Emperor Concerto – that I knew – and after the interval Sibelius 2. Now I'd never played the Brahms overture and the Sibelius, and there I was leading these works, with a new orchestra, having just looked through them that morning. A real baptism of fire. I managed to keep my head above water and Charles Groves was wonderful, kind, understanding and very able. In my one year at Bournemouth I learnt more than in the thirty years since, I can tell you that. We would do perhaps three concerts a week, all different programmes, and all live. And in the summer there was a concert every morning in the municipal Pleasure Gardens. Almost all was sight-reading. It was a great strain I'm sure, though I didn't notice it at the time, though I must have lost a lot of hair. I also got married. So there I was in an orchestra, doing what I had attempted to avoid. I just sort of slipped into it. And I was a leader already.

I blotted my copy-book in Bournemouth, unfortunately. I got a little too big for myself, wanting all sorts of changes, the best conductors, the best players. I made myself a nuisance, and after a time it was obvious I'd have to go. But I wanted so much that our music should be very, very good. Charles Groves, of course, had the same ideal, but he was more practical, more realistic. I was a dreamer, too much so. I left Bournemouth and went to sit with Paul Beard on the first desk of the BBC Symphony for a while. Then the London Symphony had a vacancy for a leader. That was '56. There had been a great upheaval in the LSO, and they needed replacements quickly. There was a tour of South Africa planned, with Joe Krips, and half the orchestra had exploded and disappeared. I was brought in to lead. That was the beginning of an ambitious period in the LSO. Shortly after, Ernest Fleishman became manager, and he transformed the orchestra. He was fairly ruthless and overstepped the mark quite a lot – as I suppose many bold managers do – but he was worth it, I think. He simply told the public that the London Symphony was a good orchestra. Nobody had done that before. But if you tell the public something often enough, in the right sort of way, with the right sort of tone, then it has an effect. The public woke up to us, and we believed in ourselves, and began to give many fine concerts. The orchestra had a bumper period. Lots of work, lots of very good playing, many records, distinguished conductors, foreign tours. It was a happy time for me – 1956 to 1962 – one of the happiest. Great colleagues. And it's still the same, I think. It has remained fairly stable and has a great spirit, that orchestra. It's an orchestra that believes in itself.

RON BARRON Young musicians in the South feel they have to get away. Dallas and Houston have pretty good orchestras, but even there the players feel cut off. In symphonic music, most things are happening in the North East, with a few pockets outside, like Chicago and Los Angeles. And even LA feels a bit out of it. Fort Worth has a symphony, semi-professional, not bad. I had a chance to stay there, go to university, probably in a couple of years join the orchestra. But I too wanted to get away. And in my last year of music school, in Cincinnati, I was ready to move on again. I had it in mind to try for an orchestra, and I was tired of being a student. My teacher was a wonderful man but we'd covered everything we had to talk about. I was itchy to go.

I was ready to try my luck. There were a couple of vacancies at the back of the union paper – Montreal and San Francisco. So I flew off to Montreal, and they liked the way I played, but didn't want to hire me right away. That same week our jazz band from music school was in Chicago for a concert. Well, I played in that then struggled out to the airport with a suitcase, two trombones, and a great satchel full of heavy

Musicians tune up behind
the scenes before a concert

excerpt books for the night flight to San Francisco. I got there at 6 a.m.
At 9 a.m. all the auditioning trombonists showed up. Nobody knew anything, no one had a schedule, so we shuffle back and forth and finally
I'm given a time to play — 4 p.m. By that time I was beyond caring. But
there was some political power-play in the orchestra, conductor against
musicians, so they didn't hire anyone. I didn't know what was going on.
Couple of days later I was back in Montreal for final auditions. They liked
another guy, but he didn't want to play second trombone. The conductor
was in the process of firing everyone, so they said, 'Don't worry about it,
perhaps we can use you real soon. Come back later.' I didn't mind playing
second, I just wanted to play. So I got the job, though I knew nothing
about Montreal, or Canada. All my teacher said was, 'Don't take any
beer with you. It's better up there.'

My teacher in Cincinnati was so proud. He'd had his ups and downs,
and his students were a real sense of pride to him. He always said he had
more pupils in good orchestras than anybody except Remington. Well, I
went off to Montreal, and it was a new life. My parents, down in Texas,
thought I'd disappeared from the face of the earth, though they did everything they could to help me. I rented a U-Haul trailer in Texas, threw some
furniture and stuff in, then I heard they were on strike in Montreal. I got
to Cincinnati, camped out in the local tavern, practising by day, drinking
beer by night. I stayed with friends, a trailer-load of furniture parked outside. Eventually I got to Montreal. I guess I was making $160–170 a week,
which I thought was an incredible sum, in 1968. It wasn't too much, but
fine for me, a single kid straight out of college. I got a black-and-white TV,
a carpet, a sofa, a mattress on the floor. Of course, I wasn't really poor or
starving, I just wasn't used to the big, expensive city.

62

It seemed to me that orchestra hardly ever worked. Easiest job ever. I watched a lot of football games and relaxed. At first I didn't want to practise, but soon I got going again and had all the time in the world for it. But the season was only forty weeks, so I had twelve weeks with nothing to do and no money coming in. You see, I couldn't freelance in Montreal because I wasn't a local union member. It took two and a half years to get a local card, and you can't blame the Canadians for protecting their own members. So for twelve weeks I went back to Cincinnati, picked up a few dates as an extra with the orchestra there.

When I look back on Montreal I see it was an ideal chance to practise, to develop aspects of music and playing that the student life can never quite teach. And just working, being independent, made the couple of years I was there very interesting. I got to know the city and made a lot of French Canadian friends. I think musicians of all nationalities respect each other pretty well, but the conductor's activities made so much up-heaval in the Montreal orchestra that there was some friction. Innocent newcomers were sometimes blamed by those who'd been axed. The locals didn't mind the Americans in the orchestra, despite the fact that we tended to come and go, using the orchestra as a stepping-stone to better jobs. It wasn't a first-class orchestra, not by reputation nor in practice. That's too bad, because it could have been. My experience in Cincinnati had been weak strings and terrific winds. I found Montreal the opposite — very strong strings and winds all a mess. Everybody was different. In that way it was like a European wind section, individual, soloistic, not ensemble-minded. There were so many traditions all at work in the orchestra, even though there were — can you believe it? — no less than twelve Italian brothers playing in the orchestra. But the players were good, individually, with lots of flair and excitement. When I first came to the Boston Symphony I thought, 'Well, there's nothing that much different here.' The hall in Boston is better, the strings in the orchestra are deeper. But as to individuals, I found here at first a lot of things that didn't blend either. It's a question of attitude. In an orchestra with a reputation you're treated well, with a lot of respect, and you believe in yourself and the orchestra. In Montreal, the orchestral musician is a nobody.

Orchestras in Canada, with good players in them, were just provincial enough to lack confidence. They tended to be insular, not to go anywhere. It was somehow the same with the Montreal orchestra. For some thirty years it had never played in the United States. When I was there it became a big deal to play in Plattsburg, NY, just sixty miles down the road. They had done a European tour and went to Japan for six days, because the government footed the bill for Expo. Otherwise, the orchestra went around Quebec and Ontario — that was it. But Canada suffers from Americanism, and in Quebec the trouble is doubled by the French background. It will take a while to get a sense of confidence, but musically the orchestra was capable enough. Conductors came through and were impressed. It takes money and energy and dedication to support a first-rate, international orchestra. Montreal is certainly a rich, cosmopolitan city — marvellous. But the Québeçois is not sure he wants an international city with an international orchestra. There's no band tradition up there, such as we have in the mid-West, where kids almost cut their teeth on brass instruments and are technical wizards by high school. The poor brass teachers in Quebec get beginners practically, and then they have to meet the French desire for perfection. That's not realistic.

I was two years in Montreal, playing second. Then I was fired, not that they were unhappy with me, but because they wanted to move first trombone down. He was a little afraid of his job. He'd been second for years, and he didn't like the pressure of first with some young upstart — me — breathing down his neck. He stepped down, which meant I had to step out. They auditioned for first, and there we were two years down the road with the same two finalists — me and the guy they'd sent away before. And again they preferred him, and this time he took the job. So it was back to the vacancies in the union paper, and there was this opening in Boston. Boston, I thought, that's only a jump away from Montreal. Down I went, goodness knows what number in a pile of trombonists — about sixty I think. By this time I'd had some experience, travelled around meeting different players — just broadened out a little. Again I was auditioning for second, and again they couldn't decide. Others came and went and I kept going back, so I knew I had a good chance. In the middle of that I auditioned in Milwaukee, but they liked somebody else. OK, so now I'm back in Cincinnati, waiting, and in case I didn't get the job in Boston I arranged to go back to university, to work towards a higher degree. That's something of a let-down after being in a professional orchestra, but people do it all the time. At last I had a final audition for the Boston Symphony, and they hired me. Five years later the principal trombone became vacant, and rather uniquely I won the position from within the orchestra.

Musicians look closely at an instrument

In Another Country

Though music be a universal language, it is spoken with all sorts of accents.
BERNARD SHAW, *Music in London* (1890)

MICHAEL NUTT

YES, I was a Rostal pupil, at the Guildhall. He said, 'Well, Michael, we've got a lot of work to do, haven't we?' I was with him for two years and it made me for life, in some respects, though of course I already had the grounding – the Flesch system of fingering and bowing which you don't question but just accept, because they work. I only questioned a fingering once, in the Glazunov I think. I went over to the A rather than go down the E string – I felt I wanted to change the tone of a passage. Rostal asked if it was easier my way. 'Well no, not actually easier, but I like the sound better.' 'Good,' he said. That seemed a legitimate musical reason, mere convenience was not enough.

In college I was very interested in English folk music. I played country dance music two or three times a week in some good clubs down in Sussex. I went on to a square-dance band, following a craze the Queen brought back from Canada, and from there to country and western music. I remember returning to Rostal's class after one of these dates. I was unprepared, before all his pupils and acolytes, and there was a deadly hush when I finished. What had I been doing? Playing country and western for a week! But I'm always one for doing several things at the same time, and when I wasn't in the Guildhall I was in a group of American musicians from the services, playing round the American forces clubs. I don't know what that did for my training on the fiddle. Sight-reading is my failing, though it's the great strength of English players in general. Suddenly we seemed to run out of time, we were at the end of our schooling. I mean, I don't know how players transpose at sight. I know it's part of life for certain instruments, but then sight-reading is part of my life. I do what I can. I'm the one in a corner, in the rehearsal break, going through the passage. 'Woodchopping', we call it in America.

I auditioned for Barbirolli after college, who suggested I might like to sit in the Hallé for three months, just to see how I got on. In the second violins. But I was planning a journey to see country and western friends in Texas, so Barbirolli offered to take me when I came back. In 1957 I went to the States, formed a band in Forth Worth, Texas, and did the rounds. We did what I seem to have been doing all my life – enter competitions. In Fort Worth I also had a sort of DJ programme of my own, an hour a day on KCUL. Something of a novelty to have a fellow with an English accent

Orchestras tour extensively: the Royal Philharmonic play in Holland

playing country and western. On Saturday nights we had a stage show, from Cowtown Palace, and we travelled around playing gigs, night-clubs, entering competitions. The big event was the South West United States Old-time Fiddler's Championship, for solo fiddle, supported by a backing group. I won that, I think partly on the English accent. That Old-time fiddling, it's a certain style of double stops and cross-tuning, in a basic repertoire of American folk-music using both old standards and new tunes written as late as the fifties. The fiddlers are, in their way, very good. They do get beyond the first position, but how they do it I wouldn't care to say! Anyway, after about six months I headed for California on the Greyhound, doing odd jobs from town to town, and looking for a honky-tonk where I could sit in with the band. I'd play for a few dollars and a share of the kitty. It was rough going. Some place in Texas there was a gun-fight. Two men were shot dead, we just kept on playing. A rough territory. Eventually I got to Los Angeles and all of a sudden I was tired of it. The girl I was going to marry, who was playing in a ladies' trio in an English seaside town, was supposed to be coming to the States, but I thought the honky-tonk life wasn't for her. So I went back to England, scraped off the cobwebs for a few months and presented myself to the Hallé. My wife, a fiddle player too, also auditioned and joined the orchestra.

66

If you wanted orchestral experience, you'd be set for life starting in the Hallé under John Barbirolli. Specially string players. An incredible training, and everything he did was just right, though perhaps we didn't appreciate it at the time. Three-and-a-half-hour rehearsals in St Peter's School, top of the stairs, next to the mill with the trains running by. We studied there in a hard orchestral school. Sometimes five programmes a week, and always travelling, travelling. One time we'd done a concert in the Free Trade Hall in Manchester, and some harmless little man approached us in the street. 'How marvellous,' he said, 'to be in an orchestra, what a lovely life.' I'm afraid both my wife and myself had had it up to the neck, so we backed him into the angle of a shop and told him just what it was like. Eighty to ninety hours a week, counting the travelling, and for £8 10s. flat, rank and file. Home at 1 a.m. in the morning, off the bus from Buxton, out at 8 a.m. sharp next day on a bus for Sheffield. Rehearse when we get there, a black winter afternoon and no heating in the hall – 'It'll warm up when the audience arrive.' All the big and little towns within range of Manchester, day after day, and Barbirolli himself did most of the work, though we had that other fellow – can't think of his name – who used to conduct as if rowing a boat, and never looked at the orchestra. But basically it was Barbirolli full-time, more so than Mehta with the Los Angeles Philharmonic, and Mehta is with us a lot. Oh, those old-timers. Hell, I'm becoming one myself.

I was in the Hallé from '58 to '61. At the same time – don't ask me how – I was doing a series on the BBC, playing country and western, a programme called 'Smokey Mountain Jamboree'. Thirteen weeks at a time. 'Where's Michael?' Barbirolli would ask my wife. Oh, he's ill, the car's broken down – I was in London recording. Very naughty. I don't know if people would stand for that now. It was hard enough to get through the Hallé work but with the other stuff . . . And then another radio programme came up. I was now playing jazz fiddle with a quartet, and I appalled my parents, threatening to give up the classics altogether. I left the Hallé and joined the BBC Revue Orchestra because I was spending so much time broadcasting in London, it seemed ridiculous to stay in Manchester. My wife had to see out her contract, then she joined the BBC Variety Orchestra, which used the same studio as my band. I'd go out as she came in. We met in the hallway.

That was a new and interesting musical phase. In the Revue Orchestra one day we'd do the backing and sound effects for a radio comedy series. Next day we might have to play the *Lohengrin* Overture with six first violins. I remember the first time I heard Alan Civil, he was doing a Mozart horn concerto with us. After a while I moved over to the Variety Orchestra to be with my wife, and we sat together on the second desk. But she had back trouble which got worse and worse, and we decided to try a sunny climate. We wanted to go to Spain, but I couldn't get a work permit, so I suggested America. I knew I could always earn a living playing country and western.

We took off for America, emigrated. We got to LA on a terrible hot, smoggy day, arriving with thirty-two pieces of luggage and our old dog, a

125 lb white Great Pyrenean. We were heading for Hollywood, the studios called. I had to join the union, of course, and I think $125 got me a temporary card. How do you get work? I asked. Just go out and get it, they said. I thought I may as well start at the top, so I called on the local union president. I told him my story, and said, 'Can you put me in touch with the fixers?' 'The what?' 'Well, the people who fix the bands for the sessions.' 'Oh, the contractors.' He was so tickled he took me round the contractors personally, ribbing them about being 'fixers'. I got to meet them, to my great advantage, because in the States these men are union officers, booking work and supervising the sessions. They can just walk into a studio and ask to see the contract for that session, to make sure there are no non-union men. On that very first day I got offered a couple of jobs. I remember the first one was a one-night gig at the Beverley Hilton. I sat next to this young fellow, the leader – or I should say the concertmaster. Easy music, long notes, that sort of thing. He said he was in the LA Philharmonic – I didn't know there was such an orchestra. 'And who are these old gaffers behind us?' I whispered. I couldn't hear a note out of them. 'These are all studio musicians.' My mouth dropped. I'd thought that Hollywood studio musicians must be the cream of the cream. But these. . . .

I did a few more things, made some contacts. Then I got a call from the concertmaster of the LA Philharmonic who had been talking to one of my contacts. Would I fill in as an extra for a tour of Canada? I went to his house and played for him, and that's how I started in the LA Philharmonic. Again, just luck. After the tour they asked me to stay on. I think my experience in the Hallé helped me get the job. I talk to musicians everywhere and they ask what I've done. As soon as I mention John Barbirolli and the Hallé they are impressed, immediately. And rightly so. Also perhaps they thought that I, being new and English, would stay in the job and not flit off to the studios. In LA, if you are well in with the studios, you don't want to give up that work. And if you're not well in, perhaps you're not so good, in which case the Philharmonic doesn't want you anyway. I started in second fiddles, and I'm still in seconds. I'm quite happy there. I've never had solo ambitions, though I've done a concerto with the orchestra. But I had one nerve-shattering occasion, because I had a memory lapse. The conductor panicked, the orchestra of course kept going, and I kept going. The audience didn't know what had happened. But that was enough for me. I'm quite happy to be an orchestral player. I've moved up through the section and moved back again. And there I am today.

I don't freelance much now. My wife has been quite ill and has had three operations. Luckily, the orchestra pays for a comprehensive insurance, so I only had to pay twenty percent of bills that run into thousands. I don't teach either. Well, I'm too busy at home, with all sorts of schemes going, welding and construction. I designed and built an orchestral gong-stand because of something that happened to me. About six years ago we did a broadcast from the UN, including a special Penderecki piece. Because I'm not one of those fiercely dedicated fiddle players, I

Zubin Mehta rehearses with the New York Philharmonic at its home at Lincoln Center's Avery Fisher Hall, New York

sometimes get roped in to lend a hand in the percussion – in the Mahler *Symphony of a Thousand* I get to do the funny things with the chains. In this Penderecki piece I was in charge of the bamboo wind-chimes. It opened with a brush stroke on these chimes, unaccompanied, held until Mehta came in and stopped them. Have you ever tried to silence those things? You grab them and they wobble on their stand, making a god-awful noise. And this was on world-wide TV. I could see every bloody camera pointed straight at me. Exhibitionism again! But I realized that every orchestra in the world has the same remarkable percussion stands made out of gas-piping, clothes stands, things that fold suddenly or collapse. So I made up some stands and sold my design all over the country. I might have turned it into a business, but the materials got so expensive. I never seem to get much done with my schemes. I'm not single-minded, I never have been. Presumably that's why I'm still a second fiddle player.

RAY PREMRU As a student at the Eastman School I went to Europe for the first time – my first time out of America. Summer of '54. The Yale Dixieland jazz band had free transport to Europe and back, playing on a student ship, and needed a trombone. I said I didn't have any money. 'You won't need any,' the fellow said, 'we'll get a minibus and work our way round Europe.' Most summers I'd done factory work, railway work, I enjoyed some form of heavy labour, but that summer I just shoved off to Europe. We landed at Rotterdam. The immigration man said, 'How long you going to be here?' 'Twelve weeks.' 'And how much money have you got?' 'Well,' I replied, 'about $12.' 'Good luck,' he said, and waved me through. In Paris we played at the American Embassy for the 4th of

Raymond Premru

July, and for the students of the Sorbonne on Bastille Day. We got as far south as Rome, picking up a job here and there. I had always been keen on England, on the literature, the history, the life and art generally, and I wanted to get to England then, being so close. But there was a serious squabble between the Musicians Unions in America and England, and we couldn't go. I went back to the States and finished college and saved money with the intention of coming to England. I'd done a long time at Eastman. I wanted to go abroad to compose and to study composition.

By chance I'd heard a record of a symphony by Peter Racine Fricker, and I thought he was a composer who could help me. He was willing to have me as a pupil, so I got on a freighter, went way across the North Atlantic, round the Hebrides, and arrived at Hull on 1 August 1956. I came to London and began to study with Fricker. It was not in my mind to settle in England. But I was a country boy in the States and I never liked American cities very much. London seemed so quiet and peaceful by comparison. If I wanted to compose, I thought I had to either teach or perform as well. And if I wanted to play the trombone that meant living in a city and probably trying for an orchestral job. I just fell in love with London, and I thought why not try to stay and work here? But I had difficulty getting a union card. I wrote music, met an English girl who's now my wife, and after the necessary year's residence I applied to the union. They had reservations about me. Was it wise to give me a card? They seemed to think I might work two weeks then skip out pockets bulging with money. If I could get a work permit I could have a union card, and if I could get a union card I could have a work permit. That old catch. At last I convinced the union to make the first move, because they were smaller than the Home Office. Well, I got the union card, but the Home Office said they really didn't need any more musicians. My fiancée, an adventuresome girl, suggested we just go ahead and get married. We spent our honeymoon in the Aliens' Dept of the Home Office.

My wife was teaching and I was doing a few private things, but it didn't look as if I was going to get much work and despondently I thought I'd better go back to America. Then I had one of those lucky accidents. I'd done some dates with the London Philharmonic, out of town, and a vacancy came up for second trombone. Steinberg was music director then. They asked me to audition, and naturally I agreed. But just before that came up I heard of another audition for the Philharmonia. The bass trombone job. Now I'd always played tenor, never bass, but in those days the Philharmonia was *the* orchestra, though I think all the London orchestras are pretty well equal now. Anyway, I auditioned for Steinberg and the LPO, and they offered me the job. I was very pleased, but I was keener on the Philharmonia, if possible. It was a strange and awkward situation. The LPO knew I was broke and hadn't a job, and would ring me up every day to know if I accepted their offer. 'Well, I'm sorry . . . just a little more time.' Somehow I stalled them until the Philharmonia audition. And to my delight I was offered that job too. I switched to bass trombone and joined them in the autumn of '58.

Setting out parts before
the concert

Most players have some experience when they get to a major orchestra. I hadn't played bass trombone, I hadn't really played trombone for nearly two years because I'd been composing and studying. And except for the student orchestra at Eastman, I'd done very little orchestral work. The Philharmonia was my first job, and the only one I've had. In those days we might get to the Kingsway Hall in the morning for a recording session with von Karajan on the box. Some standard work would be on the stands – Sibelius 2, *Sheherazade* – but pieces which I'd never played. Straightaway von Karajan might say, 'Let's just put the red light on,' first thing, no rehearsal, and we'd record straight through. So I really had a lot of homework, get the scores out, listen to records, to make up for my lack of experience. Very frightening at times, but a good way to learn the repertoire quickly. I was fortunate in my section – that wonderful section of Alfred Flaszynski and Arthur Wilson – they helped me learn the job quickly.

I think it was two years before I could slightly relax. There was so much repertoire to learn. Luckily, I learnt it with the best conductors, so many good people came to the Philharmonia then. But life with our boss, Walter Legge, could be difficult at times, though he was always fair to me. He had a fine sensibility and a brilliant eye for conductors and programmes. The concerts he planned were always great occasions. I think he made von Karajan and Giulini. He certainly gave Klemperer the freedom to express himself which he never seemed to get elsewhere. But like all of us he fell short in some ways. One day, it seemed a conductor he respected just happened to remark on the trombone section. Was it as good as it used to be? That set Legge thinking, perhaps he was mistaken in his newest recruit – me. I suddenly found that the new schedules were not arriving, though not a word was said. So I made enquiries and Legge's assistant told me, 'Well, Raymond, your future with the Philharmonia is a little bit uncertain.' I think the attitude was, if Legge expressed dis-

71

The Royal Philharmonic
play in a classical
amphitheatre in Athens,
1975

pleasure you resigned immediately. So I went to see Legge. He said he was
a bit uncertain about me and was thinking of more auditions. Would I
be prepared to audition for the job I already had? Certainly, I replied.
My first audition had been for Flaszynski, Bob Walton and Dennis Brain
in the Kingsway Hall, and I couldn't think of anything more nerve-
wracking than that. Another audition didn't bother me at all. I went to
Legge's house in Hampstead. He had a big curtain up with the judges
behind and thirty or so applicants in front. We played. The next day I
heard that I'd been reselected for my own job. Well, I asked to see Legge
again. He was very nice and apologized – he'd made a mistake, what
could he do about it? 'Give me a raise, for a start,' I said, which he did. I
think that was very fair. It seemed my teething troubles were over.

72

CSABA ERDELYI In Hungary, when we were finished at the Academy, a job was found for us. Everything is controlled by the State, and the professors who taught at the Academy were also the directors of symphony orchestras and the planners of Hungarian concert life. If they recommend a student for a soloist's scholarship, then the State concert agency undertook to look after you. In my last years as a student I began to deputize in all the Budapest orchestras — the Concert Orchestra, the Radio Symphony, and the Opera. I was sitting at the back, finding that the spirit of Hungarian orchestras was not very clean, not very professional. There were few people to respect. In time, very often the players became just state clerks, has-been talents who gave up. The job gave a modest living until the pension arrived. There was no incentive to work for anything. That was quite sickening to my young, ambitious, enthusiastic spirit. I soon decided that I would not become an orchestral player in Hungary.

The Hungarian government sent me to England to take part in the Carl Flesch competition. My performance there, and the interest of Yehudi Menuhin and Sir William Glock, helped me to set a completely new course. In 1970 I won 3rd prize, and two years later the 1st prize, the first time a viola player had won. First and last time, for they changed the rules to violins only. It seems that the orchestras and festivals that promised engagements withdrew when they heard the prize-winner was a viola. Anyway, that success led to engagements in the West and some recognition back in Hungary. Menuhin asked what he could do to help, and I thought, having seen the West only for a few vague days, that working in the West for a while might help my musical and psychological development. A vast correspondence ensued, and after great troubles with Hungarian officials I was enabled to come to England. Menuhin gave me a scholarship to come to London and have some lessons from whomever I pleased. I'm eternally grateful to Yehudi Menuhin.

I started living in London and took some lessons. On the recommendation of Joseph Szigeti, I was invited to America, to play with Serkin and Casals at Marlboro. Casals played, I joined him in chamber music, and played under his baton. It was tremendous, just to relate myself to world standards. We are rather isolated in Hungary. But back in London, after the first golden experience, I began to find out what was bad, the cold, inhuman side of a large foreign city, where I had few friends and nothing regular to do. Of course I wasn't allowed to work — no union membership. I knew, if nothing else, that I didn't want to work in Hungary, having seen the orchestras there and the kind of life a musician leads. I met a girl in London. She started learning Hungarian and came to visit the country.

I felt instinctively, even before I arrived, that London was the place I wanted to settle in. Menuhin had introduced me to the Philharmonia who were looking for a principal viola. I auditioned and apparently they were sufficiently impressed to offer me the job in spite of the forseen difficulties, that I still was not a union member. It took another year, with many, many applications, and help from prominent musicians, to get a work permit and union card. Well, every foreigner goes through this, and I was still Hungarian, holding a communist passport. I think they were finally persuaded when I told them that my wife was an English musician who had little work, and without a permit I could not support her. I got my papers in my third year of residence, and second year of application. But I'm still a Hungarian citizen, and I have to pay ten percent of my earnings to Hungary, if I want to see my family or have them visit me. That's the price of it.

So I became principal viola of the Philharmonia and had to acquire and adapt to the needs of very quick sight-reading. That is the great English tradition that we admire in Hungary. I already knew a little about English orchestras because, of course, I had played with some as a soloist. And this was a real treat compared to my experience in Hungary. Even the so-called second-rate orchestras here have a much more honest approach to their parts. They want to do justice to what they are playing, whatever their level of competence. In Hungary the notes mean something different to every individual. They are all interpreters! What is good in Hungarian music is the thing we just can't help, the full-blooded tradition of instrumental playing, which is seen and admired in the West, in the colder climates. And what we admire in England is clarity, and doing justice to the music in a self-denying team-spirit.

It is marvellous in England that orchestras flourish in every town and community — amateur orchestras. They are everywhere, part of the national scene. Not very good — amateur or semi-professional — but at the same time it is an accepted part of social life to play an instrument, more or less, to try to make music with a good team spirit. That is something to work for. It gives great pleasure to the players, and to the audience. That is not so in Hungary at all. Well, I would say that musical talent is more abundant, individually, in the Hungarian race. And individuals do emerge and get trained to a much higher level than in England. But to play an instrument in Hungary is very physical. It's immediate to take up a fiddle and *feel* the touch of the fingers, and to want to produce passionate music, specially on a string instrument. This is unquestioned in Hungary, and one doesn't have to be a gypsy to have this attitude, this kind of blood. And this is a very fertile soil for musicians to grow out of. On the other hand, to produce a team, an orchestral team, is just not in our character. Everybody wants to find his own space and is not very adaptable.

JOHN RONAYNE Now, when I left the Guildhall, I left because they wanted to draft me for military service. Hell, I said, they wouldn't give me a grant, why should I go in the Army? I was an Irishman. I wasn't eligible for grants, but apparently I was fit to fight. And there weren't any grants from Ireland, though occasionally some private funds might be provided, made up out of church collections — not, I may say, from the Catholic Church. I'd saved a little money from my time with the Radio Eirann Light Orchestra, and my poor father used to send a quid or two, which he couldn't afford. In London, I picked up bits of playing, with local

Yehudi Menuhin gave Csaba Erdelyi a scholarship which helped him to come to live and work in England

74

Young players at the 5th
International Junior Camp
at Pecs, Hungary

choral and amateur dramatic societies. I played also in a dance band on
Saturday nights, a funny combination — piano, fiddle, sax and drums.
My Radio Eirann experience came in there because I knew all the tunes.
I was interested in, well, I suppose the pop of those days, Sinatra and
Crosby, perhaps because of the wonderfully lush string sections backing
them. This dance band had no music, but the pianist had a list of about
forty numbers, and would call out a tune by name. If you didn't know it,
you had to busk. Take the middle eight, play the tune, step back and let
the sax have a go. Thirty bob a night, I think, and I used to enjoy it.

Playing Irish ceilidh music. Some players like to join in with local bands and play impromptu music

Of course I reckoned I was an experienced hand before I got to London. I took my first job when I was sixteen, in a trio at the Gate Theatre in Dublin. That was 1947. There I was working among actors, seeing people who subsequently became famous, and I thought if this is the music profession, then it's for me. Then I rose to the Radio Eirann Light Orchestra. Third second fiddle — they only had three. Soon I moved over to the first fiddle section, which was very scaring, because there were only four of us and we used to play the ballet repertoire and overtures. Wednesday nights were worst of all — a half hour of Irish ceilidh music. Now, this is usually played without music, fiddle down on the belly in the Irish style, left hand in the first position. But to me these seemed very sophisticated arrangements, written down with 8vo over it, and I'd find myself right up in the stratosphere. Wonderful training, but I used to die every Wednesday night.

We didn't touch the symphonic repertoire. I'd never even heard a symphony orchestra until I started to go to the Friday concerts of the Radio Eirann Symphony Orchestra. I'm amazed now that I could live in Dublin and be so ignorant. A string quartet I knew nothing about, I thought it was a small band. Well, when I heard the symphony orchestra it seemed fantastic, a thing that size and with all that music. I thought I'd love to be in one of those. The radio orchestra was very cosmopolitan then, whole sections of foreigners, mostly refugees from the War, glad to be in Dublin where you could still eat steak and find salmon. And soon I had the chance to deputize with the symphony. So when I came to London, to study at the Guildhall, I had some orchestral experience.

After three years in London, when the Army tried to claim me, I had to go back to Dublin. I became an extra in the symphony orchestra. It was nice to be back and bask a little in the glory of a London training, among the fine players and the fine orchestras. And I was earning money — about £7 10s. a week. My father was upset because he thought I'd reached the end of my ambition, lazing in the Dublin orchestra, doing no practice, in the dance-halls every night. After six months I found I missed London, so I sneaked back to a different address, to avoid the heavies from the ministry who were still seeking me for military service. I had to earn a living so I auditioned for the London Symphony and got some extra work, and then for the Philharmonia and worked there too, and soon I was accepted by all the London orchestras. Deputizing. The no. 6 in the LSO became vacant, which I got, and then jumped to no. 4. But the orchestra was going through a bad patch, and I was unhappy there. Also, the London Philharmonic was going to Russia. I had not been anywhere and was keen to visit Russia, where no English orchestra had ever played. The LSO refused me leave of absence, so I resigned, went to Russia, and deputized once again when I returned. Then I joined the Royal Philharmonic at no. 6. Soon the sub-leader position became vacant, and I got the job, moving to the first desk to sit with Steve Staryk. They made it a co-leadership, only because the record companies were more likely to accept a fellow if he were called co-leader rather than sub-leader.

I was still in the orchestra when Beecham died and we entered a time of trouble. Kempe, who might have pulled us through by his wonderful talent, quarrelled with the remnant of the Beecham management and left, though he came back later. In '63 we heard this rumour that we were being dropped from the opera season at Glyndebourne, though Christie himself assured the orchestra that there was nothing amiss. And next season we were dropped and the LPO was booked. We had a ten-week tour of America coming up, and many players began to be scared of leaving London for so long and coming back to nothing. There was almost no work in the book. The orchestra was falling to pieces. I left at the end of the American tour. Like everybody else I'd had enough of what was going on, and I was physically worn out. Tibor Paul had asked me to go back and lead the orchestra in Dublin, with a very nice contract. I played the last concert with the RPO in Anchorage, Alaska, and went off to Dublin for a year. It was a very nice year, leading the band in which I'd begun at the back of the seconds. I played some concertos and had an easy life — a concert on Friday night and every weekend free. It came at the right time. Others left the RPO as I did, but I was a bit of a rat I suppose.

I'd always wanted to work on the continent, I don't know why. Perhaps the continental players in the Dublin orchestra suggested it. Germany in particular appealed to me, because it was a wonderful nation of musicians. A percussion player showed me the vacancies in the back of the magazine *Das Orchester*, and I noticed a job in Munich, in the Radio Orchestra, which looked very nice. I'd been to Munich and liked the look of the town. So I auditioned, got the job and was there for two years.

The working conditions in Germany are so fantastic. I was what they call Konzertmeister, and there were two of us — sometimes they have three. My fellow Konzertmeister actually lived in Berlin, so we cut the work between us, fifty-fifty, to our mutual satisfaction. He'd have a month off, then I would. And we had six weeks paid holiday a year as well. Your cheque came in regularly every month. We had an instrument allowance, a children's allowance, and a clothing allowance. Strings and rosin were free — that goes for all German orchestras. One of the fiddles was in charge of that, he had a big box and you took what you wanted. After the almost non-existent benefits of an English orchestra it was a strange luxury in Germany. At the start, when I was there alone, once a month they paid an air-fare to see my family in Dublin, and they paid 'hardship' money for living alone. Double salary at Christmas. How can you compare that with the miserable lot of the poor old English orchestras?

It's not easy to get into a good German orchestra, but once you are in the management and the band are most conscientious, more so, in my opinion, than in London. A lot of the extras in London, who of course are present in every string section of every London orchestra for every concert, are not really interested. Not being members, they wouldn't trouble to practise if they don't know the work. In Germany I found all the players most conscientious. Of course, Germans take a great pride in what's theirs, in their music and in their orchestras. On the other hand, I don't think the Germans play any better because of their wealth and security. You play well, I suppose, if you have it in you and are interested. The thing about the English system is you are more your own boss, and you have a much bigger variety of work. In Munich I saw the same people in that orchestra all the time, though I also did a fair amount of freelance work. I suppose, in a way, my musical life in Germany was a duller life.

Life was nice, all that time off, and I was enjoying what I was doing. But my children weren't too happy at German schools, and my wife, although she is German, preferred England. Had it been my choice alone I'd have stayed in Munich. The repertoire of the Radio Orchestra was not too exciting, but I could have moved to another orchestra. Well, I decided to come back, and had to look for something. Then I heard my old position with the RPO was vacant, so I went back to that. But it wasn't the same, nothing like the old days with Beecham, and I only stuck it about ten months. I got out of orchestras and into the freelance world, where I've been ever since.

Work

The professional musician, as such, can have no special social status whatever, because he may be anything from an ex-drummer boy to an artist and philosopher of world-wide reputation . . . Take a man with a quick ear and quick fingers; teach him how to play an instrument and to read staff notation; give him some band practice; and there you have your 'professional', able to do what Wagner could not have done for the life of him.

GEORGE BERNARD SHAW, *Music in London* (1893)

American Voices

ROLF SMEDVIG

Rolf Smedvig

M Y ambitions were . . . I really didn't have any. I was just going to work as best I could. I'd seen too many friends try for orchestras and failing. They got really frustrated. I took a number of auditions myself. I just took things as they came.

I started here six years ago, I guess. We keep four trumpets under contract. I'm assistant principal, which means I usually play third, and move up to principal when Ghitalla is away. In our orchestra, no two positions are quite equivalent, so when you bring up money to the management they say, 'Well, your position is a little different, but this is what we can work out for you.' When I came into the section at a young age I thought it was just great. No, I really didn't find it difficult. I mean, I think it's good to sight-read well, but for us, in the big orchestras, sight-reading is something in the past. In the BSO we know right now what we're going to play for the next year at least — sure, we know well in advance. If something hard is coming up, you practise say two months before, then put it away, season it so to speak, and know it really well by the performance. Only in the Boston Pops season do we get any sight-reading, and a lot of times that's only because you don't choose to look at the stuff before.

After a couple of years in the orchestra I began to get very critical. I thought, 'I've been training to try to get as close to perfection as possible. How come this guy sounds like that?' Now I'm starting to be a little more professional in my attitude, to understand why certain things happen. But I love playing in the orchestra, and took to it right away. I think any sensitive musician would take to it, given a chance to play in an orchestra like ours.

ROGER SCOTT After the War I went to New York, freelancing, but I didn't care for that because I'd grown up with the Philadelphia Orchestra, and my hopes and ambition were to join it. I had a chance to go to Pittsburgh, with Reiner, and for the first time I saw the rigours of a regular season, with programmes not rehearsed perhaps as well as you'd like, travelling about, on and off buses and trains, but always expected to play well — accurate, lively, artistic concerts. After one year I came to Philadelphia, in the fall of '47. The strange thing was that in six weeks with the Philadelphia Orchestra I'd already played as much repertoire as in the twenty-eight-week Pittsburgh season. I remember the first rehearsal of *Heldenleben*. Now, I'd never played the piece, but Ormandy went straight through, stopped to balance the off-stage trumpet, and I had no idea what had happened. It was an awful shocker for me. If I'd come straight out of Curtis, I have serious doubts if I could have lasted that season. Well, I got good sight-reading experience anyway!

RON BARRON I get a lot of variety with the Boston Symphony. We have the winter subscription series, then most of the orchestra plays in the Boston Pops — that's our spring work, about eight weeks — then we come to Tanglewood for our summer work. That's the basic year. All these endeavours have been pretty successful, and the management doesn't want to change any, just make each more profitable. Now, I think I'd enjoy a little more of the freelancer's freedom, but that's the opposite of the orchestral life, at least here.

We're busy, no question about it. We give about two hundred concerts a year, and in addition many players are out doing recitals, chamber music, etc. As a principal, I'm expected to be there. They hired me to be right there, in the orchestra, and you have to go through some bureaucratic trouble to get off. I'm the only principal who plays in Pops.

Experience comes very quickly in a big job like this. I was worried, after one year in the job, about hiring someone who didn't have quite enough experience for me! I remember making that comment after an audition, then thinking how stupid I was. 'What's experience?' Steinberg said, 'you can always get that.' Small orchestras, they are the worst, always worrying about experience. Rubbish. OK, it helps to have played a piece before, but a competent musician with adequate rehearsal and preparation of the part can get the job done. In Montreal there was a big deal one time because a pianist got sick and we had to substitute Brahms 1 at the last moment, which any orchestra should know anyhow. A competent orchestra can sight-read that any time. In Boston it would be nothing, just like rolling off a log.

JOHN DE LANCIE The system of co-principals is coming in America, but it hasn't reached Philadelphia yet. It's existed on the continent for a long, long time. I know some of my colleagues will be unhappy to hear me say it, but I think it's bad — well, not bad, but not the best for the orchestra. It means that for every concert you have a change of team so to speak. I can't pretend to offer a solution. There are good reasons why orchestras have to institute this system. We now play four or five concerts a week, and that's a lot of work. And you're always expected to produce the best, so it's not an easy job.

Now, the Philadelphia Orchestra, in the '20s and '30s had a winter season, twenty-eight to thirty weeks, then two to four weeks touring, but no summer work at all. The men wanted a summer season, but the management wouldn't have anything to do with it. So in the '30s the men began the Robin Hood Dell concerts as a co-operative venture. They played those concerts during the Depression, and oh, it was brutal. Five concerts a week for eight solid weeks. One week, I know, the split-up was $19 each, for a week.

LEONARD HINDELL So many of us dreamt of getting into an orchestra, that's what it was all about. I went to the Metropolitan Opera right out of the Manhattan School of Music, at age twenty-one. And that certainly seemed to me a degree of recognition and a goal achieved. It wasn't

Leonard Hindell

security or money, but recognition that I was good. At that age I wouldn't dream of turning down a good orchestra position, principal or section. A string player might have a different point of view.

I stayed eight years in the Met. I didn't know I was going to stay that long, but before I turned around eight years had passed. I enjoyed it, but the opera repertoire gets a bit repetitious. Just sitting in the pit accompanying the singers, allowed me to coast along on my instrument. After a while there weren't too many demands, technically and musically. But I had a good time, and with steady employment I was catching up on non-musical pursuits; but then I felt if I wasn't careful, if I didn't create challenges for myself, my playing might deteriorate. I would remain a great opera player exclusively. I started giving recitals, doing much more chamber music and playing a lot of contemporary music. Then the job of second bassoon came up in the New York Philharmonic. I felt I had to move on.

There's security in the Philharmonic, and a good salary — there's a sense of freedom when you know that cheque is coming in regularly.

There are so many facets to working in an orchestra. There's something very social about it. Being a member of a big institution is also prestigious, useful if you want to open a charge account, or lease an apartment.

Our orchestra is in some ways a tough orchestra. But I think it's misunderstood. There's great camaraderie. But there are problems. I find myself thinking about life in New York, and I feel the pace and stress of life here does contribute to the atmosphere of the orchestra. Many prefer a quieter life, more easy-going. But I feel fortunate to have studied here and to work here. There's so much music going on here, the best in the world all come here. Public interest is broader. And for a musician, hearing that variety and quality can't help but stimulate you. Even the Met and the Philharmonic are considered pretty conservative in New York. Take, for example, a controversial person like Pierre Boulez. Would he be employed as music director of a great orchestra anywhere but in New York or London, I wonder?

And I want to say something about being in an orchestra that is the opposite of personal recognition. I mean the feeling of being involved in something so much greater than ourselves. I get a kick out of playing chamber music, a little solo now and then, but the bassoon pieces I play can't compare with a Brahms or a Mahler symphony. To be part of a performance of, say, Beethoven 9 is to get out of yourself and experience something really great. If you don't play in an orchestra you miss that wealth. Some of our finest wind players won't venture out as soloists because they feel their solo repertoire just doesn't measure up to the orchestral repertoire. A Telemann sonata, or the Schumann Romances are fine, beautiful, but they just are not a Beethoven or a Mahler symphony. I play Saint-Saëns or Hindemith on the bassoon, it's important to me and I feel good, but I play a Mahler symphony and I feel something greater.

MICHAEL NUTT Well, I've been in the Los Angeles Philharmonic eleven years now, and if you'd told me, when I left England, that I'd be in the same job in twelve years' time, I'd have said no way. But when they start offering you all sorts of pensions and security, money and benefits. . . . When I started, in '65, the season was about forty weeks, then you were effectively out of work. I remember working nights in a bakery. In some ways it was good, because you could plan two months' holiday in the summer. We don't have a family and we like nice long holidays. The other players would teach or freelance. Now, we work fifty-two weeks. I looked up the contract for our last pay negotiations. The basic rate starts at $440 a week. Taking $2 to the pound, that's £220 a week, rank and file. And apart from housing, Los Angeles is not as expensive as London. I often think of coming back to London, but after eleven years with that pay, that security . . .

PETER HADCOCK This is my thirteenth year with the Boston Symphony, but by no means am I an old-timer. We have Rolland Tapley in the fiddles, this is his fifty-sixth year in the orchestra. People stay a long time. Well, there isn't a lot of freelance work, freelance pay isn't very good, and in general there are many, many more players than jobs. The deal provided for American orchestral players has become good, just in the last ten years, and that makes players stay on. If you move, you know, you start to lose your pension. Players get dug in now, get rooted to one place. When I was first in Buffalo we had, I think, a thirty-week season, maybe twenty-six weeks, no pension, no pay during the summer. That was lay-off, not holiday. We all rented cheap furnished apartments. If you could get $5 a week more from another orchestra you went quick, because you were a kind of gypsy anyway, going from apartment to apartment. Now we have full-time work, benefits, security, pensions. I don't think anyone gets fired, straight out, no matter how weak his playing is. There's non-renewal of contract, which amounts to eighteen months' notice. And they let you know privately, so you can just retire if you want to. Occasionally, a player will try to fight it, in which case the management will usually buy him off. I remember one fellow who wouldn't retire. They said, 'You're not going to play next year. We'll pay you full salary, but don't bother to come in.' They carried one horn player, who was having trouble with his lip, for almost two years on sick leave. That cost them a lot of money, salary, recording sessions, everything – he didn't play a note. And they had to hire someone to play instead of him.

PAUL FRIED In the Boston Pops you are playing what a great many people like, but it gets to be a grind for us, six nights a week, and Arthur Fiedler is getting old, that fine edge can go when you're eighty-four. And it's hard playing in the open air. This is the first year we haven't done that 4th of July concert. In Bicentennial year there were about half a million people out there. It becomes a happening, not a musical event. They go just to see if they can be one of half a million. It's very strange, these things take on a quality of their own, beyond music.

String players have a harder time than wind players. They play all the time, in every concert. I get a concert off now and again, which is great.

Naturally, principals are expected to be there, that's what they're employed for. But now the work is split up a bit — we assistants are getting a chance to play. Principals need time off, and the young assistants need experience in playing first. Nobody comes straight out of music school and plays principal with the Boston Symphony. You've got to get some experience. The other thing, of course, is that jobs are extremely tight. People don't want to leave these great orchestras. Where else do you go? And who wants to retire? That's the closest thing to dying, or worse. You're a musician, and that's what you love to do.

2 English Voices

SIDONIE GOOSSENS I began my professional playing in London musicals, about 1920, I think. I started with *Chou Chin Chow* at His Majesty's, then came *Cairo*, another Eastern show, and a Somerset Maugham play, with lots of Chinese effects. After that was *Hassan*, with music by Delius. I remember also the original production of *No, No, Nanette* at the Palace Theatre. I liked the theatre pit, though it could be hot and sticky. At His Majesty's we were really under cover and could just peep through the lid. It was there, during *Chou Chin Chow*, that the Shah of

Sidonie Goossens

84

Persia saw me playing. He went to the management and offered to buy me, and the harp. Such a funny little man, little fat man.

At the same time I was doing a certain amount of deputy work in the orchestras. I think I finished with those shows because I was getting more orchestral work. Then I went into the Queen's Hall Orchestra, with Sir Henry Wood. My sister Marie was there, and I came in as second. We seemed to stay in orchestras after that. We were in the LPO and the LSO, as well as the Queen's Hall. We just went in at the deep end and did everything. I joined the Queen's Hall during the Promenade season, so I've played in the Proms since about 1921, and I'm still there. The audiences in the Queen's Hall were enormous, but not as wild as today in the Albert Hall. The banners, the fancy dress, the chanting, that has come in since the last War. On the last night Sir Henry would never make a speech. He'd take his bows, then appear with his overcoat across his arm and his hat in hand. The lights would dim and the audience would sing 'For he's a jolly good fellow', and in darkness we went out into the night.

Henry Wood already had women in the orchestra when I went to play for him, in the '20s. He didn't like women cellists, they showed too much leg. He was fussy about legs. At that time we started to wear light stockings, and skirts were shorter. Lady Wood, the old Lady Wood, came to us, the harpists, and asked us to tell the ladies of the orchestra to wear gunmetal-coloured stockings, because Sir Henry was too distracted. His eyes kept going down to those light-coloured legs.

I was glad to do anything that came along. I did quite a lot of solos and chamber music, just as it came. And of course when I started with the BBC Symphony I began to play all the concertos. That was quite enough, having to tackle every new concerto. And I did it. I had been in at the beginning of broadcasting, in 1923, in the old wireless orchestra, the 2LO orchestra. The BBC signed me up in 1927, the Symphony officially started in 1930, and I've just been there ever since. I've really done over fifty years, but the official fifty will be in 1980. They don't know what to do about it, we've got out of depths. I should have retired years ago. Well, I'm the last original player. I've had the gold watch, I forgot to put it on today, and I felt lost without it. I suppose in 1980 they'll just give me my marching orders. 'You've had enough now, you can go.' In that time I've never been a member of another orchestra, though I've played with all the London orchestras. I've just been principal harp of the BBC Symphony for fifty years.

MARIE WILSON, MBE When I was at College my father fell ill. He'd had a hard childhood, going down the mine so young, and he was an invalid in his last years. I had to earn money to keep the family. I was studying in the daytime and playing in the evenings, in the band of a silent cinema. I also played in theatres and in cafes. Then, towards the end of my College days, I auditioned for Sir Henry Wood and the Queen's Hall Orchestra. Sir Henry, I believe, was the first English conductor to put women in a symphony orchestra, to make up for the losses among the men players in

Sir Henry Wood conducting a Promenade Concert. The Proms are a wonderful training in repertoire for musicians

the First World War. That was before my time, as I didn't audition until 1926 or '27. And very nerve-wracking that was! But he accepted me, in the first violins, and I played there for three years. Then, in 1929, the BBC began to form its new orchestra, and I began as no. 3 in the first fiddles. Later, I became co-leader and stayed with the BBC Symphony until 1944–45. In the early years it fell to me to lead the orchestra in three Promenade seasons. You can learn all there is to know about repertoire if you lead three seasons of Proms under Sir Henry Wood. He was a fantastic orchestral trainer, and a disciplinarian.

In my first years with the BBC I'd played solos and concertos a good deal. And after 1945 I went back to solo concert work, though I was older then. After a while I began to feel the pull of the orchestra, and in 1948 I was invited to join the Philharmonia. That was a great orchestra. We had one famous conductor after another, and I stayed for fifteen years, very happy years. Then the London Philharmonic approached me to become their first woman player — apart from harpists. I felt it was an honour, and would open the door to women, which it has. So in 1963 I joined the LPO, and I'm still playing, having been there just over sixteen years.

All in all, old though I am, I still love playing and the orchestral life. Our orchestra is a friendly crowd, and whenever I suggest retiring the management, my friends, and even my doctor, they all encourage me to carry on as long as I can. So I still play. One's work is all-important, and I've never known any other kind of life.

RICHARD ADENEY In 1939, aged nineteen, I went before a tribunal as a conscientious objector. I don't quite know what happened, but they gave me an unconditional exemption from military service, and I was pitched straight into the London Philharmonic as second flute. In less than a year I was promoted to first, simply because everyone left. It wasn't a good orchestra, with all those wartime losses, but for me it was a tremendous training. It was a shock at first, yes indeed. Really, I didn't know one end of the flute from the other. I could make a nice sound and play solos quite well, but orchestral playing . . . I had terrifying experiences. I recall sight-reading a Brahms symphony, at a broadcast public concert, with no rehearsal whatsoever. I'd never played the work, nor do I think I'd heard it, and there I was playing first. Ludicrous. I got very good at sight-reading, though I'm not so good now.

Fatigue was a real problem during the War. All over England, two concerts a day and night journeys in between, in unheated trains, wandering through wartime chaos. I don't know how we survived, and still played. But I've always liked orchestral playing, and the money always seemed rather good. My first payment, in cash, from the LPO was two big, white £5 notes. I was overwhelmed — all that for a week's work, doing what I loved. I had no thought then about security or retirement. Nowadays the insecurity makes it very difficult, the ease with which work can dry up. A number of players now have some second line — a shop in the background. Just yesterday an oboe player told me he did very well making reeds for others, and a first trombone is pretty rich from selling

Alec Sherman conducting
the New London Orchestra
with Dame Myra Hess at
the piano

bits and pieces for brass, mutes and the like. There's reputed to be a viola
player in London who owns fifty houses.

I liked orchestras but I got terribly bored in the LPO during and just
after the War. I came to dread the Tchaikovsky symphonies, and the
Schumann piano concerto, which kept coming up. Certain pieces have
left their mark so that one can no longer listen to them. But I can't say it
was a bad life. Compared to sitting in an office, it's not boring — a bit of
rehearsal and a two-hour concert.

GILLIAN EASTWOOD At twenty-one I was offered the leader's job in the
Carl Rosa Opera. I took it gratefully, and it made me take responsibility
seriously. Those were tough, happy days with the Rosa. We would do
Tannhäuser with eight first violins, or a *Tannhäuser* matinée and *Carmen*
in the evening. We worked all right, and travelled too, being a touring

company. I found operas wonderful training. You have to listen, for a start, and look at the conductor, which some players don't think important. I know that many young players of my generation got early experience in the Carl Rosa, and I think that company did great service to music. Once in Dundee, where music was hardly known, I noticed the same white-haired old lady coming every night for a week, and even to the matinée. She was a widow and her son had presented her with a week's holiday. She chose the opera for a week, rather than go away. The pleasure of just that one person justified the whole tedious journey to Dundee.

JOHN FLETCHER I was still at Cambridge when I got into the profession, and it was staggeringly simple. I was encouraged to try for the tuba job in the BBC Symphony. I arrived in London in all innocence. It was the teaching practice week for my Dip.Ed., and in chemistry that is a terrible hassle – an awful week of filter-papers, rush and chaos. By Friday night to go to London and play some orchestral excerpts to Dorati seemed like a holiday. I played all right – couldn't do it now to save my life – and got the job. There I was, in a job and having to learn it, as happens quite often in England, where musicians are taken on for their potential, as I suppose I was. I was lucky. There was a great exodus of older tuba players, and no middle generation, so young players like myself fell in. Well, I never regarded myself as anything more than a stop-gap. And now some staggering players are springing up. If they'd been around I wouldn't have had a smell of a chance. There are only fourteen full-time orchestral tuba jobs in England, and they are all closely watched. I'm one of the oldest now. The kids coming up, wanting a job, wait for me to be run over by a bus. It's a sobering thought. I'm a believer in meritocracy, and it's not right to keep out better young players. Obviously the future is fairly uncertain.

TONY PAY When I left Cambridge I found things very difficult. I didn't have the contacts of those who'd been to music colleges. To the profession I was an unknown quantity. Then by luck and accident I began to deputize in various orchestras, playing first clarinet. Really, I got in at the top floor, without the hard business of fighting my way up. When I became principal of the Royal Philharmonic I was obviously thought of as a first clarinet, which in a way I was, but I wasn't fully equipped and experienced. Initially, I had what might be called engaging naïvety. I thought I could question conductors, ask how things were done, say anything to anyone. Perhaps that was refreshing in a way. Without some enthusiasm in an orchestra, very quickly you turn off completely on the worst dates. But my manner jarred. There is a sort of Cambridge University manner which does not go down very well with someone, say, who started playing trombone in a mining village band. The manner *is* irritating, and too direct. But my amateur experience was that players only improved by self-criticism and criticism of others, quite openly. This however is not done by professionals. But professional disapproval only made me angry and arrogant. I remember once suggesting that someone hadn't played well in tune, and I got a real earful – 'You haven't played a bloody thing in tune since you joined the bloody orchestra.' He was a Welshman with a wonderful command of invective, and he knew how to put me down. He left me devastated. Eventually I had a long talk with him, realizing that some of the feeling against me was well justified, and we sorted things out over several whiskies. At least if I was a young upstart I could drink all right! And I came to understand the business of being a professional, of having if not the best possible standard all the time, at least a high lowest standard. You can never predict the best concert, I feel these things strike from above. But you can make sure the worst concert is not very bad. That's important – a full professional standard.

Antony Pay

GARY KETTEL I was knocked out when I first started playing in the BBC Symphony. Timpani is a great thing to play in an orchestra. It took me a little while to get there. I was very cheeky and I think it got around that I might answer the conductor back, so I didn't get offered orchestral work. But after a time in the orchestra, and this is one of the reasons I left and went freelance, I felt I was getting too secure. In the BBC I think I lost a sense of value a bit, because that cheque came in what ever happened, and I could spend and not worry. Being a freelance, your own boss, gives you better judgment and sense of proportion.

Another thing about the BBC Symphony, you can be a poor player, but if you're on time and never moan at the conductor and always queue nicely for your room-key on tour, you'll have no trouble, Whereas a good player who is a bit of a hooligan gets in trouble all the time. There's more likely something done about bad behaviour than bad playing. I think that's wrong. I know, in a way, you have to keep on fine players of twenty years ago who are now a bit slow. But there were young people who couldn't play. I'd watch them from the timps at the back, and they just weren't making it. I was called to the office for reprimands a couple of times. But no one ever complained about my playing. What if I'd said, 'Look at those fellows at the back of such and such a section. I've listened and watched, and I'm sorry to say they can't play'? That would be considered a bit heavy-duty. I think the BBC Symphony lost some good young players, because the management got their priorities wrong. I resigned after a while. That was strange. I was called to the office to be bawled out, but I got my resignation in first. 'Well,' they said, 'that makes what we had to say irrelevant. Thank you for playing these years, we enjoyed it.'

BILL LANG I like the variety of work in London, but the other side of that is the insecurity. And then again, if you are insecure, at least you practise. Now some people get jobs with the BBC Symphony just for the security of the contract, and they become like men on the council, they retire on the shovel, leaning on it. Others, some of the younger fellows, and not so young either, are doing three sessions a day, and that's not too good for the playing. A string player might manage it, but a trumpet can't. The lip goes. We were doing some film music yesterday, fantastic, playing top Fs for a film called *Fist*. But I couldn't do three sessions like that a day. I'd be killed. Those screamers do it, but they wouldn't be able to play the introduction to the *Oberon* overture next day — that little delicate opening.

ROBIN MCGEE I'm out of symphony orchestras now. When I was in the Royal Philharmonic and the London Symphony I liked the people. It's strange, I got on with nearly everyone and I enjoy seeing them now. When they're stuck for a bass I'll go along and play with them — for the fun of it. I like the LSO particularly, that rather hard professionalism, very clear cut. But after many years I found the life and work of our orchestras somehow unsatisfactory. What would improve it — the German or the American system? I'm conditioned now. I couldn't *bear* to think of flogging along in a section, even as principal, knowing that my pay-packet is coming in each month, knowing that all is looked after — holidays, sickness, pension, everything — and that the schedule stretches out interminably, and that I'd be faced with Boehm, Karajan, or whoever, for years, for ever.

I rather like the musical shambles of London. But I don't think it's the best way to produce a very great orchestra. Do we need a re-made version of the 'English player'? The members of the London orchestras are frequently run ragged by insecurity, worry and fatigue, yet they can generate great spirit and fine performances. Perhaps the shambles is the essence of musical London, a city so uniquely provided that foreign companies flock over here to take advantage of our cheapness, our competence, our versatility and our quickness. What is the first attraction, are we that good or that cheap?

CECIL JAMES Pick up a copy of the paper on a Saturday morning — the amount of concerts and music-making in London is almost frightening. Years ago, when I started, there was just a fraction of that. But it wasn't a bad living, even then. I used to get £11 10s. a week at Glyndebourne, when the LSO did the opera season there, before the War — Glyndebourne was considered an honour, so the pay was a little less! I ran my little Ford 8, and put something in the Post Office Savings each week.

I had no idea at all what to do when I left the College. I just wanted to play the bassoon, and I loved the sound of a symphony orchestra. I'd go to the Proms, sit with my ears pinned back — if only I could get in an orchestra like that. I was very innocent. Well, I had luck. Beecham was forming the London Philharmonic and had pinched all the players from the London Symphony, so the LSO decided to take a chance with some new youngsters. I was asked along, as third bassoon. The thrill! Then I was invited to join as second. I couldn't believe it, I didn't know anything. Honestly, I must have done terrible things, but perhaps it didn't matter, because a lot of us were inexperienced and we didn't have much work anyway, because Beecham had pinched that too. We had to make do with what we could get, spread ourselves around. I did the *Desert Song*,

90

and loved it. There wasn't the work then that there is now, with the orchestras hammering away seven days a week and everybody dropping with exhaustion.

I stayed with the LSO until the War. After the War I was principal in the Philharmonia for about twelve years, from 1951. Players are now beginning to get all sorts of delights that didn't exist before, paid holidays, sick pay, pension plans. The great thing in the old days was 'No blow, no dough' — no play, no pay. And no pensions either, nothing, you just played until you dropped or were turned out. And for all the improvements, it's still a bit the same in our self-governing orchestras today. After all, I've been blowing the old bassoon for, what — more than forty years? And nobody's offered me a pension. But I suppose that's in the English tradition. Right back in the year dot, Queen Victoria had a Private Band, partly in London and partly in Balmoral. The musicians had a contract which offered a pension after so many years. My father and two uncles were luminaries of this band. An honour, you see. Now, when Edward VII took over he was so much in debt that the palace decided to make economies and tore up the band contracts. No pension, and you couldn't sue the Crown. It almost stopped my father being a royalist.

I used to know the first bassoon of the Vienna Philharmonic, who was also chairman of their board. We were talking about orchestras. They had nine bassoons on strength, though two had sunk to 4th or contra-bassoon, getting towards retirement. They had paid holidays, paid absences, shorter hours, more rehearsal. He was amazed at our system. 'How does it work?' he said. All that worry, insecurity, rush. Yet it does work, and successfully too. A contradiction, isn't it? When the BBC

Workers give a concert in Dresden's Zwinger Yard

Symphony first started, with secure contracts, pensions, etc., they had some wonderful players, but it was as dull as ditch-water. Bored to tears with the certainty of their lives. It took Toscanini to liven them up, they were too comfortable. Then, by the same token, the Vienna or Berlin orchestras should be dull, but they aren't. Short of murdering a policeman I don't think you can get the sack from the Vienna Philharmonic. If someone goes mad or on the bottle, he's quietly shoved to the end of the section, appears once every three months, and marks time until his pension. I couldn't envisage being in any orchestra that long.

I gather the American orchestras are run roughly on German lines, though of course they are privately financed. And I hear they actually have rehearsals before they get to the recording studio. What a luxury! The Philharmonia was, at first, primarily a recording orchestra, yet very often we'd get to the studio and say, 'What's on this morning?' I remember we did *The Rite of Spring*, with Markevitch, on mono. Later, we were doing two sessions at Abbey Road – Schubert, I think. The second morning I met a fellow in the canteen. 'You know what's on?' he said. '*Rite of Spring*.' I didn't believe it, I thought he was pulling my leg. But it *was* the *Rite*. Markevitch had a couple of free days and was going to re-do it in stereo. Well, that's a bit of a change from Schubert. We had to be quick on the draw, one conductor after another. It's funny about that. If Karajan was coming over, we knew what he wanted, different phrasing and so on. Then maybe Szell would come, another type altogether, but we dropped right in to what he wanted. I can't think of anything worse than the same conductor all the time. Look at Philadelphia – Ormandy for donkey's years. It's not too bad if you like the chap, but even the best begin to wear. With so many conductors, you say, 'Oh dear' as soon as you see them. Fancy being stuck with one of those. Terrible. Dog's life.

English players have individuality and character in their playing, and that's because they are not so regimented. They're freer spirits. It's this peculiar orchestral set-up over here, everybody has to be alive-O. You're as good as your last performance, and you can't say I'm here for thirty years and I'm bound to get better. In or out, it's as simple as that. I'm all for the thing as it goes. There's still enough work for an ancient like me, with all that goes on. I still get an occasional set of film sessions. Personally, I don't want to play in a symphony orchestra ever again. After all these years, I can't produce the sheer physical stamina needed. I don't know if I made particularly hard work of it, but I think if you ask any of the orchestral boys in England they'd say that after slogging away for several weeks, three times a day, they're exhausted. People say we are doing what we like. So we are, but it's still damned hard work.

(overleaf)
Waiting for the conductor
at the Royal Albert Hall

(opposite)
André Previn and the
Vienna Philharmonic

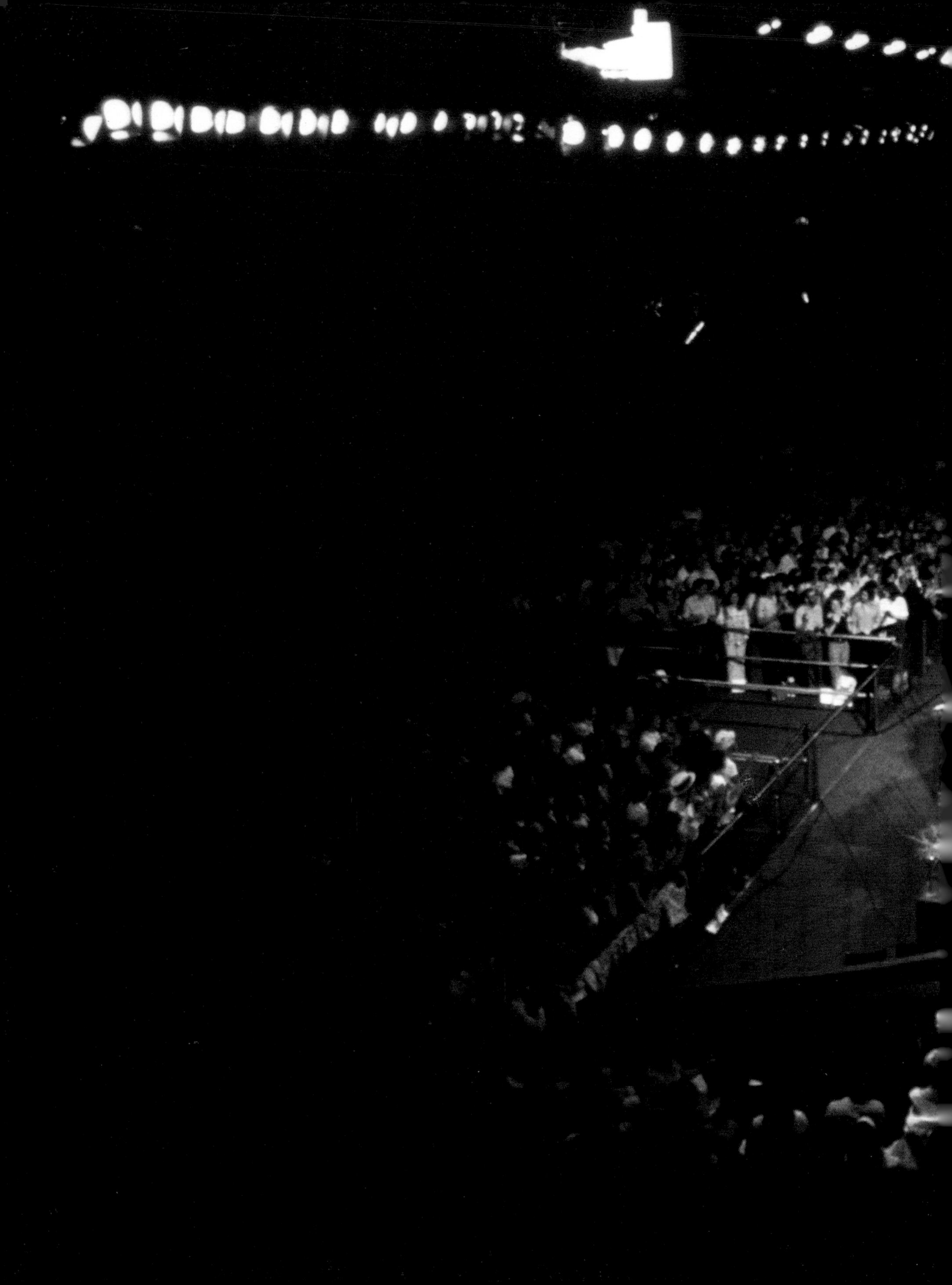

Limitations

In most parts of the world the musical profession is badly organized. Musicians must trust to luck or to their skill in business. Talent is not always the first consideration of organizers of orchestras. They are more often concerned with budgets than art.

CHARLES MUNCH, *I Am a Conductor* (1955)

Three Forms of Government
1 *Employees, merely*

ROGER SCOTT

WHEN I was a student I would go to concerts and look at the Philadelphia Orchestra, and I thought, all I have to do to be in an orchestra is to play my instrument well. But that's the least of it. You get involved in politics, fights and frailties, confrontations with the conductor. A hundred people together make for a lot of friction. We are a stable group and we see a great deal of each other, travel together, eat together, and above all play together. And to make good music you should come together in conformity and sympathy.

Travelling from concert to concert can involve a lot of hanging about

(opposite)
In concert

Surely, there's frustration in our kind of set-up, with a board of rich patrons, a management, and then players who are just employees. My teacher couldn't understand why I left the Marine Band, with its security and pension — which the orchestra didn't have then. I told him I wanted to feel free, to tell the conductor to go to hell if I felt like it. That's a court-martial in the service. Yet here we are in the orchestra, still pitted against the management many times, recrimination on both sides, nastiness over contracts, perhaps even a strike. Backstage, we argue among ourselves, maybe don't talk to colleagues at all. Yet we have to perform, and we *do* perform. We are professional musicians. Not only that, but we can't short-change the public who've paid good money to hear a composer's work faithfully done.

An alternative to our system is self-government. I don't know how we'd manage that in America. I spent one summer in Israel, playing as a guest in their self-governing orchestra, and I saw them operate. At their annual general meeting the floor was red with blood, most awful personal accusations and vendettas. We fight enough among ourselves, just facing up to the management. I can't imagine how we could be self-governing. I served on our Player's Committee for a couple of years. Never again, thank you.

JOHN DE LANCIE The big American orchestras have established pretty good lives for their players. I would say that our musicians, with the help of the union, have developed a rather secure profession, and that they get a good middle- or upper-middle-class income. It takes a pretty wild situation to get a man sacked. It's damn near impossible to fire anyone. And the kind of work-load that the London orchestras do was ruled out years ago. I don't think there's any place where orchestral musicians work as hard as in England. I find that kind of a paradox, in the one country of self-governing orchestras the players accept conditions and work that no musician in other places would take from his employer.

American orchestral musicians are just employees, the hired help, nothing more than that. The men in the orchestra have absolutely nothing to say about choice of conductors. Nothing. And nothing to say about anything artistic, decisions, nothing, there's not even an advisory committee. Other orchestras have an Artistic Committee, but Philadelphia is probably the last bastion of the old, rigid dictatorial system. Ormandy may choose to share decisions, but if he doesn't choose he won't. What's the alternative? Self-government is something that has never happened here, in any place. And I'd say that's because there isn't the *slightest* chance of government subsidy. Oh, a little piddling amount occasionally comes out of some cultural committee — window dressing for the Great Society! Back in the Depression, when like so many others throughout America the San Francisco orchestra folded, the city government passed a bill providing that one penny, I believe, in every tax dollar could go to support the orchestra. Oh my lord, what a revolutionary step — Communism! No other city followed, and though I believe it still exists in San Francisco to the best of my knowledge it has not made *that* much difference.

RON BARRON This split-up of the orchestra, into the A and B groups — what does it lead to? We are all so suspicious we wonder what plot the management is hatching. Ideally, to hell with it all, and just let's make music. But you get so conditioned to thinking about money. And only in recent years have orchestral musicians begun to make a reasonable wage. We want the security of the year-round season, but then the work load gets heavy, and you may become a machine in your musical production, just go through the motions. Wasn't that nice? Very often it wasn't, but with a hundred of you up there it sounds OK.

There's a danger in civil service mentality, but I think we have a lot of it now anyway. Show up, do the playing, go home. Sure, it could get worse, and there might be some government, bureaucratic overlay, which is terrible, and might produce the thing I'm afraid of — just production-line music. Even now, we can just coast along, knowing how hard it is to get fired, but still we don't quite have civil service attitudes yet. It's hard to balance the needs of music and the requirements of a job. And for me personally, unions have gone a little too far now. We want, and feel we have a right to union protection, on the other hand anybody who doesn't keep in mind the need to do the music right is at fault. Music is not quite like other jobs. We are supposed to be giving an artistic performance. Supposed to be.

GARY KETTEL The people in the BBC Symphony, I'm surprised they are still there, because they are such nice blokes. It seems to take a certain kind of mentality to be happy in a management orchestra, like the BBC Symphony. They seem to need to be safe. When we went on tour, a few of the lads would dump the luggage first thing and look for a nice little bar or restaurant, but the regular BBC types would immediately queue for the room-key. A friend of mine used to say that if the plane came down in the middle of the Sahara, first thing you'd know there'd be a queue. There were some terrors for caution in the BBC. I remember one bloke on a tour of Paris — what a gastronomic delight! Well, this fellow had a case full of Tupper Ware boxes with sandwiches and salads for four days, so he didn't get food-poisoning and didn't spend his subsistence. I found that orchestra definitely wasn't for me.

RODNEY FRIEND Well, everybody complains about work. But orchestras in America have an easier time. Of course they do, with seven weeks' paid vacation, free days every week. That sort of schedule is unheard of in London. I recall, in the LPO, playing five weeks at a time, without one single day off, running from one end of London to the other. I'm an Englishman and I support my English colleagues in every way, but the orchestral conditions there are not satisfactory. Outstanding musicians can make a very nice living there, and still work in orchestras, but that is not typical. In the New York Philharmonic, with good vacations and up to five weeks' unpaid leave, every member has a chance to do other things, solos, chamber music, or just relax.

2 Self-government

TONY PAY It's difficult to have a self-run orchestra. Often the players on the board have a poor idea, or worse, a wrong idea of what the orchestra should be doing. Their prime interest, and I suppose it has to be that way, is to get enough work to give the members a decent living, often at the expense of the quality of the work. We are so under-financed we have inevitable conflicts between commerce and artistry. It is ridiculous that our orchestras have to spend time kow-towing to record companies, chasing commercial work, being in studios playing rubbish. And still the orchestras can't keep their good players, specially string players.

TOM STORER It's a typical English way of working, our self-run orchestras. A good old compromise, unwieldy and rather inefficient. The players employ the manager and keep a tight watch on him. It's said that a good manager can do what he wants with us, a bunch of amateurs. But however good he is, he's still an outsider, a non-player in a tight-knit group of musicians. And the abilities needed to manage an orchestra are rare. Your business can never make a profit, decisions have to be as much about artistry as commerce, you are constantly losing money and having to find more to be lost again. I'm afraid our orchestras go through managers like shoes.

The London Symphony has been self-governing since 1904. I can't conceive of any other way to run an orchestra, but I've never been in any other orchestra. I only hear the bad side, about orchestras abroad, about the BBC Symphony, and I don't like what I hear. We are self-reliant and responsible only to ourselves, and we can say exactly what we think to conductors, managers, and members of our own board. I can't imagine having to watch what I say, or being pushed around by a bureaucracy.

In a self-governing orchestra, players discuss the right way to play a piece in rehearsal

JOHN FLETCHER We have bouts of musical chairs in London every so often. One person moves and suddenly it's all-change, like stirring up ping-pong balls in a barrel. In 1968 I moved from the BBC Symphony to the London Symphony, from the civil service system of the BBC to the self-government of the LSO. Self-government survives partly by default, partly because it does actually work. People only notice when things go wrong — 'Oh lord, musicians making a mess of their own affairs again!' But I've always been terribly impressed by the wisdom and maturity with which the LSO has made the vital decisions, though certainly I don't agree with everything. An observer at our board meetings would see just how far true democracy can be taken. Democracy is really the abdication by the bone-idle to the few who can be bothered. Orchestras are full of those quite happy to leave things to others and then moan like hell at what's done. Now, the civil service, as in the BBC Symphony, is where everybody abdicates responsibility to a management, and spends all day getting an acid stomach and crying about 'them' and 'us' — a totally hopeless mentality, it seems to me.

ANTHONY CAMDEN At its best, the self-governing orchestra is unbeatable, at its worst, terrible. I look at the London Symphony today, still very much alive after seventy-four years of self-government, in the league of great orchestras on a fraction of the money available to any major foreign orchestra. The London orchestras get around £150,000 a year each, more or less. Berlin has about £2½ million a year, and a bit more if they want; Vienna gets about £2 million, Paris about £1½ million.

I'm the chairman of the LSO at the moment. All the decisions are hard, both administrative and artistic. But I think the most responsible part of the job is to try to plan the future course, to take effect long after my three years on the board are up. In the beginning I found it a terrible strain, playing and being the chairman. I hadn't been on the board before and I wasn't up to date with policy. We had no manager, the orchestra was going through something of a crisis. We weathered that crisis, and now it's not such a strain. I know what I can do, physically, and I make sure my playing doesn't suffer. Just because I'm chairman doesn't guarantee me my position as principal oboe. Recently a London orchestra removed a principal player who was chairman at the time. Members of the board have to travel with their colleagues, live among them, talk with them, above all make music with them. The balance between commercial and artistic policy is terribly difficult. In a lean period we have to chase work, in a fat period get rid of it. We tread carefully between work of artistic worth, and work which is financially profitable and which ensures the players' income. A player only gets paid for what he does, piece-work.

ROBIN McGEE I was talking to a producer at Decca records, and I asked how the London orchestras were? 'Oh, all much the same.' That's the way I feel. Given the right conductor, they all play about the same. In fact, in a large piece, like *Heldenleben*, they *look* the same. There are only so many good horns around. The producer was not enthusiastic, 'The strings are not satisfactory, every orchestra has passengers.' I'm afraid that's true. So many fine string players in London opt out of the orchestras, and it's not always a question of money. Our orchestras fight madly for funds, cut corners, undertake dubious work, drive players too hard. Music, where orchestras are fighting for existence, is a cruel business, and artistic standards do often slide. The strange tension of English music! Pressure and insecurity. It's the making of our players – I wonder if it's the un-making of our orchestras? If you took those away, in twenty-five years would our players be so competent, so professional, so quick? But that is achieved at what cost to lives? I left the orchestra, I had to.

3 Autocratic

RAY PREMRU When Walter Legge decided to make an end of the Philharmonia in 1964 it was very difficult for us. We'd been ruled by one man and now we had to take over the reins ourselves. Confronted sud-denly with a shut-down, our principal clarinet acted very quickly to try to keep us together. Naturally, we wanted to stay. We had no other place to go. Klemperer stuck by us, and we still had a little bit of recording work. We took the title New Philharmonia because Legge wouldn't let us keep the old one. We've got it back now, though I believe we had to get it from a Chinese gentleman in Philadelphia. I'm glad we've dropped the 'New', it sounded like a soap-powder. In one provincial town I saw a poster with the NEW about two feet high, and 'Philharmonia Orchestra' underneath in small letters.

ALAN CIVIL I was in the Philharmonia when Legge suspended it. That was an orchestra for eruptions. Tremendous arguments which Legge's secretary had to sort out. Legge would never discuss contracts or money with you. He was the boss, which was correct. His secretary had to do all the negotiating and nasty business. The number of times I threatened to leave. Then off we'd go to lunch, to sort things out. We used to joke about the 'free lunch', which meant trouble. Sometimes one returned from lunch to find one's job gone. Oh, there was a lot of dirty dealing, not for nothing it was called 'the cloak and dagger orchestra'. Yet I suppose, in a way, all orchestras are run in this manner.

When the Philharmonia crashed there was no preparation. Some of us were told just the previous evening, before the newspapers got the story. Bernard Walton, principal clarinet, immediately formed a committee to keep us alive. I was a member but Walton did the donkey work. As soon as the word got round that the orchestra was likely to fold, the LSO made a bid for several key players, which might have been a nice gesture to those players but didn't help us in our fight for survival. We managed to stay together in our new, self-governing form, but the first couple of years were bad, because there was no work. Recording companies weren't too interested. Legge had sold off our old name. It took us years to get back to health, and even longer to get the old name back. Klemperer stuck by us. I liked him very much. Well you see, Legge, in a way, had

Walter Legge who ran the Philharmonia until it was reformed as the New Philharmonia in 1964

kicked Klemperer in the teeth. He had been made conductor for life, then suddenly his orchestra looked like disappearing. That's why Klemperer was furious. Yet even today I still think Walter Legge was a great man. His judgment of players and conductors was extraordinary. Everything he did with the Philharmonia was an occasion, a grand event.

Sir Thomas Beecham

JOHN RONAYNE I was still in the Royal Philharmonic when Beecham died. In fact, in a sense, I think I helped get Kempe to take over. It was a funny situation. I'd played for Kempe in the LSO, and I thought he was fantastic, which he was. Then, when I was in the RPO, Beecham wouldn't let other good conductors near the orchestra. Like many great men he wanted no competition. So when Tommy was away for long periods, avoiding the taxman, we were getting very bad conductors and our earnings were suffering. We weren't getting the recordings or the concerts with these men. So we asked Beecham for better men, such as Kempe.

Now, when Beecham died the money was on Sir Malcolm Sargent taking over, because Lady Beecham liked Sargent. I remember the principals were invited to the flat in Baker Street, and Lady Beecham asked us about a successor. Three or four names came up. Barbirolli, but that was impossible because Tommy never let him near the orchestra. Sir Adrian Boult, but he was getting on a bit – though of course he's still going strong! And then Sargent. When he was mentioned the principal oboe said, 'I'm leaving as soon as he's appointed,' and someone else added, 'I think that goes for all of us.' Kempe was suggested, but Lady Beecham said we could not have a German, after all we were the 'Royal' Philharmonic and the Queen Mother was our patron. It was left like that. Later, we were doing something with Kempe for TV. We all loved playing for Kempe and he obviously liked conducting us, but no one knew what he thought of this awkward situation. So in the long dinner break I went to see how he stood. I asked for a few words, he looked at his watch and said, 'Yes, but I'm expecting a call from my wife.' We began to talk, then he got up, closed the door and we went on for an hour and a half. He thought Sargent was to be appointed. 'You must realize,' I said, 'the band don't want him. They want you.' He was very modest, but I think he did know that. I told him there was little we could do. We had been run by an autocrat and having lost Beecham we were pretty disorganized. He didn't really understand how English music worked. At the end he said, 'I'm invited to lunch with Lady Beecham.' And I think our little talk must have given him the confidence to stick his neck out, because the next we hear he's been appointed chief conductor.

A Judgment

RODNEY FRIEND In management orchestras, as in the United States, I see a rigidity, a lack of opportunity to move, and a distance, a coolness, between the player and his employer. In self-governing orchestras I see over-work, insecurity, poor conditions, but a terrific team spirit. I must admit, much as I admire the marvellous playing and the wonderful conditions of the American orchestras, I adore that team spirit. You are responsible ultimately for your own fate, and that makes for strong morale. In London, each orchestra is working for survival against keen competition from four others, so first or last chair, you play for all you're worth. You play to please, which doesn't necessarily happen in the one-orchestra town, with its secure body of musicians — New York, Philadelphia, Boston, and so on. Their morale comes from self-respect, which depends very much on whether the conductor is using the players' skill to the best effect.

Stress

The daily existence of an orchestral musician presents difficulties that only the love of music makes endurable.
CHARLES MUNCH, *I Am a Conductor* (1955)

1 Discontents

Hugh Maguire

HUGH MAGUIRE I suppose, like all young string players, I'd hoped to do better than become an orchestral player. But one becomes ensnared, it's just the way things happen. You fall in love, you want to buy a house, a car, you're not prepared to make the sacrifices so you drift into earning money. You become a sort of musical prostitute, and I suppose that happened to me. It seemed fairly easy to get into an orchestra, I was a good enough fiddle player. It seemed fairly easy to make quite a lot of money. After my studies, around 1950, I went off to Paris, attempting to avoid the orchestral fate. I had been playing, as an extra in the London Philharmonic, with the great conductors lost to England during the War, but there were also the other conductors whose names I dare not mention. And it dawned on me that there were very many bad conductors and very, very few good ones. So in the orchestra one spent most of one's time in purgatory. I was determined then *not* to be ensnared. I didn't want to sit in an orchestra, but I was afraid that would happen if I stayed in London. Most of the conductors were no good, that was the point of it. It wasn't so much the players' attitude in the orchestras, although too often they sat with their legs crossed, fed-up, saddened and disappointed men. I was a little afraid also to become like that. But the chief reason was the miserable conducting.

ROGER SCOTT It was the strangest thing, when we went to China a while ago. We were directed to a table for communal dining, and you found yourself sitting next to somebody you would normally never sit beside. You managed a few words to a colleague you hardly knew or could not stand. It was a great leveller, both amusing and revealing. Then we came back and reverted to old habits and prejudices. I first saw these conflicts in the Marine Band during the War. People sat on the same stand and didn't talk to each other, I thought that was terrible. I

104

imagine that happens in New York. It's pretty bloodthirsty there — that's a rough orchestra. That's why I left New York, when I was freelancing. I saw people only existing for pay-day. I was young and idealistic, I wanted some musical satisfaction for myself, and also for the audience. I wanted a little credit, too. Now, here in the Philadelphia Orchestra, we do get some. Ormandy can be very gracious. He'll give me a bow after the Mahler 1 solo. He'll give the cellos a bow, let's say after the nasty business in *La Mer*, and the violins, or the winds, after a difficult passage. You may say he's a hypocrite, but it's still a recognition of your skill and gives you one reason for enduring the routine. If you are constantly beaten down, or badgered, as some conductors do, you figure, 'Why should I work like that if he gives me no credit?' There's more to music-making than that, just being paid for a job.

I think the very nature of our big orchestras breeds some problems. We've worked up to security, a year-round contract, and we have a very small turn-over of players. You think twice before you move, and that's very hard on the young musicians. The competition to get into orchestras is frightening, just frightening — 100 to 200 applicants for each position, you name it, bass drum or piccolo. And once a young player is in he might get nowhere for years. We lost a young bass player this year, after he'd been here six or seven years. He thought he was going to set us all on fire. Frankly, I'm sure he felt he'd have my job in a few years. Well, in six years he moved from 9th to 8th bass, and that was only because of a retirement. It's got nothing to do with ability, simply seniority. Our policy is to throw a new player to the back of the section, and there he waits, sometimes for years, not playing in Mozart or the smaller pieces.

A Hungarian Quartet relax together during rehearsal by playing cards

He may languish there, far away from the conductor's beat, bored and unsettled.

I don't know what the answer is. As teachers of the next generation of orchestral players, we all get depressed. We are turning out fine students all across the country. What are they going to do? They've used the freshest, most inquisitive years of their lives devoting themselves to an instrument, which they've thoroughly mastered. Then all of a sudden, no work! There are just no openings.

ALFIO MICCI It frightens me to play alone in public! But that's not true of many of our string players in the New York Philharmonic. A lot of them wanted to be soloists, and perhaps they are unhappy at having to settle for orchestral playing. Well, when you have auditions, and there are a lot to choose from, you're going to pick the very best. But I'm not sure you need anybody that good in an orchestra. I sometimes think eighteen soloists in the first violins doesn't produce the best section. Eighteen potential virtuosos are not going to make for ensemble, and eighteen violinists asserting themselves make it very hard for conductors.

Well, I do have a feeling that discipline in our orchestra leaves something to be desired. I sometimes wonder why some of the men come into the orchestra because, you know, they really don't seem to want to be there. A lot of them act up and it gets very rough, hard for our concertmaster, very hard, and I sympathize with him. I don't know what's going to change us, if anything. No conductor has managed it. I don't know what the beef is. The salary is good, conditions are good. In general, artistic policy and conductors are quite good. I think our conditions are far superior to those in England. Our contract protects us with some pretty tight rules for time off, for travel, for touring. We've got our own comfortable hall — I was amazed to hear that London orchestras don't have their own halls. Sure, our management makes some beauties of mistakes, but do the men think they could do better? If we had the English co-operative system life would be much tougher. I wouldn't care for that.

JOHN DE LANCIE Nowadays, in America anyway, a conductor can't ask a string player to play alone, though of course the wind player, who only plays one part, can't hide behind the section. It's a mixed bag, whether that is good or bad. It gives the tutti player an easier ride, but it can intensify the bad feeling between string sections and solo winds. The solo player is exposed. Also, the management has another weapon against principals. The union agreement only covers basic salary, while principals negotiate their own, which may be fifty percent or more above basic. Now, if the management or conductor doesn't like a principal, his salary can be reduced to minimum and the union won't interfere. That can be a weapon to drive a player out. And if he's unhappy with the music director or the policy, but wishes to stay because jobs are tight, it can be an awful long time before he sees a change. Ormandy, for example, has been with the Philadelphia Orchestra forty-two years.

106

Part of the brass section of the Royal Liverpool Philharmonic Orchestra

ROLF SMEDVIG I've always played in many groups and I take every chance to play solos. I don't want to play third trumpet for the rest of my life, though it may be, because of lack of openings, that's all I manage within an orchestra. But I still have — perhaps idealistically — other goals, which I haven't really spelled out but which I hope will emerge from things I do. It's not easy to fit in other work, like our brass quintet. It gets harder and harder to fit in a couple of free days, or to take off for a tour. We do get seven weeks' vacation, but that's the time for the brass quintet, and in the last two years I haven't really had two days' vacation together. Every year I seem to book something in. 'Wait a minute,' I'm beginning to say, 'I want some time off.'

LEONARD HINDELL I find I do need a rest, but I also feel, both musically and for my own ego, that I need to do things that get me out of the orchestra. I'm taking my vacation on Monday, but I'm using it to play for five weeks at the Waterloo Festival that Gerry Schwarz runs in New

Jersey. There'll be some fine playing, some teaching, all very relaxed. You feel you are participating in something, getting feed-back more directly than in the big orchestra during the regular season, specially as I'm second bassoon and therefore not a solo player.

I sometimes feel I do little but play, eat and sleep. I meet my responsibility to the Philharmonic, then I start practising or rehearsing for something else, and much as I enjoy it I feel that's my whole life. In a way, music to me is still a hobby and a love. My first love. So many of us find that in our early twenties we are pretty one-dimensional practising, studying, listening to every concert in town, buried completely in music. Music is love, politics, ambition. You have to be more than good. So one strives for that standard. Later on you may catch up with the usual business of life – marriage, family, other interests. But music still runs alongside. Now, I'm really tied up at home with two children, and I feel a little jealous, like I'm not doing what I want. It's a conflict. If I play a lot I'm happy, but then I feel I want to be, and should be, sharing time with my family. Yet if I do too much of that I feel I'm missing out musically. A great irony.

What of the future? Age and failing powers are a problem for every orchestra. Retirement is a double-edged sword, for some players are playing better than ever at sixty-seven, and some should have gone, from the musical point of view, long since. We are not a co-operative, we are not involved in management decisions. I feel it is not our place to voice doubts about colleagues, though we may know ourselves that a man is no longer up to Philharmonic standards. Every large, enduring artistic institution can stand some falling off from the highest standards. The orchestra survives, and eventually weak links are replaced. I regard the orchestra – I don't know if this is the right attitude – I regard it as my place of employment. We musicians are not represented on the board, we do not make artistic decisions. On the other hand, we do make up a community, and we look on the troubles of colleagues more sympathetically, more broadly perhaps, than a music director would. We live with the orchestra for twenty-five, maybe even forty years, and we take account of not just musical standards, but also livelihood, security, loyalty. And pity too.

2 Penalties

TOM STORER How many times have I been asked if my job in the orchestra is part-time. Part-time! The public has no idea of the strain. On the last tour of America I fell ill. On the last night I had a massive heart attack in Philadelphia. I had the presence of mind, at three o'clock in the morning, to get myself shipped down to Jefferson Hospital in a taxi, and what was more of an achievement, to get myself admitted. Anyway, I promptly died on them, technically dead for six minutes, so they couldn't get rid of me, and I was in no state to answer questions. No one knew what had happened to me. When the orchestra gathered for the bus next morning I'd disappeared. They dug me out at Jefferson and the LSO came up trumps. 'Don't worry about a thing,' they said. 'Just sign for everything and we'll sort it out later.' It terrified me, watching the dollars click

108

The London Symphony Orchestra van which was specially adapted to the needs of transporting musical instruments

up — so much for the cardiogram machine, so much each pill, each injection, each blood-test. The bills were not cleared until the orchestra did a successful tour of Mexico and used the profit to pay off medical debts.

But our American orchestral colleagues were marvellous. My wife flew out, on insurance, and our LSO principal bass suggested she stay with his old teacher, Roger Scott, principal in the Philadelphia Orchestra. Unfortunately, he forget to tell Roger, so he poor fellow, had a sudden call from an unknown woman, expecting to stay. With typical American kindness he drove in, collected my wife and carried her off for a month, though he knew neither of us. My attack happened on April Fool's Day, and I'm just past the second anniversary of my rebirth!

JOHN FLETCHER London *is* exhausting, body-destroying, and can be soul-destroying as well. Financial insecurity induces people to work at that pressure. You take everything because if you refuse they don't ask you again. I've certainly found that. But most people grab as much as they can today in case it doesn't come in tomorrow. That's the driving force, and perhaps the other extreme is worse, complete security until sixty-five. Whoever heard of a superannuated football team, full of ancient, pensionable players? If you can't play football you go, and so perhaps with music. It's a cruel way to look at it.

Nowadays there's a little more compassion for those in trouble. But that needs resources. The Berlin Philharmonic can afford to give six months off, to rest and play long notes in private. With our slender resources we can't do that in London. So we hustle along. Things might be peaceful for a while, then suddenly things go berserk, everybody falls

109

down dead. It's the pace and the irregularity that is at once so ghastly and so fascinating. Such pressure can affect orchestral standards, but there's no rule. Sometimes terrific pressure can produce stunning results, though for brass players fatigue is a very great problem. You can never predict a concert. You can turn up at some awful place after a tedious bus ride, on a filthy cold, rainy day, nowhere to eat, nowhere to change, freezing water dripping through the roof, stage too small, busted chairs creaking all over the house, and for some reason — anger perhaps — the audience gets a better concert than one done in the comfort of the Festival Hall. And on tour the orchestra can get terribly tired and woebegone. Then suddenly some godforsaken hole in America gets a concert the like of which we haven't heard in ten years.

GILLIAN EASTWOOD I remember, on a recent tour of Italy, we had a terrifying trip from Naples to Palermo, earthquakes under the sea hurling the boat all over the place. *Everybody* was ill. We arrived about eleven o'clock in the morning, yet every member of the orchestra was on the platform that night for the concert. 6,000 people stood to hear us, and how the orchestra responded! The playing just got better and better. That's spirit, and I think it's maintained by the way we habitually work, by the struggle for survival. But this constant fight does impose very great strains on the players.

Moving from city to city
while on tour can be
exhausting

JOHN FLETCHER Certainly, our orchestral players don't seem to last to a ripe old age. Someone will retire, on a minuscule hand-out, and the next thing you hear he's dead. He's been geared up like a working pit-pony just to keep going, and as soon as you take the treadle away he collapses. To get good musical results is really a punishment. What is the answer? You can be as addicted to that sort of working as to alcohol. The session boys, running around three sessions a day, in studios morning to night, what can they spend their money on, apart from drink?

BILL LANG There was an article in the papers a while ago about the drinking on the London Symphony tour of Japan. Well, I was on that tour and I didn't see anything much. But, yes, nerves and strain do lead to drinking in orchestras, and nowadays there's a lot of drinking everywhere. Brass players like to drink beer, though I don't care for it. It relaxes them. I used to drink, and I've found that if you enjoy a drink, it's fine. But if you're drinking for a purpose, because you are afraid of the job or the instrument, then it's fatal. It's *fatal*. I know a few who do that, and I've even told them it's fatal. I think I'm entitled to tell them because I'm much older and I've seen bad things happen to players through drink. You can understand how it happens, delays in travelling, boredom in buses and trains and at airports, things go wrong. You can't always be on parade. But drinking before a concert is another matter, that's usually out of fear or nerves. You start doing that, you fall down on the job, and you don't last very long.

MARIE WILSON I've often been asked if there's any prejudice against women playing in orchestras. I can only speak for myself, but I have never encountered any. I think that if a woman can do the job as well as, or better than, a man and – most important – behaves at all times in a pro-fessional way, then there is usually no prejudice. I have had some recog-nition. I was awarded the MBE, and I've played in two coronations. Young people today appear to have loads of confidence and great technical skill. But discipline seems less evident than in my early days, before the War. And there seems to be less time for reflective work, owing to the pace of work today and the general stress of life.

CSABA ERDELYI Life can be so unpleasant, rehearsing all over London, playing anywhere. It would be so much more human to have a base, one hall for rehearsal and concerts. We do rehearse in Henry Wood Hall a lot. It is a very handsome hall, but it has difficult acoustics, and when we go to the Festival Hall for the concert we have to re-rehearse to balance for the new acoustic. Otherwise we are like gypsies, tramping endlessly to Walthamstow and Bishopsgate – Oh god, to play in the bathroom is better than that. I still think the poverty of orchestras is unbelievable in a city like London. With this poverty, there is just no free time, and this affects me most. On the continent or in America, if one is a principal it is acknowledged that one must have some time to work at your playing. The *sportsmanship* of English sight-reading, with no time to rehearse or digest! I think it is tremendous, and I certainly didn't have that habit from Hungary, but it is nothing to do with music. Nonetheless, it is a necessary equipment to be an orchestral musician in England.

JOHN RONAYNE A musician's life in London is nothing else but his life in music. He can't afford to have any other life, the demands of time, energy and money are so fierce upon him. To an extent, I like the English way – the variety, different places, different people, different music. But as I get older I think I would settle for an orchestra in Germany. They look after their players. People here are thrown on the scrapheap, or fight in the freelance jungle. It's of no concern what happens to them, and many decent players fall by the wayside. Some old colleagues of mine in the Royal Philharmonic, what do they do now? I never see them or hear them playing anywhere. Did they wish to end like that? I'm sure they would rather have stayed out their time and retired on a pension. Or at least get a little recognition for what they had contributed. My old colleagues, if they'd been on the continent they'd still have a place in musical life, a reputation, a position in a music school, even if troubles had interrupted their playing careers. What are they reduced to in England – impecunious men scraping by on private lessons?

CECIL JAMES My first entry on my first appearance with the Philharmonia, it was the *Rite of Spring*. The bassoon begins, starting cold, and it's difficult music. 'If I mess this up,' I thought, 'I'll wreck the performance for everybody.' I remember it was as if I'd been living on a diet of molten lead, nerves at the end. And when you come out you are still quivering, you can't switch off. No wonder orchestras are torn by tensions, soured by animosities. The pressure of playing, of making music live! I recall once a secretary got caught in the studio, just as we were about to start a recording session with Karajan. She found herself stranded right in the orchestra, and she said later she had no idea about this sudden generation of electric tension, the fellows she had seen in the office often enough suddenly transformed by the red recording light. And at concerts we look very grand on the platform, all dressed up like elegant gents. Does the audience know that some players are at the last extremity of fright? You might rehearse time and time again, but the danger of going wrong always exists, and the occasion is so important. You are gathering yourself to give a *performance* of great music.

ALAN CIVIL I wouldn't recommend the life of an orchestral musician as a wonderful life. It's a very strange life, at least here in England, so much is unreal, some hardship and a lot of frustration. Musicians are not paid too badly, but the pay still doesn't compare with other jobs that are a lot less wearying, a lot less difficult and a lot less valuable. As always, the wrong people are squeezing money out of music, not the players. It's the old story, write it, arrange it, conduct it, record it, but don't play it.

Instruments

'Italian violins are the old masters of the musical instrument world . . . they have been appreciating – predictably – from 10 to 20 per cent a year over the last decade . . . it is indeed a very good time to enter the market.' Joseph Lufkin of Sotheby Parke Bernet doesn't see only violins, of course . . . he also handles early lutes and mandolins, pianos made before 1830, virginals, flutes, recorders and harps . . . Mr Lufkin will be pleased to help you . . . he will also be delighted to help you add to or start a collection...

Advertisement in *The New Yorker*

The String Instruments

ROBIN MCGEE

FOR certain people – in and out of the musical profession – string instruments have become just articles of merchandise, speculative commodities. They get sent to the places where they fetch the highest prices, sold in fashionable auction-rooms. And players, for whose use the instruments are, are left fishing. The good instruments are going into bank-vaults, museums, pension funds. Absolutely crazy. What kind of artistic world is it that would withdraw the brushes and paints from Leonardo, hoard them in a strong-box, and expect him to do his pictures with some old muddy colours and the frayed end of a rope?

A list of string instruments owned by, or donated to, the Los Angeles Philharmonic Orchestral Association, for the use of orchestral members:

Violins
Tassini (1756)
Montagnana (1737)
Tononi (no date)
Guadagnini (1775)
Guadagnini (no date)
Stradivarius (1711)
'Earl of Plymouth'
Stradivarius (1728) 'Perkins'
Stradivarius (1729) 'Jack Benny'
Landolfi (1754)
Pressenda (1832) 'Jack Benny'
Amati (1617) 'Winslaw'

Violas
Gasparo de Salo (1550)
Gasparo de Salo (1570)
Gand & Bernardel (1877) 'Heifetz'

Cellos
Stradivarius (1684) 'General Kyd'
Guarnerius (1706)

ALFIO MICCI Violins are so expensive, they've gone completely out the window. About ten years ago I bought a Galliano, and that was from a fellow in the orchestra who was going to buy something better. That's how it works. Most of the men in the New York Philharmonic have, not Strads, but good instruments. It's nothing to pay $100,000 for a really fine violin, and you don't make that sort of money in an orchestra. Some orchestras have collections to loan out. We've talked about it many times, but never acquired any. And you really don't need Strads to have a good sounding string section. Those instruments are for soloists who need to project, to carry right through the orchestral sound, which is the last thing you need in a string section, to stick out like that.

JOHN RONAYNE How does a young fiddle player start today? How does he find a decent instrument, and then how does he pay for it? I have a Carlo Guiseppe Testore, not one of the greats, but a good workmanlike maker. I've had it at least fifteen years and when I bought it, it cost £800. Now I think it's valued at £13,000, maybe more. About eight years ago I got a second fiddle, a German one for £65. Hills recently told me it's worth £1,000 – in eight years! The young player now will have to go for a modern fiddle, and there are some good ones, but that can cost £1,000 or more. My old fiddle is a bit temperamental, subject to weather. If it's a muggy day it is reluctant to sound – something to do with the wood. Most players like to muck about with their instruments, move the sound-post, put on a new bridge, try new strings. But I reckon you should let an instrument settle down and then leave it alone. For about twelve years I had a bridge which seemed to be buckling a bit, but the fiddle was going well and I just didn't want to change that bridge. A new one shakes everything up. The old instruments seem to stand up to heat and humidity quite well, unless you go to India in the hot weather, but I think you will find that most orchestral players don't take a decent instrument on tour. The risk of damage is too great.

ELEANOR GOULD I play on a modern viola, a Carl Berger, made in New York in 1950. A nice, solid instrument. Many violas have a very nasal quality, which I don't like. This has a very forthright tone – matches my personality. I could never hope to get hold of a good, old instrument. In the States it's just too expensive. I mean, I was fortunate enough in my bows, because they also have gone sky-high. My Hill bow is worth about $3,000 and my Sartori nearly as much. I guard them with my life. I was lucky to have gotten them before the price went really jumping. And instrument insurance in the States, that's almost impossible. Some orchestras take out policies to cover their players, but for freelancers, particularly in New York, all insurance was cancelled some years ago. The union raised such a stink that a scheme was worked out, but only with one company, with a $200 deductible, and such a huge premium that I couldn't possibly afford it. So I have no insurance, and that is not unusual for a freelance. The theft rate in New York is tremendous. My apartment has been broken into five times.

American master violin-maker, Mario Antonio Frosali, looks at the body of a violin

Frosali checks that the neck of an instrument has not warped with time

The North American climate can be hard on instruments. When I was in northern Michigan, where there's practically no humidity, anything that's glued just falls apart. My viola was constantly opening up. I finally got some equipment, glue, clamps, and so on, so I didn't have to go nearly 500 miles to Detroit, to get it stuck together. A fellow told me that all modern string instruments have a settling, because the belly wood is softer than the back. So the angle of the neck and fingerboard changes, making an uneveness up in the positions. It may be a big job to correct it, so I thought I'd take it to Ghent. I know I'll get good attention and good prices there. Belgium is not cheap, but prices in New York . . . Re-hairing bows, you know what that costs in New York? $25 a bow. I used to re-hair every three months, automatically, and change all my strings too. But the cost of strings now. Astronomical. I can't afford to change like that now.

TOM STORER My best cello is a Grancino, made in 1721, bought in the days when it was feasible to get decent instruments. I paid just about a year's salary for it, long ago – about £500. And now at £7,500 it's still worth about a year's gross takings, so I suppose pro rata the value is about the same. I think the London Philharmonic has some funds to help young players buy instruments, a very good policy on the whole, but in the London Symphony we've never been so provident.

115

Young players today tend to be earning their living on instruments we older players rejected as students even. And of course in an orchestra one needs a second instrument anyway, as a spare and to take on tour, though I took my old one on tour for fifteen years without a scratch. Being old and stable it stood up to temperature changes better than some modern instruments. If anything cracked on tour, it was nearly always a modern bass. But a valuable old instrument is a liability on tour, and when I took to motorcycling I had to get a spare. I bought a Scottish cello, 1916, made by a man rejoicing in the name of Smellie. There are some good modern instruments around, and a lot of fiddle players in the LSO are using modern violins. But they're not cheap. Well, the wood alone for a fiddle is going to cost over £100. It takes about three weeks working time to make one violin, let alone the hours hanging around waiting for the varnish to dry. And craftsmen nowdays don't work for dustmen's wages — or I should say the wages dustmen used to get! However, there's a renewed effort to teach the craft of instrument making. Now some serious young men are taking it up and doing pretty well. They buy old windmills in Suffolk and ship crate-loads of viola d'amores off to America.

An instrument seems to become stable at about 100 years — partly the wood and partly the varnish. The oil-based varnishes of a good instrument oxidize very slowly. Linseed oil, drying naturally, takes about 100 years to oxidize completely. Then it becomes very tough, almost impervious to any solvent, and helps enormously to preserve the stability of the instrument. And the wood seems to settle down in that time too, the resins becoming finally stabilized. Perhaps I'm lucky. My old Grancino is very untemperamental. If there's anything wrong it can usually be traced to me.

ROBIN MCGEE The bass player doesn't have to go chasing Italian instruments. The English makers — names like Lott, Fendt, Kennedy, Forster — are very good, and some of the German basses are good too. Fortunately, I've got a nice English bass, among others. I don't think it's yet got to the stage where experienced professionals are playing on very poor instruments, but my students have great trouble in finding basses. In fact, I persuade them to sell to one another at greatly deflated prices, rather than join that speculative rat-race, pushing prices up, and making all musicians suffer in the end.

Strings

CSABA ERDELYI I believe in gut greatly — natural fibres. Wood, gut and horsehair, those are the essences of string instrument sound. That makes for real sweetness, touching the soul. But every instrument is different, and I wouldn't say 'gut only' as a rigid principle. I've found for instance that the bottom string, the C, on my viola sounds very well with a nylon-covered string. It lasts longer than a gut, but I find it soon loses its freshness. But there are always fashions, actions and reactions in these things.

Sitting during a break in rehearsal surrounded by basses

I think modern instruments stand steel strings much better, and the old ones breath easier with gut. The volume of sound is much the same, depending on the instrument. Gut might sound a bit weaker under the ear, but the projection, the flying of the sound so to speak, is more immediate with gut.

TOM STORER I used always to have gut strings, even in the orchestra, because the Grancino doesn't like metal strings. They lack flexibility, elasticity, and their unvarying pressure choked the instrument, drying out the sound. Then I started using the Tomastik covered strings. They are not as subtle as gut, but they have the consistent quality of metal without the relentless pressure. They're a bit bright and crude, but a fraction of the price of gut. And when a set of good gut strings for a cello can cost up to £50, it becomes a question of economics.

ELEANOR GOULD Most viola players use a steel string on the A, but I don't care for it, it's too harsh. I use silver or aluminum wound strings. I like a gut A, which is fine for baroque music, but if I play the Bloch Suite or the Quincy Porter Concerto, where you are way up on the A, gut won't take it. So I compromise with a wound string, though that takes longer to tune if you don't use an adjuster. There's no movement back to gut in American orchestras. Many players use steel strings.

ROBIN MCGEE Every problem is enlarged on the bass, starting with carrying the thing, and it goes on from there. If you're out of tune it's by that much more, and there's so much room to play out of tune. If you squeak the whole hall knows. And the usual disadvantages of gut strings are worse on the bass. I use metal strings because they solve a lot of those problems. Metal just goes on until it breaks. Gut is unreliable and fiddly, it gets hairy and has to be oiled and trimmed. The cost is high, though even a set of metal bass strings now costs £40–50. With the few notes that we play, I think metal gives us an easier target area.

Relaxing with the
newspaper during a
rehearsal break

The Woodwind
Flutes

RICHARD ADENEY I have a couple of silver flutes, in the French tradition, though made in Japan. They are rather like Datsun cars, solid, mass-produced, well-built, but not very exciting. On the new flutes the relationship between the notes is more accurate than on the old. An old French flute possibly has a very nice sound, but the actual positioning of the key-holes is slightly out, whereas the modern Japanese get nearer and nearer to being just right. Otherwise nothing much has changed in the flute. The bore is the same. I think Mr Boehm got it pretty well right in 1832.

I took one of my flutes to Mr Cooper of Clapham Common, a kind of virtuoso doctor of the flute. He makes very good instruments, but extremely expensive, and only one every year or so, so there's a vast waiting list. But I took him my head-joint and he altered the mouthpiece, making the sound much more interesting, and he replaced the Japanese lip-plate with his own. Some players like to mess around, change the shape of the holes with plasticine and solder, which looks awful but sounds marvellous. But I don't tinker like that, I just hope for the best. Modern flutes are not difficult to come by. I've just got one fairly cut-price – £850. I was offered a new American gold flute for £5,000, but I'm not altogether sold on gold. It's a wonderful feeling to play on it, and easy to adapt to, though some flutes are difficult. But I don't know if gold makes a difference. Really, it's how the instrument is made, not what it's made of. But I'm not quite sure.

118

PAUL FRIED I've had one flute for the last twenty-two years, the Powell I started on when I was eleven, and it's pretty hard to beat it. It's an old Powell – number 751 – made by Powell himself, so I feel it's like a Strad, a gem of an instrument. In America we generally use Powell or Haynes flutes, though more and more are buying Japanese instruments. Many would like an English Cooper, but he doesn't make a lot of flutes. The Powell is a French style instrument.

I play mostly Powell. The lower register you have to work for, but the middle and upper are very fluid sounding, easy, and that's what I like. Recently I bought a Muramatsu gold flute, and you know the Japanese are always refining things to the nth degree, so they've made a very fine instrument. I think gold does change the tone, giving a warmer sound, which is not quite so successful in the orchestra. The art of the instrument maker is in the cutting of the head-piece, and I'm still looking for the right head-joints for the type of sound I want. I have to be confident that it's a free and easy sound, I like that kind of re-sponsive instrument. Gold tends to be warm, but the tone is heavier than silver. Silver has that cutting quality that most orchestral flautists find they need.

Oboes

JOHN DE LANCIE The problem of reeds is a very difficult one, and it's absolutely essential for an oboe player to learn about them. I started when I was about nine, with a teacher who was willing to help me with reeds. At that age it's a little difficult to get into, unless you have a leaning to-wards mechanical things, which I didn't. I know it was a terrible shock for me when I went to the Curtis Institute, at fifteen, with no reed-making experience, and I suddenly found the whole business an awful mystery. I must admit I came very close to giving up.

ANTHONY CAMDEN The problem with reeds, the big problem, took all my time in my early professional years. You see, to finish each oboe reed will take the best part of an hour. Well now, if you take twelve pieces of cane perhaps only one will finally be usable. With experience, looking at the cane you learn to judge a good one, though it may not be so. You measure the thickness, look at the closeness of the grain and the shine on the bark, twist and test elasticity. From that you know the useless ones and throw them away. Then you are down to say six out of twelve, all looking as if they might happen a little bit. You might soak those to test absorption, flex them when wet, watch for changes of colour, and discard some more. After all this testing you might be left with three out of twelve, hoping that perhaps two will work and one will be very good.

My students find it difficult, and I do at times, to get a proper bevel edge on the knife, like a razor-blade, to cut the tip of the reed as thin as a wafer. If you get that wrong it might need a couple of hours work on the oil-stone. And one's gouge must give true measurements, not too wide at the top which flattens the upper notes. And the staples must be of the right thickness to suit the temperament of the instrument. If a reed has nothing wrong with it — the right cane, well-shaped, well-gouged, supporting itself at both sides — it may last me a couple of months, but that's very rare, perhaps three times in my life. I'm lucky because my saliva is not very acid. For some players, with acid saliva, a reed will not last more than four days. And for me also a reed will sometimes collapse in two days. I usually keep about thirty spares in my reed-box, any one of which can be made to play in about five minutes.

There are different schools of oboe sound. The Americans use the dark-sounding French Lorées, though I don't think the French use them now. English players are beginning to play French instruments, but a lot of us still use our English Howarths. I do. It has great projection, and a good one seems to have the ideal measurements. I think it copes best with the problems thrown at a London oboe player. For example, you might find yourself grovelling around the bottom of the instrument for a milk ad on TV, *pianissimo*, written really too low for the oboe. And a lot of continental instruments are just flat at the bottom, or produce too thick a sound to control properly for the microphone. For our great variety of work, concerts, recordings, sessions, we need an exact instrument, very correct, which speaks easily with a clear sound. The Howarth fits the bill very well. In an orchestra, people want to hear the oboe carry a line, phrase the tune. Other instruments are for virtuosity, but I think oboe players are regarded for sound, though of course the technique must be there.

Clarinets

TONY PAY Today, there are so many different models of clarinet available. Styles in sound change. The pendulum seems to swing between a sound that was quite focused and compact, and a wider, larger sound. The compact sound was in favour perhaps until the War, and then players like Jack Brymer and Gervase de Peyer altered the sound, playing on English clarinets. Now the swing is going the other way and players are getting interested in the more focused sound of the continental instruments. There are national schools of clarinet playing, and you should adjust your playing to the music — some players don't — and that means you need a wide range of possible kits. I try to steer a middle road, realizing that the middle road always has pit-falls. If I have to play like a German clarinet, I can't do it quite as well as a German player, and if I have to produce a more open sound I won't quite get the sound of a wide-bore instrument. But we are coming to accept a wide variety of clarinet sound now. I like also to have a fair amount of resistance in my set-up, something to blow against, as we say, with the diaphragm doing some of the work, not all the control at the reed.

The usual orchestral clarinets are A and B flat, also E flat and bass, though I try to avoid the bass. I also try to vary my instruments. The C clarinet, which sounds quite different, I find very useful, and a lot of composers have written for it. Ordinarily, most players would just transpose it on the B flat. But it has a nice sound and an agility that you don't get on the others. I recently did *Falstaff* on a C. It was brighter in the section, and I think that's what Verdi had in mind.

ALAN HACKER Instruments interest me very much, their history and development, their construction. A clarinet to me is much more than just going to Boosey & Hawkes for the latest model. There's a difficulty with modern woodwind. The best instruments were made about a century ago – hand-made by craftsmen. Quite good ones are made now in large numbers, machine made, the best being French, but they don't have the special quality of the old ones. I think you have to try to go one better than mass-production, and that means a lot of delving into odd corners and old shops.

And if you haven't a good reed you can't play well, one must stress that. A good reed allows you the maximum range of dynamic and tone colour, to play, in other words, in the most vocal way. In the orchestra you have to keep some kind of pattern with your reeds, ready to move on when one goes. The trouble is reeds get better and better the more they are played until all at once they go. They get too bright and lose the fundamental in the tone, and you're just left with a lot of fizzy upper harmonics – a tone with no support. I have a rather nice old reed-case from the 'twenties – it says 'England's greatest Manufacturer of Clarinet, Saxophone and Motor-horn Reeds'. I buy maybe twenty reeds, scrape them and lick them, then practise, going from one to another, because the more you play on them the more the character appears. Then I select the eight best and put them in my case. Then I'm ready. I think most players just try to get a good reed, but I like to have one reed for Debussy and another for Mozart. Recently, at a Festival Hall rehearsal, my young daughter criticized my tone, and I had another reed to go to immediately. In fact I used one for Mozart, then for the Berio Concertino I changed to a slightly harder, more aggressive reed. But of course in a symphony orchestra, the idea – and this is fundamentally wrong – is to play the music of some 200 years in more or less the same style. My attitude is rather different.

PETER HADCOCK This business of characteristic instrumental sound is very strange. Any time somebody tries to figure out an historical sound he may be right or wrong. I think ultimately it comes down to what *you* want to sound like. I can play practically any clarinet, any mouthpiece, and, you know, after six months I'm going to sound the same. I change mouthpieces and it seems to be great. Three weeks later I'm back with my old sound. And in general also my students might want to change but they just can't. Most players in the States use French Buffets, a few others too, but all French system. It would be hard to say just what is the tonal difference between French and German instruments, because I think it's more a question of the player than the instrument.

Waiting . . .

Bassoons

CECIL JAMES I started the bassoon at fifteen, but now you get kids playing at ten. There's a good reason for that. I play on the French system, but now nearly everyone plays the German system where the closer lay-out of the keys means you can get by with a smaller hand. Nowadays, of course, I'm a sort of freak, playing on a French instrument. This has a narrower bore which makes it a bit tricky, rather like the old French horn, but when it goes it has a most beautiful voice. But treacherous to play, accidents can happen. The German system gives you a more sporting chance.

I'm a bit biased about the bassoon, I still prefer the French instrument, well played. The German is a duller, vaguer sound which doesn't appeal to me. But the French is going out now — oh yes, it's had it. It's had a bit of a revival in America, for special purposes, where they call it 'the new sound', and some of their players are playing both, which is very clever — the French instrument for French or baroque music, then back to the German for big orchestral works. Here in England, the specialist orchestras are either using the French bassoon, or authentic baroque instruments, and the results are splendid. My instrument is now so old I always say it's practically baroque anyway.

I always maintain that the reed is about sixty percent of good bassoon playing. If you have a reed that goes well then your worries are lessened and you can address yourself to the music. I make my own reeds, though that is not general with English bassoonists. My father didn't, but I was shown how to do it, and was driven to it during the War. The oboe reed is vitally important, to vibrate the column of air, but I think the bassoon reed is more an integral part of the instrument. But the bassoon reed, being larger, gives you a little more latitude than the oboe reed — not too good but not too bad. Archaic method to use in this scientific age, isn't it? relying on the luck of the cane. They were doing it in Egypt thousands of years ago. Picked something from the roadside, scraped it, and with luck it went.

Cecil James with his
bassoon reeds

The Brass
French horns

ALAN CIVIL The horn does have a reputation for difficulty, though nowadays you can get working models, you might say, which ensure that all the notes that used to be bad on, say, Alexander horns are easier to get. The tubing has been ironed out and the notes are in the centre, as it were, but in doing this they've somehow made a metal instrument without much character. People playing these horns tend to sound all the same to me. That's my own prejudice, and I find them difficult to play. I like a horn with a bit of a problem that you must work out for yourself.

Facial make-up, mouth and lips and teeth, are important. Sticking out teeth, or the wrong size, can affect the horn sound. Also thick lips are not always good. You could say get a larger mouthpiece, but there's a limit to size, if you want to keep a characteristic sound. But now sound is a matter of personal preference. At one time a horn sound was a horn sound, but now there's so much variation and everyone is right.

Well, I keep on playing the old hand-horn, the natural horn with no valves. It gives you extremely good lip flexibility, and you still have to listen for your notes before you play them, and know exactly where you are going to pitch them. Many young horn players, notably in America, at an early age get a huge American Conn double horn. They know nothing about the beginnings of the horn, the harmonic series is all by-passed. They have a gross 4-valve instrument that comes out like a euphonium, or baritone horn, as far as I can hear. And the hand positions are so important, the right hand is not there just to hold the horn up, you have to humour the notes with the right hand. Now, many of these kids achieve a sort of perfection, but it's up the wrong alley-way. There's something missing, because they are ignorant of the real nature of the instrument. So I go on with the old instruments, trying to get the essential sound in my head.

Ordinarily, I play on one instrument, though I may change, depending on the music. I have a descant horn for Bach or anything high. It takes some of the misery out of the higher octave, but the danger is that the sound will come out like a bugle. People play on them all the time, which puzzles me, because the sound is not that good. My normal horn I bought in 1948, from Alexander in Germany. It cost me £44 – I'm still playing it. And I've had possibly fifteen other horns since then, which I've tried and discarded. Now the Alexander is really on its last legs, it's clapped out. All the valves leak, there are patches on it, it's thin in the bell. I think if it packs up, I shall have to pack up too.

Trumpets

ROLF SMEDVIG When I was growing up, the ideal orchestral trumpet sound that students had in mind was that of Herseth in Chicago. A beautiful big, open, full sound, that blends very well in section playing. So the big, wide-bore Vincent Bach trumpets are usually played in the

States. I play a Vincent Bach generally for large trumpets, C or B flat, though for smaller trumpets I might use Yamaha, Selmer and so on. It's hard to become a specialist when you're in an orchestra, because the music from week to week demands different instruments. The piccolo trumpet, for example, we don't use much — only in the Rite, in a Bach suite, or the Brandenberg — but we are expected to have one and play it.

BILL LANG The brass in English orchestras is a bit mixed up at the moment. I think the chief difficulty for trumpets is that the other brass instruments have changed so much. The wider the bore, the safer the instrument, and that's what many players have gone for. The old French horns, for instance, led a rather dangerous life with their narrow bores, but played well they had a wonderful pure sound. Now trumpets, which are more or less as they were, perhaps with slightly bigger bores, seem out on a limb in the new orchestral brass sound. Trombones are sounding like horns, horns are sounding like hooters, and the trumpets are trying to find out where we are.

The first decent trumpet I had was a Vincent Bach, from America. Vacchiano from New York was coming for the Edinburgh Festival, and

The Green Park Band

Barbirolli asked him to bring me this trumpet. Vacchiano would only take the American price — well, that was forty percent cheaper than in England. It was £90, not much now, but more than I could afford then. So Barbirolli bought it for me and I paid him back at so much a week.

Trombones

R AY P REMRU English players used to have very small-bore trombones, known as 'pea-shooters', not, I think, generally used elsewhere. Then, about 1951, the marvellous trombone section of the New York Philharmonic came for the Edinburgh Festival, playing on large-bore instruments, and English musicians began to play these trombones, for a rounder, more flexible sound. There was a general change-over to larger instruments, and now in England we use virtually the same equipment as the Americans, I myself have two American trombones and a British one. Denis Wick, the principal trombone of the LSO, in conjunction with Boosey & Hawkes, has developed an excellent bass trombone, based on a new technique and able to play in several keys — a slide trombone with two independent valves giving a number of combinations and allowing tremendous facility. The strange thing is that in the 'fifties the American instruments swept the board here, but now Americans are copying the Wick/Boosey instrument.

R ON B ARRON The slide is still the most natural way of controlling air flow. The natural form is a length of pipe with a slide introduced to change the length for a chromatic range. Air goes through the trombone with the least amount of curves and hindrance. Even the valve that most trombonists use, the rotor valve to lower a 4th, introduces some stuffiness.

Usually, now, the tenor trombone in B flat seems to be working out best. The old English bass trombone was in G, which never took hold in the States. In ours, the idea is not additional length, but size. They are all pitched in B flat, same length as the tenor, but size and bore are bigger, and they'll have the F valve and maybe the double valve. There are so many ways of approaching that second valve that you almost have to ask, 'What are you doing? What key are you in?' There used to be an alto, often in E flat, a tenor also in C, and in Eastern Europe the F bass. Bartok's famous glissando in the *Concerto for Orchestra* is for an F trombone. He starts on the low B, just below the low cello C, and just whistles up to F, which you can't get on a B flat instrument. So since 1944 bass trombonists have been up to all sorts of funny business, with pedals and bits of string to pull the valve while working the slide. The trouble is the F bass trombone is hard to find, and being a small-bore instrument, it doesn't sound too well with our big B flat tenors on top of it.

I try to use different instruments for different music. Home base for me, so to speak, is my Conn 88H, which I've had since high school. I keep coming back to that, an easy, free-flowing instrument. I guess it's been around since the 'forties, that model. I like my Conn and I use it for the softer, more melodic, chorale-like pieces.

Harps

SIDONIE GOOSSENS In Europe we all used to play on French Erard harps. Years ago Lyon & Healy extended the sound-board, and then harps began to get bigger. At first, we could never afford these American harps. Then this desire for largeness – I don't really know what started it, if the new music demanded it – led the continentals to make bigger harps. I think the Obermayer is the best. But it's another sound, bigger, boomy, and perhaps fits the new music best. I still think the Erard, with gut strings, has the more beautiful tone. I have two Erards, but I also bought an Obermayer – I had to, rather like keeping up with the Joneses. My sister Marie, who is coming up to eighty-four but still does quite a lot of recording, is told by engineers that her Erard gives them no problems – 'You do the work for us and we don't have to turn the knobs.' It's a much cleaner sound, much. I proved it a while ago when we recorded a trio written for us and Leon, for his eightieth birthday, 'The Art of Leon Goossens'. Foolishly I took my Obermayer while Marie was playing on her Erard, and I thought, when we heard the playback, 'Oh what have I done?' I had to tone mine down while the engineers fiddled about in the box. Marie's Erard sounded just beautiful, but my harp was all twangy. I was very upset. Not many orchestral harpists play the old instruments now. On our last European tour I think I saw only one, an Erard, in Zagreb I think. An old one is no disgrace, and the new ones are terribly expensive – about £8,500.

Harps

Playing

The Violin Sections

*Violins are able, nowadays, to execute whatever they will. They play
up to the extreme height as easily as in the middle. Passages the most
rapid, designs the most eccentric do not dismay them. In an orchestra,
with sufficient numbers, what one fails to perform is done by others.*

HECTOR BERLIOZ, *On Orchestration*

HUGH MAGUIRE

THE responsibility of the orchestral leader, the concertmaster, is a
slightly problematic question. I can only speak about myself. For a
while, as a young man, I sat with Paul Beard, leader of the BBC
Symphony for very many years. We were never close. He was a good
deal older than I and, I suppose, a bit suspicious of me. I was a young
fellow with a hell of a lot of hair — all gone now — and a bit of a whizz kid.
I fancied myself a bit. And though I didn't greatly care for Paul's fiddle
playing, I realized he didn't half know his job. I learnt an immense
amount from him, about how to get round a piece in the simplest possible
way, how to cope with difficult passages, what to aim at, dynamic control, doing effective bowings easily understood by everybody. Nothing
fancy. The bare minimum of effort to get the best results. An economical
way of working.

I always thought the leader's first duty was towards the composer. But
a conductor may be more interested in himself than in Mr Beethoven.
That's a great problem for leaders. In a way, you must split your loyalty,
between composer and conductor. If a conductor seems dishonest with
the music, you might have to go into secret conclave with him. This
doesn't happen often, and sometimes it's just not worth it. Your views
will make no inroads into his conceit. But always you must remember·
that the conductor is completely in charge. You must not bother him
unnecessarily, even though you have to represent the body of the
orchestra. It is a skilful art, which you practise more by example than by
interruption. A leader who talks too much is fairly useless.

A leader also has a responsibility to the orchestra — questions of
loyalty and protection, keeping people happy and sitting with compatible
partners — simple matters. And more important, he has complete responsibility for bowing. But if I see the first viola doing something different, I
don't bulldoze him into my way, I'll see what he has to offer. It's highly
democratic among the string principals, this business of bowing. None-

127

theless, the way one bows is extremely important, affecting the style of the whole orchestra, specially in the classical repertoire — where the division of the bow is, what accentuation to use. Unless that is done sensitively the music can sound terribly distorted, because small errors of judgment become magnified, terribly magnified, depending on the size of the orchestra.

JOHN RONAYNE It takes a lot of tact to lead. In England we have a great hassle with bowings, because our orchestras have to hire parts, which the leader has to re-bow each time, scrubbing out the amazing aberrations of the man before. Now the tradition here, at least with the great conductors, is that they don't interfere. I never remember Beecham or Kempe saying anything about bowings. The leader and the string principals are the experts and it's up to them to get it right. But when I went to lead in Dublin, in '64, the conductor Tibor Paul, a Hungarian ex-clarinet player, thought he could do it all. I remember in Beethoven 6 he produced a miniature score with some very bad bowings which had belonged to a famous old conductor of the Berlin Philharmonic — I forget who. I told him frankly they were bad, but he was the conductor and if he wanted them, we'd do our best with them. 'Forget it,' he said, 'do it your way.' I got on quite well with him because I found I could put my cards on the table in private. You must *never* fight a conductor in front of the orchestra. I've seen leaders do it, usually about bowings, and refuse to give way. Well, it's terrible for a conductor to lose face in front of an orchestra. And orchestras, of course, love to see conductors in a fight, and see them lose too. That's why the conductor-baiters are so much appreciated by their colleagues. Everybody waits for the fun.

Pierre Boulez discusses
the score with John
Georgiadis during rehearsal

Leaders also can't afford to lose face. David McCallum, a famous leader, said to me, 'I've only two bits of advice. Don't talk unless you have to, then people will listen. And never demonstrate. Explain in words, if necessary, but don't get up and play.' And that's true. For some reason if you demonstrate you never play well. You're half talking and half playing, it sounds bad and makes a bad impression.

HUGH MAGUIRE Sometimes I'll be asked, 'Well, how do you follow a conductor?' Have I ever looked at a conductor's beat in my life? I'm not sure . . . One looks at the conductor, the whole man. The message comes from the balls of the feet, right through to the top of the head, not just what he does with his hands. I think to look for musical guidance just from the stick is idiocy, up the wrong track altogether.

ALFIO MICCI I'm on the inside of the 3rd stand of first violins – no. 6. We have a rotating section, the men working towards the back and then coming forward again, but rotation begins behind the third stand. I'm frozen where I am. All the string sections rotate, except the basses – I've no idea why they don't. The players behind me, who are moving around, get a turn to be off occasionally, in the smaller pieces. That's nice for them. We who are frozen at the front get more money, but it's not that much and sometimes we wonder if it's worth it. It would be nice to be off once in a while.

Certainly it's difficult to play at the back of a string section, much easier and more pleasant towards the front. Perhaps that's why people at the back get a bit restless and discipline gets out of hand. They are distant from the conductor and it's hard there to get the feeling of what's going on. You have to play softer to hear what's happening, being so far away, but I sometimes think too much sound is coming from the men at the back. Well, in our orchestra all the string players are very experienced. You could rotate the whole section from the concertmaster back. Not that our concertmaster isn't a very fine violinist, but there's none of us who couldn't actually sit on the first stand. In our big American orchestras you can't really say that one player is inferior to another. It used to be that way, but not any more, because competition for places is so fierce.

GILLIAN EASTWOOD When I first started in the second violins I found a certain challenge. The first violins always have the tune and we have our *chuk, chuk*. Then suddenly we might get two bars which are solo. I found that challenging. And lots of times, playing along, we find a lovely note which is rather important, and we can bring it out. You can see the conductor's face change, and he'll smile at us – 'Ah, it means something.' I love it. The business of seconds being inferior to firsts is ridiculous. A very good second fiddle section gives an important richness to the orchestra in the middle. And I know Maestro Giulini, for one, feels very strongly about that. Very pro second fiddles. Well, the first violins really are the king-pins, they have a most particular importance. The function of the seconds

Gillian Eastwood

is more structural, vital but not brilliant, and members of the section must feel that and enjoy their role.

It's a different business playing in seconds. Our parts are easier, in some ways. We don't have to play so high, and when we do we groan, 'Oh dear, I'll have to get the rust off that string.' But we have our own little problems with bowing across the strings, difficult manoeuvres, quick accompanying passages. A second has to be strong, because we work harder in the lower part of the instrument, lots of tiring *tremolando*. We have to be careful about fitting with other sections, altering our sound slightly, for example, with violas. And we may set the tempo going, which needs careful rhythmic control. First violins often aim for brilliance and effect, but I think we should try for sound and depth. Playing an under-octave to the firsts, we should be slightly firmer, as it were, because the lower part stabilizes intonation in octave playing. To help intonation, some conductors want seconds slightly louder than firsts.

We all say what hell it is to play at the back, of seconds as well as firsts. I know that's true. I have one very experienced player whom I can keep about the fifth desk. But if you've someone very strong at the back, and the section starts playing from there, people don't know where they are. That can be absolute hell for me as principal. But a very, very experienced player on last desk, who knows exactly how to adapt, that makes a principal very happy. The secret of a good section is to know your players, and where to place them.

MICHAEL NUTT I think you need a certain kind of mentality to be happy in the second violins. Perhaps lackadaisical, an acceptance of your state. I don't worry that I'm not playing the tune, I'm a cog in the whole machine, maybe modest but important. I think some of the younger players are often frustrated in seconds. They work and work until they get into the first violins. Fine. It doesn't always happen like that because every opening is up for audition, for outsiders as well.

I get very cross when I hear talk about the wonderful LA string playing. You see, my other orchestral experience was in the Hallé under Barbirolli. And our LA string sections are nowhere near that for discipline and ensemble. In LA individual players could run rings around the Hallé players, no doubt about that. But as a string section, no. If I have one grouse about the Los Angeles Philharmonic it is that they don't play as an orchestra, because the strings don't play as sections. Everyone has his head down on his fiddle, he's right and the next fellow is not as right as he is. They don't think as a section. I'm happy to be a second violin, I know my place and like it. Many of our first violins are frustrated soloists. Also, we're rather isolated in LA, and lack contact with other good orchestras. Perhaps we are too inclined to believe our local review. But I suppose every honest musician knows that what he's doing could be a lot better.

String players in England have said to me, 'Oh Giulini is going to LA? Every day will be a different bowing.' And we have terrible problems with that already, because the fellows in the front can't make up their minds. They seem to have no clear notions about the best means of sound production. Although we have a big music library, with parts already marked, conductors come along and want it their way. Recently with Barenboim we were getting so messed up that by the time the marking got back to me — 4th desk — I just had to put my fiddle down and copy the bowings over the shoulder of the person in front. 'Why isn't he playing?' Danny asked our principal. 'Because every time I start playing,' I said, 'somebody alters the bloody bowings.' I'm a bit naughty like that. Oh, bowings are a big hassle. With Stokowski you did as you liked, so long as it sounded nice. I don't think I agree with that, because our bowings were so disciplined under Barbirolli, everything was very carefully worked out. And, by golly, if he said 'at the point' he wanted it in the last inch. Herr Spitz, the Berlin Phil called him. And for a vigorous up-bow he wanted the whole string band with arms swinging in the air. Not just for the sound, but also to promote a kind of corporate feeling, and to give a visual pleasure, a sense of élan and gaiety.

I agree with older string players that now, in general, left hand technique is often amazing, but bowing technique is poor. I think most experienced orchestral players will agree with that. But bowings have to be right, they are an essential part of style and sound production. And a concertmaster can't just bow to suit himself, he must consider how best a whole section can realize the demands of the music. Or else his string players just get frustrated.

The Viola Section

Viola players were always taken from among the refuse of violinists. Hence it arose that the viola performers knew how to play neither the violin nor the viola . . . But, little by little, the viola will, like other instruments, be confided only to clever hands.

HECTOR BERLIOZ, *On Orchestration*

ELEANOR GOULD The viola section is middle ground, a middle voice, and I like to be there, to listen to what's happening all around. On the top, or the bottom, so much of the spectrum is beyond you. In the middle you are more at the balance of things. We have to be able to go both ways, sometimes playing with the upper strings and sometimes with the bass. And the viola has to make the adjustments, musically and bowing-wise, to the particular passage. That's interesting. I don't try to sound like the upper strings when I'm playing with them. If I want to sound like a violin I can play one. Nor do I think the viola has, as it were, two separate registers, high and low. A chest voice and a head voice. I don't think you can chop it up like that, and it shouldn't be chopped up in singers either. There should be a blend, a progression.

I hate this free bowing, I think it's sloppy — I know Stokowski liked it. But you can't sound a unified section unless you do things the same way. Conductors decide bowings very often in the States — piano players! — and the reason is, I think, because string section leaders haven't made a stand, either not caring or not thinking it important. Now when I'm principal there are times when I bow with the cellos and people say 'that's strange'. Cellos usually bow the reverse of upper strings, but if our parts are with them there's no reason why we shouldn't bow with them. But generally, of course, the violas will take the bowing from the concertmaster.

CSABA ERDELYI The viola itself, yes, it is an awkward instrument, because it is a great strain to hold an instrument above the heart. The position is unnatural and needs very good blood circulation. The violin, being lighter and shorter, is not so strenuous. Those extra inches we have to reach with the left hand create a position that makes body balance difficult to find — an equilibrium. The stop is bigger than the fiddle stop, but we don't have to play the stretches of a Paganini *Caprice*. The average hand will have no problem fingering the notes on the viola.

My notes were difficult when I joined the orchestra in England, because I was used to playing things thoroughly practised, not music that I had to sight-read, with almost no rehearsal. It *is* a rat-race, for everybody, even those who can do it. And therefore I think the musical value of these performances can suffer very much. It's a miracle that English orchestras, living this way, can produce exciting performances. If one could only find a balance, maintain the commitment and excitement, and just let the players go more deeply into the material, then we would have really glowing performances. The orchestras do repertoire works time and time again, but always badly, *always*. Beethoven 5 — one rehearsal only for a Sunday evening concert at the Albert Hall. Of course everybody knows the music. Then there comes a good conductor who gets two rehearsals and a Festival Hall concert, and everyone is amazed that we just don't know the piece, because it is full of the dross of not playing it properly, just skipping through and surviving on an artificial brilliance.

Oh, being principal is a great strain for me because there are a dozen people behind playing the same part and looking for clear direction — what bowing, what style? Bowing is difficult for me as principal, coming from an Hungarian school, because it seems to me that so many English string players have faulty bow technique, so that people end up in a certain part of the bow and feel uncomfortable. There are some bowings that are no problem to a harmonious technique, but in some places I find it difficult just to bring the section together, and so they feel there is a clash of style. Some say I'm just odd, and they can't follow me. On the other hand, I think I have shown many times that my way would work better. But again, there is just no time to sort it out.

I do believe that often the violas should support the bass. The viola bow is a heavier and clumsier bow than the fiddle bow, and the articulation of our part, musically, has more in common with the cellos. The obvious example is where the violins are playing 'on the string', and the cellos, by nature, are playing 'at the nut'. Good. But where should the violas go? So often one adapts the fiddle bowing which becomes clumsy and dragging on the viola. But with a slightly more percussive style, the thicker strings of the viola would respond better, speak quicker and improve the rhythm. We are the mediators, the traditional role that composers have assigned us. The viola used to be an undeveloped instrument, maybe just filling the chord, but now, perhaps since Berlioz, we are taken seriously and given more equal parts and opportunities.

The Cello Section

Violincellos together, to the number of 8 or 10, are essentially melodious; their timbre, on the upper strings, is one of the most expressive in the orchestra. Nothing is more voluptuously melancholy, or more suited to the utterance of tender, languishing themes.
HECTOR BERLIOZ, *On Orchestration*

Tom Storer

TOM STORER When I first came into the orchestra, a very keen young man, I was disappointed by the lackadaisical attitude of the back desk players. It was much more important to be first in the coffee queue than to make a right entry. Then I too became aware of those little matters that make life irksome in the cello section. There are mechanical problems. We need a nice floor to dig the spike in. We loathe stone-floored churches, or hard wood-blocks and parquet — and people with good carpets loathe us of course. The shape and height of chair is more critical for us than anyone else. Almost no hall has decent chairs. The Philharmonia has its own, fantastically expensive, but we haven't managed to persuade our orchestral porter that he can carry ten chairs on top of everything else. Even in the new Henry Wood rehearsal hall, specially created for us with

133

consultation at every level, we found the chairs impossible for cellists. And as the cello is not very portable, we tend to leave the good one at home and keep the second-best with the orchestra, which I suppose has some bearing on the sound. Not that we play on bad instruments — respectable English or French cellos by little known makers — but they are possibly less good than the instruments of other string sections.

Since the cello is not held under the ear, in the orchestra it can be hard to hear yourself, and sometimes impossible, in the full tutti sound. It used to be said of fiddle players that if you could hear only yourself, you were too loud. But if you can hear your cello at all, you are possibly playing too loud. We are very intimately related to the basses, and a bass section can make or mar the life of a cellist. And intonation with basses is always a headache. There's a certain kind of approximate quality with bass intonation. So often one gets a rogue bass, not bothering too much, and that wobbling away an octave below upsets all that you can hear, because of the overtones. Bassoons, or woodwinds generally, are seldom a problem. The differences in tonal quality absorb small discrepancies in intonation. And luckily, in London, we play with woodwinds of the very highest standard — the problems are more likely to be in the strings. We live very amicably with woodwinds, our friend the bassoon in particular. You have to be good natured to play a thing like that.

LYNN HARRELL I soon felt all the usual complaints in the orchestra. You can't hear yourself, you can't play in tune because the pitch is wavering around, you're losing your individuality, you can't make head or tail of the conductor. I saw this, and I tried to deal with it.

We'd often talk about this balloon of a fantasy, which we'd constantly pop, that a soloist has so much freedom of expression which you lose in the orchestra. But in a cello section, say in a big cello passage of a Brahms symphony, one man plays a wrong note, he has two ways of approaching it: one, it's not important, it will be covered by the rest of the section; or two, he might think that the section has studied and practised as if it were in a sonata, and the wrong note has ruined the work of the section. It's the sense of responsibility. Well, looked at like that, section playing suddenly becomes creative, important. Whether you can be heard as an individual or not, you still have the responsibility to the music. The composer wrote the part for a string section, for ten cellos, not for seven playing and three faking.

I think so much bad practice in sections is habit. There was a back cellist in Cleveland, a lovely man, but suddenly his job was on the line. Szell decided he was no longer up to it and, with the management, wanted to fire him. They told him they were going to listen to him. Now, he hadn't taken an audition for twenty years. He came to me, as principal, a much older man than I, and said, 'Lynn, what do I do? I've got to play for them.' I suggested he prepare some solos from the orchestral repertoire. He played them to me, and they weren't good, really not good, faulty intonation, bit scratchy, some crazy phrasing. So I asked if he could practise as if preparing a solo recital. 'Pretend,' I said, 'these excerpts are

134

for a solo recital. Pretend this second movement of Brahms 2 is the beginning of the second movement of the F major sonata.' 'I would never have thought of that,' he said. 'I mean I'm just one of the ten cellists in the section, not a soloist.' He had a tenth attitude to what he did, so he reduced his playing, over the years, to a tenth of his real ability. Now his job was on the line and he'd have to rediscover his talent. Yet somehow he had not been able to apply before the more rigorous standard of a solo recital to the business of playing in an orchestra. He could do it. He practised diligently, played the parts well, and passed with flying colours.

Events like this made me think how to work successfully as principal. How the hell was I to get on their side, a young cocky kid, with half the experience of some of them? Three ex-principals sat behind me in the section. There was no way I could just turn round and give orders. I couldn't make any direct statements about how to play. And in looking for other ways to run a happy section I began to understand some of the problems. There's a lot to discover. Well, I knew that playing principal was hard, and playing in the section wasn't easy, but it took me a long time to discover the full horror of back stand playing. I was appearing as a soloist at a festival in Ames, Iowa, and Zubin Mehta asked if I'd like to play in the LA Philharmonic the night before. I said sure, because I hadn't played Mahler 5 in about five years, and I love that piece. So I slipped into the back stand of cellos, right in front of the trombones. It was awful. In the loud parts I couldn't hear myself *at all*. I could have been playing any note, and I wondered if it would have made any difference. But I know, from being up front, that it does make a difference, though the back stand player just has to trust that he's right. That was in the loud parts. In the soft bits I couldn't hear the front of the section, nor the violins. And I

Rodney Friend, concertmaster of the New York Philharmonic takes a break with music director, Zubin Mehta

135

couldn't even sense very clearly where Zubin was gesturing, because I was so used to being under the conductor's nose. That was a tough, tough night's work. I told Zubin, 'Playing at the front is difficult, playing at the back is impossible.'

It can help to have strong, experienced men at the back. There's an old-world notion of ensemble — Szell had it and it's ridiculous — that the principal leads and everybody else follows. Well, if that's true, by the time the impulse gets to the back the guy there is going to be an eighth note, a quaver, late. But experienced players at the back, with a strong sense of music-making, know where to play in the beat, even to anticipate it, so that the sound from the back of a large section coincides with the attack from the front. This creeping along after the principal doesn't make sense. The other day we were doing a Paganini Trio with Pinchas Zuckerman, and we had this little duo, in the trio section of the minuet. Pinky said, 'It seems a little late to me.' Well, I thought we were absolutely together, but I knew what he meant. He meant me to forget about following him, to take a bit of initiative as if I were leading, and the problem was solved.

The Bass Section

Some are so injudicious, nowadays, as to write for the heaviest of all instruments, passages of such rapidity that violincellos themselves would have difficulty in executing them. Whence results a serious inconvenience: lazy or incapable double-bass players, dismayed by such difficulties, give them up at first glance, and set themselves to simplifying the passage.

HECTOR BERLIOZ, *On Orchestration*

ROBIN McGEE In recent years bass technique has been extended vastly. I look at my students at the Academy and I see they are very good note-getters, though obviously they lack experience. Today, a lot is expected from the bass. I was about to say unreasonably, but a composer writes what he wants to, whether you can do it or not is your problem. Contemporary music is certainly taxing, but the difficulties in the usual repertoire are still quite severe. If you can get round all the Beethoven symphonic bass parts for example, you can handle most things.

I use cello fingering, so I'm stretched all the time. I have to practise or I'm sure things would deteriorate faster than if I used normal fingering, which leaves out the weak third finger. But to use all the fingers, if you can do it, gives a great advantage in coping. It's more strenuous, and the bass is a fairly energetic instrument anyway. It's not all grotesquely sweat and blood, but it can be hard work, it's a big instrument. Of course we don't play all the notes of a fiddle part, though we sometimes wonder if we've been given the fiddle part by mistake. I think it's more important to be musical on the bass than to be very technically brilliant, more so than on other string instruments. Our business is fitting in, on the bass you have to *place* things so carefully. To play a bass line you're insane if

(opposite)
The double bass player

136

you're not absolutely tuned in to what's going on. Some bass players are not that aware, and I sometimes think it comes from them only playing the bass. I think I'm very fortunate to have a musical background that covered other instruments before I got to the bass.

The principal bass must look out for ensemble and dynamics. One hopes the players will sort out the note-getting process themselves, because you can't help them there. I think performance is built on an ability to play extremes, but it's too easy to be a happy mezzo-forte all the way through. The excitement in a Berlioz piece, for instance, is in the terrific contrasts of mood and dynamic, which he writes in very clearly, but they take a bit of effort to put into practice. In an orchestra, often when you think you are playing very loud, you are not, and similarly with softness. One has to exaggerate, to get it across. And ensemble in the bass section is difficult. The bass is inclined to be late because it speaks slowly and one tends to play late because of the time-lag. Placing is tricky. But one adjusts to these matters by experience. If the section is musical, very little needs to be said. They know what to do. But if they're not the right guys, then you've got problems.

The large symphony orchestra generates nerves and tensions. The size of the thing! And always this terrible time-lag, trying to play with someone 50ft away, or more. For a bass, even a bit of *continuo* with principal cello is nerve-wracking, because we are so separated. We all talk of the dog's life of the back desk players, but they *are* at a disadvantage, at the mercy of the orchestra and the conductor. In England, it's these things that drive people out of symphony orchestras. One seems to have a critical period of orchestral playing – long or short, I think I lasted better than most. Then you have to try something else, even though the orchestral repertoire is so rich, in fact the greatest. You do a cycle full of bad conditions and poor conductors, and at the end you see people coming up actually learning conducting at your expense. That's hard to bear.

ROGER SCOTT Sight-reading is not a strong tradition here, because we play the same programme a number of times. In fact, I sometimes feel if we play a programme only twice, it's an awful lot of work for so short an exposure. Now, about the most we play a programme is four times. I was really shocked when I heard that the London Symphony plays a programme once, and that's it, on to the next one. Well, the players become marvellous sight-readers, but I should imagine that ensemble and section routine would suffer by that.

One thing I found, coming to Philadelphia all those years ago from Pittsburgh, in Pittsburgh there would be mistakes in every concert. You don't make mistakes in Philadelphia. For example, piccolo and clarinet might tune together before a certain piece, or the harp might deliberately tune with the celeste, which is often a little weird. We work this way regardless of who's conducting. And there's a tremendous *esprit de corps* in the orchestra which no conductor has been able to throttle. New players assimilate it as if by osmosis. When I first arrived I watched my teacher lead the section, and suddenly it was my responsibility to lead,

(opposite above)
Practising the cello on the train

(below)
Checking a violin

above
The New York Philharmonic
meet the Japan
Philharmonic baseball
team before the game on
a tour of Japan

below
Eugene Ormandy

and to men who were older than my father I'd have to say, 'Do this, do that.' Naturally, there was a little resentment at first, because I was so young, then they'd say, 'OK, we'll do it.' And in return I took the blame, as section principal, if anything went wrong. If a conductor went after a bass player I'd step in. That goes with the job. But if you can play you're respected, if you can't you're not.

Sure, it's nice for a new player to be helped in the middle of the section, with experienced men on each side to prevent him from making false entries. We don't do that here. We just throw him to the end of the section, almost without exception. When I came in I was on the 4th stand, and another new man was by himself on the last stand. It's sink or swim and most swim very well. You're new, inexperienced, absorbing a new style, puzzling out the conductor from a long way away, trying to hear, and no one makes allowances for you. But you learn. I think very highly of our section now. I know all the ways of our players, we play a very similar style, and I think we have a very high level of intonation, and a good concept of sound and dynamics. We have a concerted approach, perhaps unique, because so many of us are from one particular school. We all play with French bows, and most of us have studied with either of two people. We get very little complaint from conductors.

When I first came here our library was rather small and we rented parts a lot. Now our library is large and we rent as little as possible. Obviously it's better to have your own parts and have them marked. But I share a room with our librarian, and time and again he'll hear from a guest conductor, 'Here's a marked score, and I want these bowings in the parts by first rehearsal.' I don't know if this is general elsewhere, but I feel they think they can impose it here. Well, harking back to the old days of Ansermet and Beecham, they came with their own parts meticulously marked. I remember Sir Thomas prowling around, picking up a part and making a minute change for the next rehearsal. Of course, some music, the Russians in particular, can only be rented. But our rental parts are stamped 'Philadelphia Orchestra' and they come back to us with our markings. And when Ormandy goes to Chicago, Cleveland, or wherever, he asks for those parts to be sent ahead, so he can create the Philadelphia sound with his own characteristic bowings. Well, it's upsetting to be presented with a new set of bowings just before a concert. I try not to do this, and the men in my section know my tricks well enough. I always try to find the simplest bowings that work. I learnt early on that you couldn't bow for the strongest player, because a weaker player either can't do it or can't adjust easily. I remember in my first days as principal I was approached by a colleague, a good player, as old as my father, but not very quick. Ormandy had put a new bowing in the *Euryanthe* overture on the morning of a concert and this man just said he couldn't change in forty-five minutes. 'Hide,' I said, 'just duck behind where he can't see you, and come in when you've worked it out.' It was a rather complicated bowing for thirty years ago, what we call a back bowing, and his old schooling in Germany had never taught him anything like that. So my instinctive reaction was to protect him.

141

The Flute Section

The sound of this instrument is sweet in the medium, rather piercing in the high notes, and very characteristic in the low ones . . . It may be employed in melodies, but without equalling either the artless gaiety of the oboe, or the noble tenderness of the clarinet. The flute, then, is well-nigh devoid of expression, but may be introduced any-where and everywhere.

HECTOR BERLIOZ, *On Orchestration*

PAUL FRIED In America the A is 440, though it's usually a little sharper, about 443. It's too bad, I like a 440 A, the lower pitch is a little warmer. But I think most conductors, and violinists, would just as soon have the slightly higher pitch for a more brilliant sound. In Germany, it's way high, I couldn't believe how high it was. That can be a problem for woodwind players, it sure can. On the flute, if the head-joint isn't cut quite correctly, for instance, if you push in too much you distort the whole register. And in a hot hall, where pitch is rising anyway, it can get so high you can't get up there at all. I think it's even worse for the oboe and some others, you keep pushing the instrument in and you're cutting off the middle. Of course we woodwind players always complain that strings tend to tune a bit sharp, but I don't think our string sections in Boston are bad in that respect. Boston and Philadelphia, of all the American string sections, are famous for their warm sound. And string sound is the basis of all orchestral sound. We can get the good string players here in Boston, because though they work hard, they have a much better life in the orchestra than freelancing, which is really tough.

It's strange, listening to that Tchaikovsky piano concerto, you get very tired of it, but playing it, playing first flute, you get very involved. Playing and listening are always such different feelings. To sit on that stage with a hundred or so people, playing some virtuoso piece like *Pictures at an Exhibition*, that's a most exciting thing — those waves of sound emerging from very ordinary human beings.

RICHARD ADENEY Flute is the easiest instrument to start and reach a reasonable standard in a short time. An oboe sounds ghastly until he's good, but an amateur flautist can sound very nice. As on all wind instru-ments, the most difficult thing is the control of pitch. All too easily it can go a bit up or down, and unless you're thinking about it all the time, you'll be out of tune. An orchestral flautist is expected to play piccolo, alto flute and bass flute. I can play quick pieces on the piccolo — the fingering is the same — but some things, like the very high, gentle noises in some Shostakovich, I find exceedingly worrying, whereas a full-time piccolo player would take them in his stride. And the intonation is rather different, not more difficult, but strange. I get by, but I'm not really very good at it.

In the section one thinks all the time about intonation and balance. It needs a lot of noise to be equal in tone to an oboe or clarinet played

Richard Adeney

loudly, and to cut through the full orchestra sometimes you have to play terribly loudly. Big sound is important in an orchestral flute, whereas in chamber music you would go more for sweetness of sound. And in the orchestra you have to watch out for certain individuals. You get to know those in sympathy with you. A first flute develops a very strange close relationship with the first oboe, almost a sort of love affair. You sit next to the oboes and play so much with first oboe in unison and octaves. I always got on very well and comfortably with my first oboe. Perhaps I wouldn't know what to say to him at a dinner, but I formed a very close, musical bond. With certain players you develop almost a second sight and can anticipate what they're likely to do, what sort of sound and phrasing. You may know, as well, that a certain oboe has a slightly flat F, so you must temper your F a bit flat too. Luckily, the silver flute doesn't go flat in the long rests. Just blow down it and it's all right again. Of course the whole wind section tends to go down in pitch together, and then we just complain that the strings are sharp!

The Oboe Section

The oboe is especially a melodic instrument. It has a pastoral character full of tenderness — nay, I would even say of timidity . . . A certain degree of agitation is also within its powers. But care should be taken not to urge it into utterances of passion, anger, menace or heroism; for then its small acid-sweet voice becomes ineffectual, and absolutely grotesque.

HECTOR BERLIOZ, *On Orchestration*

JOHN DE LANCIE I feel very strongly that musical performance is divided into two distinct categories, the physical and the intellectual. I don't believe you can develop the physical too early. You know, the first few years are going to be abominable. But if the kid can bull his way on little by little he manages to cope with the instrument, with breath and lip control, even at quite an early age. It's my experience, at least in teaching, that the later one gets into it, the harder it is to develop really outstanding dexterity, on any instrument. On some instruments — cello, double-bass, bassoon — the small hand may not be able to manage the stop. And even on oboe or clarinet the hand might be a bit small at eight or nine. But in general the earlier a musician gets going the better. I firmly believe that when I went to the Curtis Institute at fifteen, I had more technique on the oboe — just technique, not musical ability or understanding — than at any other time in my life. I had dexterity, being able to move my fingers fast with the fewest mistakes.

ANTHONY CAMDEN If the reed is not quite right, and the red recording light has just come on, then playing the oboe can be terribly hard. But I learnt from my father the value of relaxation. Nothing bothered him, not even the reed for a bassoon concerto he had to play that afternoon.

Playing in a cold church can have a bad effect on instruments, especially those in the woodwind section

I think that's good psychology, being reconciled to the inevitable problems of the instrument.

No oboe can be absolutely in tune. But a good ear and a thorough knowledge of your own instrument should see you through. Slight wanderings of pitch have to be continually corrected with diaphragm or lip. Either one has a free reed and controls it at the lips, or one controls from the diaphragm. If you let the diaphragm sag and don't draw the air from the very depths, then your upper notes will definitely come down in pitch. And of course, in long rests, the instrument tends to go flat. My policy — I'm sure everyone has a different way — is to make my reeds so that when they go right into the socket they are slightly sharp, just a fraction. Then I play most of the time with the reed pulled out a tiny little bit. Now if I have a long rest, say sixty-three bars in a slow eight in a Mahler symphony, and I have to come in on a low E natural for a solo, then I can push the reed in fractionally rather than try to lip the note up, easing the reed out again when the instrument has come back to pitch.

In the section, I think it's most important to be able to be both negative and positive. If you play strongly, with a big vibrato, and you come to a passage where someone else — the clarinet — has to be positive, and you can't get out of the way, then you ruin the whole shape. Oboe sound can so easily stick out, so you must be able to play with a negative sound that is just part of the structure, just adds to the chord. When clarinets are just purring quietly, then it's very hard for the oboe to hide under that. For me, clarinets are the most critical section. Flutes and oboes are very much together, in thirds, in unison, answering phrases. The clarinet is different, a single reed, with a different kind of vibration. We use vibrato a lot, but in English orchestras the clarinets don't use it that much, so it's difficult to balance with clarinet sound.

144

The oboe speaks quickly, sometimes too quickly, which makes it hard to articulate really quietly at the start of a phrase. And we must watch out for strings, because they are inclined to creep up, a bit sharp, and it's sometimes our responsibility to see they don't creep too high. Then the winds are thrown out, and the whole intonation of the orchestra goes haywire, and this is specially so if the bass departments go sharp. If bassoons, basses, and to a certain extent cellos are in tune, the chances are there's no problem in the orchestra at all. But if people have to creep up, either by lip or by pushing, that puts the scale out, affects the temperament and makes odd notes stick out. Fortunately, in the oboes we can hear what's going on all right, every note of our own playing is clear, and we can thus pay attention to others, to get the balance. And with a good conductor who is aware of balance, you find you can actually hear the things you expect to hear. Only when the conductor has disregarded balance and tonal structure, in rehearsal or concert, then you suddenly lose where you are.

The Clarinet Section

*The clarinet is an epic instrument. Its voice is that of heroic love; and
if masses of brass instruments awaken the idea of warlike troops . . .
numerous unisons of clarinets, heard at the same time, seem to
represent loving women, with proud eyes and deep affections, who
sing while fighting, and who crown the victors, or die with the
defeated.*   HECTOR BERLIOZ, *On Orchestration*

PETER HADCOCK Playing first and playing second are different — not very different, but certainly different. When I play second, no matter who the first is, I try to play with him. If he's six measures ahead and a half tone flat, I try to be with him, and that's what I want from a second when I'm playing first. But when I'm playing first, I'm concerned with the whole orchestra, and specially the other woodwind sections, and I don't want to be dragging around a second clarinet. I've got problems enough.

I've never felt that the clarinet is the odd man in the woodwind. Being a single reed, it is a little different, and I try to avoid not being as expressive as, say, the oboe. An oboe will tend to use more vibrato, and if I'm not careful the straight sound of the clarinet might make me an outsider. And clarinet I think — everybody will say this of their instrument — but the clarinet I really think is about the most difficult to play in tune. It tends to do the opposite of others. Flute, French horn, brass — play loud and it goes sharp. Clarinet goes flat. Flute, play it soft in the low register and it's going to be flat. But clarinet is going to be sharp. Unbelievable what you have to do to make the thing stay in tune — you're putting down what seems like eight extra fingers just to make it, you know. And playing some of those solos that want to be heard, but not to sound forced, you tend to pinch more to try to avoid playing flat. The whole thing gets to be a problem.

Cecil James *(right)* talks
with Jack Brymer

TONY PAY The trouble with any reed instrument is to learn to make do on reeds that are not ideal. As Jack Brymer says, when you just begin that important solo you realize that the cane in your mouth is not your friend. Weather, humidity, atmospheric conditions affect it. And you do too – how much is physical effect and how much you? A complex phenomenon. Staying in tune is hard on all wind instruments, but the clarinet is an acoustical compromise – 'Oh yes,' says everybody else, 'but so is my instrument' – and it's impossible, theoretically, to build a clarinet in tune. There's a lot of correction to do. For a schools concert in the Granada Cinema in Harrow at nine o'clock of a winter morning, the problems are very different from the crowded Festival Hall at night. Temperature difference can be as much as 20° F, and that very much affects the instrument.

We play in general as part of a complete woodwind department. Clarinets are often a crucial part of wind chording, and it's important to be able to take that chord apart and work out the clarinets' contribution. Woodwind sections will get together and try things over if ensemble seems wrong. And it's not always clear-cut right or wrong, context can determine a note also, and that needs to be understood. People are usually very sensitive about intonation, something they are hardly conscious of since they play as it feels right. Questions on intonation can lead to friction very easily. But if one understands that intonation is often a case of convention, then a note can be flattened or sharpened without stirring antagonism.

Composers often write low clarinets with cellos and high clarinets with upper strings. Our low register is best for colouring – the upper register is rather bland. I try to sound closer to oboe than flute in the high register, I think that is more interesting. We play a lot with flutes and oboes, and the blending of wind sections can be tricky. In good orchestras, reedy clarinets tend to go with rather smooth oboes, and vice versa. In the old days of Beecham's Royal Philharmonic, the open English clarinet went with a reedy, but not thin, oboe. In general it doesn't work to have two sounds that are very, very characteristic trying to play in unison, and unison playing is a problem in any orchestra. Though we belong to the woodwind, often we can't hear flutes and oboes too well because they sit in front of us. The rule is that those who can hear well adjust to those who can't, with the proviso that negotiations are always possible. We do try to play in terms of a tempered scale, but strings can do that more easily, and are inclined to play their leading notes sharp if it feels right. Now sometimes we can't do that. Whatever I do I might not be able to get a flat leading note in a certain key as sharp as a string player would easily and naturally do. These are problems that not all string players understand. We feel that they want things sharper than we do, too sharp, though that's given the lie when you hear clarinets being notorious sharpies. Strings want to sound brilliant, and creeping sharp they land the wind in grave trouble, specially if the day is cold, and we are at the limit of adjustment, all pushed in. We can't get any sharper.

The Bassoon Section

The bassoon is of the greatest use in the orchestra on numerous occasions. Its sonority is not very great, and its quality of tone, absolutely devoid of brilliancy or nobleness, has a tendency towards the grotesque . . . Its low notes form an excellent bass to the whole group of woodwind instruments.

HECTOR BERLIOZ, *On Orchestration*

LEONARD HINDELL As an instrumentalist, I feel frankly if I'm very busy, playing a lot, and I don't have the ideal amount of time to prepare, I feel I can get by and put together something in the short time available. But ideally I might want a week instead of a day, not just to learn the notes but to feel I can make a statement. And even a week is not very long. To play to an audience, the idea is not to play properly, note-perfect, but to make a statement. With orchestral parts this doesn't apply to quite the same degree. You are just a small part of the whole, your job is to play in tune, the right notes at the right time. To have some degree of imagination, certainly, but also to be the tool of the conductor, to be flexible enough to play in the way he wants.

CECIL JAMES The bassoon is not a popular sort of instrument. The public don't really know much about it, and sometimes not even if they've heard it. Well, it's a darn difficult instrument to play, I've always found it so. It has such an extended range – three octaves and a fifth – and every bassoon, whatever make or system, is always a fight, to get good intonation and good quality of sound. Also, it's not very loud, though you expect it to be. But it's equally difficult to play quietly. Difficult instrument, with no popular acclaim.

Control comes from the combination of lip and diaphragm. Breath control is most important and strangely enough – perhaps people think about it now – it was certainly neglected when I started. Nobody thought then whether you give a vibrato from the lip or from the diaphragm. A player once came to me for a sort of a master class. He made a very small sound and wanted to make it louder. We did a three-hour lesson and at last he said, 'What really is the secret of a big sound?' And I believe I replied, 'Well, *you just blow the bloody thing.* That will be £5.' Yes, the energy required is tremendous, a tremendous amount of breath. My wife plays the oboe and we've argued all the years of our marriage about the relative strain of oboe and bassoon. I always say, how do you manage a concerto on the oboe, or some long obligato in the *St Matthew Passion?* You couldn't last for that time without breaths on the bassoon. The oboe needs a large volume in reserve, like amperage for a light, and you let it out in dribbles. But the bassoon uses up the air, you can't keep a reserve. All bassoons are Boehm system now, they are covered in keys like moon rockets. But that's one of the advantages of the German bassoon, you have lots of alternative fingerings. On the French system you've only got one fingering.

I always maintain that first bassoon is only as good as the second will let him be. What I mean is, if you have an excellent second — and there's an art in playing second — then intonation problems don't exist, he accommodates you. A second who doesn't agree, or who phrases in another way, makes life very, very difficult. I think it's the large size and large range of the bassoon that make things so hard. There's more to go wrong. In a draughty hall we also go a little bit flatter than anyone else. The bassoon is a slowish speaker also, decidedly so, specially down below. You must start well on the beat, or else you're out. I began as a second bassoon and was lucky to have a helpful first. Then, years later, when I'd worked my way up, he was getting on and came to the Philharmonia as my second, and we never had any problems at all. Poor old second bassoon, he never has a chance to shine. You admire the first in the flashy bits of Tchaikovsky, but who's noticed the second, how well he's done his supporting role? Yet the bassoon is part of the backbone of orchestral sound, like the foundation of a house. A bad bassoon runs like poison through the orchestra. If the bassoon is a bit off, other players start pulling or pushing their notes, and the whole thing goes absolutely sour. So it's important that even the unglamorous second bassoon should be spot on.

We always feel slightly odd-man-out in the orchestra. And this is made worse by our difficulty in hearing, sitting at the back with a not very loud instrument. The acoustics of certain halls are very tricky. The Festival Hall, for example, is terribly hard for us if we have to play with the fiddles, the sound just doesn't come back. In Brahms 3, the slow movement, the first bassoon just can't hear what the strings are doing. People are so far away from each other, subject to that time-lag, yet they have to come in together. It's a marvel that a symphony orchestra ever gets off at all, isn't it?

The French Horn Section

The horn is a noble and melancholy instrument; yet the expression of its quality of tone, and its sonority, fit it for any kind of piece. It blends easily with the general harmony.

HECTOR BERLIOZ, *On Orchestration*

Alan Civil

ALAN CIVIL We've got more horn players than ever before, lots of playing, and lots of girls playing too. And the standard has shot up. Every orchestra in England has a good first horn. Well, when I started, admittedly in wartime, the standard was appalling in some orchestras. They used to say, if you knew how to get the instrument out of the case you had a job. Three notes out of five, that was good, very good. There is now, I think, an English school of playing, and it's a mixture of French sound, from Aubrey Brain, with the technique and display that his son Dennis added, plus a bit of the German style stemming from the Borsdorf family. I think it's a good sound and a good style. Perhaps there have been some wrong steps. At one time the London Symphony horns congratulated themselves on their 'American sound' which Americans couldn't recognize. They were playing on very wide-bore instruments that produced an owl-like whoop, a constipated owl, which didn't carry at all. We called this sound 'the creeping mist', a tuba sort of sound with no detail or definition. You need a bit of edge, I think anyway, but not to the extent of French players, who get more edge than tone, with vibrato as well.

Technique can sometimes get in the way of true sound. To me, the huge vibrato of the Russians disguises the true intonation of the horn. And the French, still using piston valves instead of key-valves, affect the quality of the sound by the rapidity of execution. The horn doesn't seem able to keep up. There's a thin edge between serviceable technique and the point where it goes, as it were, beyond the capability of the instrument. In a sense, that's true of most instruments. Once technique leads to excessive speed and facility it's hard to get true sound.

I never talk too much to the players in my section. I hope they'll be listening and following, and that's what usually happens. It's very easy to become a nagging principal. Often when it comes to the performance it's the first horn that makes the balls-up! A horn player is on a very fine line of suspense. But one does get together with the other brass principals and discuss how a passage should go, length of notes, where to come off a note, things like that. But playing with your colleagues so much in a good orchestra, you get to know what will happen. You know the notes to humour in order to be in tune with a certain player or a certain section.

There's a tremendous amount of boredom in orchestras, any orchestra anywhere. Many players in England get out – play solos or chamber music, or join the session boys. But playing the horn, I've always been a great believer in belonging to an orchestra. And you must sit on the edge of your seat most of the time, you must be generally worried. Complacency is very bad. Some horn players, bored to death with the repetition of endless Beethoven, go into freelance session work, where the horn writing is a few simple-minded glissandi and things. Awful. Then everything goes wrong, sound, technique, musicality, everything. They get a strange sense of what constitutes a solo. The fellows with nothing to play, just padding, come across a couple of notes solo and suddenly it's a gigantic problem. I think you have to be in the front line all the time, playing without fear of splitting notes. Play the music boldly, the best that's around.

The Trumpet Section

Notwithstanding the real loftiness and distinguished nature of its quality in tone, there are few instruments that have been more degraded than the trumpet.

HECTOR BERLIOZ, *On Orchestration*

William Lang

BILL LANG There's a lot of pressure in playing the trumpet and the lip can go fairly easily. A few years ago we had conductors who would repeat and repeat, you couldn't reason with them, they wanted everything all the time. But that's part of the job. You need an easy temperament for the trumpet. When I first came to London they wouldn't even tolerate what we call a 'bumper' – a helper for first trumpet, so he can take it easy on loud passages and save himself for the performance. I had to do everything. But now they'll use a bumper for a hard programme. It makes a difference, you have no idea how eight bars – four bars – can make a difference for a first trumpet.

Now, on the continent, for something like the Bach *Suite in D* – which we regard as repertoire – the trumpets are given a week off, perhaps more, to prepare. And for the *B Minor Mass* they might get a month. Perhaps that's too much, but three days before certain works would be nice. About a year ago, I had to go back on first for Katchaturian. Well, the Russians like everything larger than life. We did recordings and concerts – honestly, I had to blow like the very devil. The day after all that we had the Rachmaninov-Paganini Variations, with some terribly delicate trumpet, so hard to do after blowing like a gale, like circus-playing. I had to get the lips soft and you can't do that by blowing. You try to play quietly until the lips come back and vibrate. I could have done with some time off then.

It's rare that we can do it, but I like to sit in line with the trombones and then we have a better chance of hearing. But mostly we get the trombones behind, blowing right into the ear, and then, with the best will in the world, your own sound builds up, until you're probably playing too loud. Conductors don't seem to take account of seating problems. Laziness really. They get used to a certain lay-out, so that with the eyes down on the full score they know already where each section is. But if you can't hear what others are doing, you can't blend your notes into the general sound. Some of the brass get a bit lazy too. They put the instruments down on the stands during the bars rest, and of course they go flat. I never use the stand. I put my trumpet under my coat on a cold day and keep the mouthpiece in my hand. Well, pitch wanders about anyway during a long rehearsal or concert. Perfect pitch is no good to us, we need good relative pitch. Then again, in a big band, the time-lag is a great nuisance. First fiddles sound behind to us, then the principal viola, in front of us, will stand up and accuse us of being behind. Trumpets speak quickly but some of the other brass is rather slow. You deal with all these problems by experience, but really, the difficulties we face in performance often have little to do with the music.

The Trombone Section

The trombone is the true chief of that species of wind instrument which I have designated epic. It possesses, in an eminent degree, both nobleness and grandeur. It has all the deep and powerful accents of high musical poetry.

HECTOR BERLIOZ, *On Orchestration*

R O N   B A R R O N   Any brass instrument, over a long period, really becomes an athletic endeavour. If you're a bit low, unrested, it just become stagnant. You use too much embouchure, too much strain on the facial muscles, not enough reliance on the air column to support the structure. That aspect of it can really tear you down in a hurry. The theory is to use the maximum amount of air available, and I try to get students — myself as well — to draw air from as low as possible. But there are different approaches as to how you use the air. It's what works best for you. Whatever you do, of course, you must remain relaxed. If getting air in and out is a tense process, no matter how much air you get, it won't do any good.

There's a lot of pressure on the mouth and teeth. I try to go regularly to the dentist, and luckily I have a normal mouth, no unusual crevices, no fangs to stick out and cut the lip against the mouthpiece. I try to use just enough pressure to keep the seal around the mouthpiece, so you use the air-flow most efficiently. Just concentrate on gathering the air and letting it through the instrument, don't think about the metal at all. Isolate and then forget technical processes, and then the problems become musical. Unfortunately, like so many worthwhile things, getting to that simplicity is the hardest of all. Everything between the lungs and the end of the bell gets in the way. And if a fellow gets good results in an unusual way, don't bother him with orthodoxy. You just can't tell Louis Armstrong and Dizzy Gillespie that they shouldn't puff their cheeks out like that! But the athletic aspect of trombone playing is a constant battle. I complain a lot and my wife says, 'Do something about it,' so I go out and try to play soft-ball, be active and keep in trim.

We get along pretty well together in the section, and we try to use comparable equipment. For example, when we were in London in '76, for Brahms 1 we used our Conn trombones. I've always liked consistency of sound, as I was trained to appreciate in Cincinnati, and as I hear out of British sections, nice, evenly matched, everybody thinking alike. And the Conn sound blends pretty well, even with the Holton bass trombone. It's important, in a section, not only to have a similar concept of sound, but also to have equipment that matches up. In brass, you really have to satisfy both requirements. Well, after this London programme there was an encore — Seiji Ozawa chose the ending of the *Miraculous Mandarin*, wanting to show off trombones and some of the loud, driving parts of the orchestra — and for that we picked up our Vincent Bach instruments and played those. I asked Ray Premru, from the Philharmonia, who was in the audience, if it made any difference. And Ray thought it really did, the Bachs giving a much brighter, harder sound, while the Conns were more mellow. That was in the Festival Hall. I didn't mind playing there, though it was hard to tell, the orchestra being out in the open like that. Perhaps it's good nowadays to have a hall a bit bass-light, specially with our loud, powerful American orchestras.

R A Y   P R E M R U   In the orchestra, I just play bass trombone, and there's a difference in sonority between bass and tenor. But the bass must be fairly flexible, blending in some works with the tuba and making the right octave sound, and then in other pieces making a lighter sound, as if there were three tenors in the section. In the Mozart *Requiem*, for instance, sometimes my part is definitely bass, and in other places rather tenorish. To gradate the sound, to find the right sonority for the right combination of instrumental colour is quite a problem. The trombone, specially the bass, requires a lot of breath and a lot of strength. After a period of hard work, then the job becomes very, very wearying. Add to the playing time the travelling, up to three hours each day in London, and you soon become tense and lose concentration. The lip also is a problem. If you have several days off — when do we get that in London! — you can't just leave the work at the office and come back to it. Like athletes, we must do the calisthenics, as it were, just to keep in shape. I do find I can take one day a week off, and the embouchure will benefit from the rest. But take two days, the flexibility starts to go, and you work twice as hard to get it back. I don't think the public realize how much discipline is involved. 'How marvellous just to go out and play' — that word 'play' implies the antithesis to 'work'. We don't just 'play', we work and work in order to be able to play.

One problem we have here in London is that no orchestra has its own home, so we play all over the place, in strange halls, where it's hard to judge your balance. It's so much easier for American or continental orchestras to come to terms with the acoustic of their own hall. For us, even the new Henry Wood rehearsal hall, luxurious and beautiful hall that it is, has some acoustical problems which I'm well aware of, sitting at the back of the orchestra. And when I had to conduct a rehearsal of my *Concerto for Orchestra* there, I felt the problems from the front. I saw people playing a passage, but I couldn't hear it. Yet London orchestras are supposed to play well, adjusting their playing, in good and bad halls, all over town.

When you're sitting at the back, as the trombones do, and the farther away the harder it is to hear, you do tend to rely on the point of the beat. If it's not there, and you are just trying to listen and play as you would in chamber music, then you must anticipate and hope for the best. You get a feeling for what's right from orchestral experience. In the Philharmonia I think this has changed over the years. Von Karajan didn't seem to want anyone to play on the beat. Starting a quiet brass chord he always implied that he didn't want to hear 'pah', he wanted the equivalent of an up-bow, the sound rising out of nothing. Of course that's very difficult for the brass, but in the Philharmonia we got used to it. Then with Klemperer, I think we always played behind the beat. A lot of people would have had trouble playing with Klemperer because of his physical handicap — he should have been dead three or four times. But he knew what he wanted and managed to convey it to us, and though we played behind the beat it worked. Now with Maazel and Muti, both very positive, I think we play on the beat. So much is intuition, very often one has to *feel* what to do. You tune in.

The Tuba

It must be well understood that this instrument is not adapted to shakes and rapid passages. It can play certain measured melodies. . . . It has at once something of the trombone and of the organ.

HECTOR BERLIOZ, *On Orchestration*

JOHN FLETCHER A weird instrument, the tuba. A lot of people don't quite understand its function, and I must say I don't either, because it changes. For heavy German music we need a big deep sound which the whole brass section sits on. But for English or French music something more agile is required. Other wind and brass sections are divided into high and low players. The tuba has to cover four fully-working octaves and plunge from one end to the other with no warning. A Berlioz overture followed by a Prokofiev or Shostakovich symphony means a rapid movement from the dizzy heights of the treble clef down to the deepest basement. For all this, one should use different tubas, but most people in England, because of the great variety of our work, use a compromise in-between size.

John Fletcher

Waiting, loitering around, is a problem. The lip goes stale, with a sort of horrible polyurethane glaze on it, the tuba goes flat, and you sink into a lower mental state. With an orchestra in full flight, you get a communal buzz, a high adrenalin flow, but to be just outside and then to come in, it's like jumping on a merry-go-round going full-tilt. Time drags, in rehearsal, having nothing to play, so I usually take something to get on with. The tuba is the only one of its kind in the orchestra. It's plonked alongside the trombones for convenience, but the sound doesn't have very much in common. We've got used to the blend of three trombones and a tuba, and I accept it, but tuba can be used as part of the brass section, and also as a fifth horn. Berlioz established the tuba in the conventional orchestra, replacing the opheiclide. The trend was towards more weight of tone, which the tuba gives. But now, with the current mania for instruments and mouthpieces that are, in my opinion, too large, the tubas are making such a heavy sound, they've gone right away from being brass instruments and sound more like ships' hooters, with about as much artistry as those are capable of.

Much of our job is fitting in with others, but there's a young generation — I suppose I'm as guilty as any — that wants to be important, make a telling contribution, and plays far too loudly, and the result would be amusing if it weren't so annoying. But the bell of the tuba shields you from the sound, and I can't at all judge my dynamic when I'm playing. I always thought I had difficulty in making a big sound — they call me 'the whispering giant' — yet listeners have told me I'm too loud. Conductors often wave me down. On some recordings we've made, especially on EMI with Previn in a fairly general acoustic which I like, the tuba is far too ponderous. I didn't think so at the time, I was just doing my best.

153

(opposite)
Practising the violin at the
last minute

Percussion

*These instruments are of two kinds: those of fixed sound, and
musically appreciable; the second includes those ranked only among
noises to produce special effects, or to colour the rhythm.*

HECTOR BERLIOZ, *On Orchestration*

GARY KETTEL In a symphony orchestra, the best thing for us to play is
timpani because there's more in the repertoire for it. Many orchestral
percussion parts are very boring, but there's a lot of ironmongery to get
around. There's the triangle, cymbals and bass drum, side drum, tenor
drum, glockenspiel, tubular bells, xylophone, castanets, tambourine,
whip wood-block, temple-block, and that's about it for the ordinary
repertoire, though the music of the last few years includes a lot more. Oh,
and then you get the odd effects like wind-machine, thunder sheet – in the
Alpine Symphony – and anvil. A lot of conductors insist on a real anvil,
but unless you're a blacksmith it doesn't sound right. We use lumps of
railway line, or bits of drainpipe, or scaffolding tube can sound good.
Effects are often not what they seem. You've got to use your loaf in percussion and be ready to improvise.

In the last few years I think percussion players have got a little over-
assertive. The idea is to be a bit important, because orchestras considered them bangers and tappers of no account. But there's more skill
to percussion than people think, just getting a triangle or cymbal to ring
properly. But I think a lot of the fellows now play too loud. I like extremes,
and you can do that in percussion. 'Was that a cymbal?' – so quiet. Yet
with the same instrument you can raise a horrible racket. I look on percussion, specially in romantic music, not so much as a thing in itself, but
as a subtle extra colour. It merely adds to the texture.

Gary Kettel

(opposite)
The harpist relaxes during
rehearsal

With tuned percussion the pitch is fixed. Pianos are quite often tuned sharp, I don't know why, but I find the fixed scale percussion are generally OK. And when you go abroad, to a different A, you take your own percussion in the van. Intonation on timps is another matter, though the tuning gauges make it easier now. You set the notes beforehand, then just look to see if the pointer is at E, or whatever, and hit it. They are reasonably accurate. But a good player will take account of variations in pitch throughout the concert, and also consider the tempering of the scale. An E in C sharp and an E in F are a bit different. So I think, in the bars rest, you should always listen and adjust. Some players just look at their gauges, and a couple can play very accurately like that, because they know their drums.

I wish more orchestral musicians these days would use their ear-holes, rather than try to watch conductors waving about vaguely. Even Boulez, despite his reputation for exactness, got nervous in concerts and rushed. He could do a 3/16 and a 7/16 and do an 8 against it exactly, but when it came to a simple, rigid tempo, he didn't have natural time — he'd be no good playing drums in a rock group. Sometimes we'd say, 'Excuse me, we think that's rushing.' 'No, no, I assure you zis is not ze case.' We'd do it again and he'd get it right, because he was concentrating. 'There you are,' he'd say triumphantly, 'it was ze same as last time.' You could never get the last word with Boulez. Now very often, if, say, cellos are playing with drums, they don't listen to the drum-beat, they follow the conductor who's starting to hurry. Going with the beat is sometimes wrong, if you listen carefully. I said that to the orchestra a couple of times and just got jeered down. I suppose the trouble is, in the big orchestra, you can't hear too well what others are doing. Well, I've also done those semi-light music sessions with the Royal Philharmonic, rhythmic numbers with drummer, bass guitar and guitar. The rhythm is going *chuk, chuk, chuk* in their ears, and the fellows are still sitting with eyes riveted on the conductor. They've got the beat pounding in their ear-holes! That's beyond me.

Claudio Abbado rehearsing
with the LSO

The Harp

Nothing could be more in keeping with the idea of poetic festivities, or religious rites, than the sound of harps ingeniously introduced.

HECTOR BERLIOZ, *On Orchestration*

SIDONIE GOOSSENS No doubt about it, the harp is hard to play, and not just to play but to make a good sound. Sometimes a wonderful technique only produces a tinkling tin sound. A harpist must have a good sound. It's partly the strings, you must look after them. I use all gut, except for the lowest ones. Gut is temperamental, but the sound is much nicer. The harp, of course, is a non-chromatic instrument, with the peculiar headache of having to make complicated pedal-changes, and many composers just don't consider that at all. They write as if for the piano and we have to make grotesque contortions to get anywhere near the notes. They expect us to play chromatically. Schoenberg, for example, is almost impossible to play. His single harp part, we nearly always have to divide it between two players because one physically just can't manage it. It's the same with Berg sometimes, they just haven't thought about it. But Schoenberg is the worst, just *wicked*.

For us, in the orchestra, I think the worst problem is tuning, and if you're not in tune you might as well pack up. Some harps hold their tune quite well and others not, but I find one of the secrets is to tune and leave it, don't fiddle about, let the strings settle. And of course our tuning is fixed so we can't temper our notes up or down, as certain other instruments can. Henry Wood used to say, in a *Carmen* suite, flute with harp accompaniment, 'Flute, you must adjust to the harp, the harp can't change.' I think orchestral players are better now, at listening to the harp. Boulez has always insisted in the BBC Symphony that the whole orchestra tunes by sections, no matter how rushed we are. Then we have no problems. People groan, but it's discipline. Brass players fool around, but Boulez knows they'll be in tune when the time comes.

Harpists spend a great deal of time waiting. We have many, many bars' rest in all orchestral harp parts, but my concentration never lapses, I'm afraid I listen all the time. At rehearsal, I never dare do anything else, not even crosswords as a lot of them do. I would get too interested and miss my entry. I try to tell my pupils that, always to follow and listen, and that way you get to learn the music. What's the good of only knowing the little bits you play? On the harp, we play so little we'd have a very patch-work view of music if we didn't listen all the time.

A View from the Platform

And I saw a man holding a stick, and I believed he was going to
castigate the bad violins. And he made a noise as if he were
splitting wood, I was astonished, and the vigour of his arm
terrified me. And I beheld they called it 'beating the time,' and
though it was beaten most forcibly, the musicians were never
together.

F.W. VON GRIMM, *Correspondance littéraire* (1753)

IN my time I've played with just about every conductor of reputation, starting with Elgar. We had Richard Strauss once or twice – very stiff. And Weingartner, extraordinary, we did the *Planets* and he just could not beat that 5 in Mars. He got muddled like anything, really embarrassing to see the great man standing there flapping. I played for Toscanini who, at least with us, was not as fiery as his reputation. Koussevitsky was much worse, often quite nasty. Toscanini was serious. He would be very nervous before he came on, sort of praying in the wings. He walked on almost with his eyes closed, hands clenched, then started very carefully, very quiet gestures. He was not demonstrative, but when we did *La Mer* I don't know how he got that crescendo at the end, it worked up so gradually but became the biggest crescendo I ever heard. I'd never played such a performance.

Furtwangler was the funniest chap to get wonderful results. He had this weird old wobbly beat, yet somehow you knew that when he got down to the third waistcoat button it was time to start. Klemperer was another fellow with a strange beat. I found him wonderful to work with though he would get very cross, terribly ratty. If someone was slow to mark in a bowing he'd be shouting, stamping, 'I said to mark the bowing, not to write a book.' He had a fine sweep and control, and a lovely sense of rhythm and pulse. Sadly, he got a bit deaf and shaky. You'd be thinking 'poor old Klemperer', then suddenly the veil of infirmity would drop and he'd be wonderfully vigorous again. He fell asleep once, in a recording. The score fell from his lap, where he sometimes placed it, fell off with a crash. Frightfully embarrassing, we just fizzled out, stopped playing. The leader just had to shake him gently, whisper 'From letter B, Dr Klemperer . . .' He was old and had suffered severe illness.

I was a young bassoon player when I first went to Glyndebourne, and Fritz Busch was already quite old. When we gathered at the very first

Rehearsing under difficult
conditions

rehearsal John Christie made a speech of welcome. He said he'd tried to get the Vienna Philharmonic, but he knew we'd do our best, implying you know, that we were only second best. Anyway, Busch soon saw that he'd got a very good orchestra, and we idolized him. For years after, Busch would wait until Christie was present before giving out rehearsal times at the start of each season, and then he'd say, 'Ten o'clock for my marvellous orchestra,' and then with a big wink, 'but *not* so good as the Vienna Philharmonic.' We loved him for that dig at Christie.

When we prepared for the Proms with Sir Henry Wood, he had everything planned out and timed to the minute. He had his big watch on the music-stand, and at 10 a.m. precisely his baton went down. You learnt things so thoroughly with him, but in the most economical time. Our Wagner nights, whole acts from the operas, we did that on just the morning rehearsal. Before I knew him he had the reputation for being a tartar. He took my teacher to lunch, which was always a bad sign, and she had her notice when she got home. But he changed. He met Lady Jessie and she changed him. He had been badly dressed, awful clothes. Jessie got him a new evening suit, instead of the mouldy green one, and he flourished yellow gloves and a cigar. She changed his clothes and he became human, and began to look after the orchestra. He began to give us a dinner after the last night of the Proms.

Arthur Fiedler is so old, it's so difficult for him now. He gets himself up for special concerts, but day in day out his concerts are, oh, unbelievable. He's very, very old. Sometimes for Pops concerts we go out to Fitchburg, Worcester, places like that, and there's always a clause if Fiedler is sick, the concert is cancelled. He's the star. The audience come for him, not for the music. Well, that sort of thing happens at Tanglewood also, say when Bernstein comes, then there'll be 15,000 people at least. A lot of it is just a personality trip, and with Fiedler it's particularly upsetting because he is now so bad. If any of us in the orchestra played the way he conducts, we'd be fired for sure. Yet nobody cares.

For many years San Francisco has had an illustrious opera season, a big, big deal, though that's about all they've got. I remember when I was twelve my teacher took me there and got me into the pit. Artur Bodanski, considered one of the great Wagnerians, had come to do *Walkurie*. There I was in the pit, about twelve years old, and every few minutes, or so it seemed, this conductor was screaming and swearing at the men in the orchestra, actually during the performance. Calling them the worst things. I thought I was going to hear music, but when I got home all I could think about was this abuse, this endless abuse.

I had a heart attack in 1959. I was still recovering when Klemperer came as guest conductor. Well, the programme had a lot of oboe in it — a *Brandenberg*, Beethoven *Eroica*, Mozart 41, I think — and I felt I could only manage half the programme, so I went to ask Klemperer if that was all right. He simply said, 'No.' I was rather surprised, but I thought perhaps he hadn't quite got the circumstances, and knowing that he'd been through a heart attack himself, I thought I'd appeal to his feelings. 'But Dr Klemperer, let me explain, I'm still recovering from a heart attack.' The answer was still no. That made me blazing mad. I saw his daughter outside as I left the room, and I told her 'so much for your father's humanity.' Half an hour later she came to find me and said, 'My father has reconsidered.' Yes, he was a good conductor, but nobody is *that* good.

The leader of the old Philharmonia told me that when he was leaving the orchestra he went to see Klemperer. He'd done so much with the old man, even played his trio, and he felt some kind of relationship with Klemperer. He was sorry to be leaving. After his last concert he felt he should go and say something. He said, 'Dr Klemperer, after all these years this is my last concert with you . . .' And Klemperer replied, 'What you want me to do, cry?'

Sir John Barbirolli

One of the fellows in the Hallé fell in love with a young woman — a singer — and they had quite a time together for a while. Then his wife heard of it, and there was a hell of a row. She went to see Barbirolli, hoping he could intervene, you see. She went to his room in the Free Trade Hall at the interval, and he was having his usual whisky. 'What can I do for you, my dear?' he said. 'It's my husband, he's got this young woman, and I don't know what to do.' And there she was sobbing away. 'You know,' he said, trying to comfort her in his kindly way, 'there's nothing to worry about, *he's playing better than ever.*'

Barbirolli was a lovable fellow, very human. He was always careful not to pick on anyone by name, give him a hard time. Once we were recording for Pye and a fiddle came in wrong. 'Cretin,' shouted Barbirolli, then immediately added, 'some of you.' He was lacking in confidence really, perhaps because of that bitter experience in New York. He liked to have all the band there, whether they were needed or not, in case he had to change a piece at short notice. He'd take the trombones all the way to Harrogate, just for the National Anthem. But he liked music — he really *liked* it.

I must say Karajan, and I think Haitink too, really made their names in England, on our orchestras. Karajan was at first little known. They were not keen to let him in, on account of a dubious wartime past. I remember we did a Balakirev symphony with him. He said he wanted something 'like the crack of a whip', and everyone in the orchestra went 'Now, now, now!' You know, he is a very clever man, he never made that kind of mistake again.

I've always greatly respected von Karajan, simply because he treated you man to man. The first time I played for him we were doing Don Juan. I was a new face in the orchestra, very inexperienced, I'd never played the piece,

Herbert von Karajan *(left)*

though I'd studied it and practised my part. Well, in the beginning the strings sweep up, then there are the basses and the bass trombone, which has the phrase on the beat, and it has to be there. Von Karajan made some loose, ethereal movement which the strings understood and first fiddle led them up the sweep. But I couldn't see or feel a downbeat at all – he just had his arms in the air, he wasn't going to beat it like a bandmaster – and I missed my entry. I think most conductors would have stopped and made a song and dance. Von Karajan simply looked over, as if to say, 'I know my job, I hope you know yours. I won't say anything now, but when we come to the recapitulation you'll know what I'm doing, and we'll see what you do.' When the recapitulation came, of course, I was ready and played it. He just glanced over again, as if to say OK, but not a word was spoken.

Von Karajan was fine. Well, he was a real man, a real general man, he drove fast cars and flew an aeroplane, as well as being a fine musician. I could get on with a man like that.

When I auditioned for Krips on bass clarinet, I knew nothing about it, I'd played it for about three weeks, and I got the kind of tone that has *nothing* – no breath, no overtones, no personality, nothing. Even close to it sounded like a distant fog-horn. The others auditioning sounded like bass clarinet players – they had buzz, and air, and things like that, and sounded good. But Krips didn't know that. He thought I sounded best and hired me. After a while I found out about the bass clarinet and began to sound like the others. I don't think he'd have hired me if I'd sounded like a decent player.

Josef Krips was the first tyrant I came across. The big temperamental act – a big baby really. He was a martinet, but he entertained us greatly with a curious manner of speech, an English that was a direct trans-lation from Viennese German. But he opened my eyes to what orchestral performance could be, and to the relationship that could exist between a young, impressionable player and a conductor who had something to offer, for all the bullshit that surrounded him, and that was voluminous. He was a fine, sensitive musician in a limited repertoire, and he had standards of orchestral playing that I had never really met before. He had curious mannerisms, which they all do. A great actor, with those thyroid eyes, large specs, and bald dome. I was very frightened, the first concert I did with him. He liked to play the contemplative – I don't know if he was. He would compose himself on the box, eyes closed, hands clasped across the belly, meditating. Then the eyes would start open, magnified to the size of goldfish behind the specs, and the stick would shoot out. This hit me like needles in my chair. I was too paralysed to play at all.

Szell scared the stuffing out of me, I was shaking like a leaf when I first played for him. I was once talking to a very famous singer about Szell. When she did the Verdi Requiem with him, she didn't sing very well because she couldn't relate to this unbending man. He took her aside during the rehearsal and said, 'When have you sung this before – if ever?' That upset her. I also find that I have to relate to a conductor if I'm going to play well for him. I don't actually have to like the man, but I must have some to and fro communication. And there's a kind of old conductor that I'm afraid I couldn't tolerate at all now. I heard a recording of Toscanini in rehearsal, and he was *screaming* at the orchestra. It sounded like one of Hitler's speeches, in Italian. We wouldn't put up with that now – I certainly wouldn't.

I was really frightened of meeting Fritz Reiner. He had a dreadful reputation as a tyrant. We were doing sessions up in Walthamstow for RCA Victor and we recorded Brahms 4. I was on to lead. I was so worried about this chap, I went along early to prepare myself, and there he was already, the image of that Hollywood heavy, von Stroheim. Moreover, he had one of those neck-halters on for some injury – grotesquely terrifying. He was introduced to the orchestra, and he was wonderful. No trouble at all. There's a passage at the end of the 1st movement of the Brahms – for string players Brahms is not always comfortable, you feel it's piano writing – a very awkward passage, leaping right to the top of the E string, up an octave. After we'd played, Reiner turned to me, 'How do you finger that?' Without thinking, luckily, I showed him, and it was all right. 'Good,' he said, 'yes, that's the best way. I thought you went across the strings.' He was frightening but a real performer. He did everything with his hands.

Beecham did everything with his eyes. Wherever you were sitting you had this wonderful feeling of contact with him – you personally, even at the back of the seconds. But you can sit under the nose of a bad conductor and you get nothing, *nothing* at all.

Beecham hated sharing the platform, and Heifetz of course was no more interested in conductors than Tommy was in soloists, so they didn't get on very well. On one occasion, when they were appearing together at the Festival Hall, Beecham decided on some sabotage. In the cadenza of the concerto, first he had a prolonged fit of coughing, then he produced a tin of cough-sweets and spilt them all over the platform.

The last time Beecham conducted us, in Portsmouth, we were doing the overture to *The Magic Flute*. We just rehearsed the chords, a beast for any conductor, then he called a halt. It was Cup Final day, so he had two TV sets of the largest kind wheeled in and we all watched the football game with Tommy. Another time, recording the *Messiah*, he obviously thought the band wasn't happy enough, so he suddenly produced two bottles of Scotch for the coffee-break at 11.15 in the morning. We loved him very much. We knew he was very ill, after that Portsmouth concert, but when I heard he was dead I was nearly in tears. On that day, a Saturday, we had a concert with Fistulari. Now he was a nice man, not a bad musician, but apt to get confused and certainly no Beecham. It was a Tchaikovsky programme at the Festival Hall, all Tommy's pieces. We rehearsed it, and the orchestra was so depressed, doubly so because we were doing Tommy's music with this other fellow. We were going to play one of Grieg's little string pieces, in memory of Tommy. We began rehearsing it with Fistulari, who was one of those showy conductors, lots of waving about. I felt so awful that I phoned the manager after the rehearsal and said we could very well play the Grieg by ourselves, without Fistulari. So that's what we did in the evening. I remember looking round at the wind section, just sitting there, waiting for the little string piece to end, and some had tears running down their faces. The memory of a great thing now finished.

There's something about conductors and football. I believe Celibidache played well, perhaps even for the Romanian team. Isserstedt was mad about it, and Beecham liked it too. Kempe's thing was electric trains. He built a fantastic lay-out, and I can imagine him marshalling those trains about, for he was a wonderful controller of the orchestra, and a very great accompanist. He enjoyed it too. I recall Geza Anda doing the Tchaikovsky concerto, which can be difficult to accompany, and Kempe was like someone driving a racing-car, following the piano round the bends.

Kempe was at his best as a guest conductor. When he took over the Royal Philharmonic, reluctantly, as he said himself, he told us he was there just to rehearse and make music. 'If you have other problems,' he said, 'please don't come to me.' He knew it himself, he was the last person to see to the day-to-day running of an orchestra. He was extraordinarily talented, but he lacked something. I think it was belief in himself. Someone described him as half-arrogant German, and half-kindly, sensitive musician. There was a battle going on in him always. He never did very well in Germany, which we could never understand — some of the Berlin

Phil told me they thought him too cold, which he certainly was not with us. Apparently in England he was a different person. I was told he had a Saxon accent. That's equivalent to a conductor here speaking broad Liverpool. Someone with a scouse accent wouldn't do anything here. It's an awful thing to say, but it's true.

Rozhdestvensky did Shostakovich 4 with us. He certainly knew it, and he was a lot of fun to watch, he was fun at rehearsal. But he seemed satisfied with practically anything. In some of those fast passages — he had four rehearsals on it, maybe that's all — any note at all would do for him, he didn't care.

Rostropovich tends to get a distinctive sound when he conducts, and he wants everything either as loud or as soft as possible. The orchestra sounds kind of ugly sometimes. He was here doing the Verdi Requiem. And at first everybody was wild about him, but you start to realize after a while that he really doesn't know that much about it. He does seem to be naïve and enthusiastic. But he loves music, he reminds me of Krips in that respect. He really looks as if he's having a great time.

I'm frightened by how skilful Riccardo Muti is with modern music. He knows precisely what he wants and how to get it. And he communicates to us how to do it, because we don't do that much of it in Philadelphia. We don't understand and we're rather rigid, as I'm sure many of the American orchestras are. But he can explain — 'I do this in 3, and this in 8, there'll be a pause here . . .' — and suddenly it becomes easier to play. You don't have to like it, but you come to grips with it and walk away thinking, 'Well, I didn't do too badly.'

A light moment in rehearsal when Riccardo Muti holds up a picture of himself — with a beard

Music-making

The principal merit of a good orchestral player consists in being subordinate, and willing to increase, by that subordination, the perfection of the whole.

LOUIS SPOHR, *Grand Violin School* (1833)

RODNEY FRIEND

A GOOD music director is the most important thing. When you put a hundred musicians together in an orchestra there's no way you can have rigid discipline. You've got a hundred highly-charged, complicated artists in one room and, you know, it can be electric – danger points everywhere. So somebody must be in control, and it must be someone who is respected, a master musician. Otherwise he's murdered, specially in New York. Well, English orchestras work with a lot of different conductors. I think English people have a history of dignified behaviour and they carry that into the orchestra so that they are never really offensive. But they can be cool, very cool, which in a way can be more hurtful than shouting. Orchestras themselves differ greatly in temperament, thank goodness, and a good conductor may work well with one orchestra and not with another.

A Working Partnership

The London impresarios, now those are the men to get the most out of time! It's the English who have brought the art of speeded-up rehearsing to a degree of splendour unknown to other nations.

HECTOR BERLIOZ, *Evenings with the Orchestra*

MICHAEL NUTT Beware the conductor who talks too much. Play the damn music! Then point out what's wrong, and play it again.

ALFIO MICCI In New York we have four rehearsals — two-and-a-half hours each – for every programme. Now new works, as we often did with Boulez, may take three of the four rehearsals, just getting the notes right. We'd read the rest of the programme. I'm not sure you need four rehearsals for every programme, it depends on the orchestra and the works. And sometimes four is not enough. But we're locked into this rigid schedule, and if a man is allowed four he'll invariably take four. Then the orchestra does get restless, with standard repertoire, and if we still need to rehearse Beethoven 7, measure by measure, we shouldn't call our-

166

selves the Philharmonic. But it happens, and it can rankle a bit. Conductors talk away, I don't know why they persist in it. A musician, he doesn't need to talk, he can express what he means with the baton, with his arms and body. Talk and talk, pick and pick, you get no feeling for the whole shape, and that's when discipline can break down. Also, stopping and starting tires the orchestra tremendously, putting the fiddle down, marking the part, trying to hear what the conductor is saying. It's incredible the time wasted.

Well, Stokowski, if he had four rehearsals, he'd play the programme through four times. That was it. Even with a new work, by the time you got to the fourth rehearsal the notes would fall in place, because orchestral players are not stupid. A conductor who stops for a wrong note is only showing off. The player knows what he's done, we have good ears too, or we wouldn't be in the Philharmonic. Stokowski would worry about balance, but the players could look after the notes. I think what orchestral musicians resent most, it's being told things they know. But I must say we don't get *bad* conductors with the Philharmonic, not incompetents.

Testing the acoustics in the Fairfield Hall

TONY PAY One says English orchestras are under-rehearsed, but it depends on what you mean by rehearsal. We all know there are certain things that are just not worth going over, and the job of the competent conductor is to sort out these things, which will come right if he refrains from tinkering, from those matters which really need attention. So many conductors niggle at the superfluous, or demand the impossible. One said to us, in a miserable hall at ten o'clock of a freezing morning, 'Can we have the winds in tune please?' And he got a resounding 'No.' The point was there was no way we could get it much better just then. We might have improved a bit, but it just wasn't worth bothering with in a rehearsal. And in a sense it's good to hang back a little in rehearsal, then in the concert you suddenly find yourself borne on a wave that is far more exciting and powerful than anything in the rehearsal. That exhilaration can inform everything you're trying to do, a euphoria that makes you capable of things you didn't even know were in you. Conductors, in England anyway, need to understand this before they begin rehearsing.

We say in England, for a repertoire piece, leave the details to the orchestra, let the conductor indicate the interpretive shape in rehearsal, and then pull the whole together in the concert. Here, it's undoubtedly true that a man good at pulling things out of the bag at the concert, although he lives dangerously, can get better results than a man who grinds away at meticulous and minute detail. We are used in London because we are quick and we are cheap, and though that may not be the best way to make music, it endows British players with certain virtues. They have wide sympathies, can take fairly easy to various styles and are wonderful sight-readers. We are chameleon-like, perhaps because of the relative weakness of our own symphonic tradition. In Germany, so I hear, an orchestra has to be told everything. A conductor doesn't need to do that in England, nor do our orchestras take to the hectoring, pedantic approach of the mid-European tradition.

Of course, in new or more complex works, strange pieces that aren't repertoire, you do need to understand the piece more fully to give a good performance. For that time is necessary, and I don't think British orchestras have that time. I sometimes wish I saw better how my part fitted in with the rest of the music, and that I wasn't on tenterhooks trying to work out what was happening. It's hard to know what importance to attach to conducting technique, to a precise beat. Remember Furtwangler — conducting is so much a question of musicality and personality. Really, in a good orchestra, once you know the kind of gestures a man uses, you make adjustments for personal eccentricities. As someone said of Reginald Goodall at the National Opera, the whole performance hung upon some player making a decision in every bar. His lack of clarity put the responsibility right in the lap of the orchestra, yet they were prepared to play for him because he was dealing at a higher level. He was saying what happens when you've got all the notes together, but he rather left it to the band to get them. It depends on the piece, how closely the players will want to hang on the beat. If you watch some orchestras they play almost a quaver, sometimes a crochet behind what the man is doing. Obviously these things are a convention. For the great chord in the slow movement of the *Eroica*, Kempe ended the downbeat with a large judder. No one quite knew where to play, so our new principal cello piped up, 'Why don't you just go like that?' giving a firm, clear beat. 'Oh dear,' we all groaned, but Kempe just smiled, and did as requested. But in the concert he was back to his old, juddering beat, and he got the effect he wanted. We played it together anyway.

JOHN DE LANCIE Now, there is something that has radically changed, even in my lifetime. When I started most American orchestras played only three concerts a week, perhaps only two, and always the same programme. And we had maybe seven rehearsals for each programme, so a thing like quick sight-reading wasn't the greatest necessity for an orchestral player. However, you spent a lot of time preparing your parts before you came to rehearsal, which there is no great tendency to do any more. These things have changed because of the pressure of work, and because the men have organized themselves in the union. And the impact, the fingerprint of a great personality is not so apparent now. A man has to stay with an orchestra many years before that can be achieved. So, to a degree, a long stay by a music director is good, though it has its dangers. Formerly, we had an age of autocrats — Stokowski, Koussevitsky, Toscanini — and I don't think that was bad. Their orchestras played in a certain way. In fact, one of the complaints I've heard from conductors coming to Philadelphia is that they can't get the orchestra to change — 'I just stand there and the Philadelphia Orchestra gives its performance of a Brahms symphony.' But a strong man can impose his ideas and style.

JOHN FLETCHER The adulterous life we lead in London, with many different conductors, is to some extent good. I think we are reasonably conscientious, trying to get at what a man wants. But of course if there's little time, he gets something like the last man got, unless he has very real talent. There's no point in getting married to one conductor just for its own sake. The liaison must be beneficial for orchestra, for conductor, and for audiences. There are cases of conductors being given plenty of time to bed themselves in and then having nothing to offer. This has happened far too often, without mentioning names, and I think we are simply wary of giving one man too much work. A lot of times one doesn't really know what a conductor wants. Many don't seem to want anything in particular, so we just do what seems right to us. There are not many conductors with whom I'd like to work half the year. It's not that I think they're bad, it's just that after a while you want to shake music up and look at it differently. We get a nice variety. They all come through London, and I think the public here is very lucky.

ROGER SCOTT Ormandy has been with us I don't know how many years. He's a perfectionist and he keeps after us, rightfully so. He hones the razor and the razor just keeps on cutting. And I believe our orchestral playing has remained so high for all these years, because he's constantly after us. If you don't play well for a guest conductor, he's gone in a couple of days, he has no power over you.

Both Stokowski and Ormandy have dwelt on the richness of the Philadelphia strings, and to me there is a lushness in our sound that other orchestras don't get. Last year, we were down to eight or even seven basses. Ormandy came to Saratoga, took one look at seven basses for Beethoven 9 and raised hell. I'm delighted if Ormandy agrees to have extras, because I do like to have a full section. If one is out you feel it, if two are out it's pretty thin going, because our orchestra has a concept of big sound, and we carry bigger sections, I think, than most European orchestras — four trombones, twelve cellos — and seven basses is weak, by my standards. Now, our new principal guest conductor Riccardo Muti comes in, and he'll spend time systematically pruning away the fat, and some of the men really don't understand. My answer is that he's just trying to get us to play his way, not our way. We learnt that he didn't want, at certain points, as much as Ormandy. Later, in the big climax, you couldn't play loudly enough, it had to be shattering, but elsewhere the finesse was very apparent. And for a conductor of his stature we'll try to do this, whereas for a lesser man we probably won't change our style. With Muti, we did a Mozart Divertimento with only eight first violins, and I never heard our violins play like that in their lives. He coaxed them, he didn't badger them. I mean, here's a young man in his late thirties working with old, hardened professionals, and they were backstage practising! One of my friends said, 'I just want to do my best, that's all.' He was being inspired to play better than he normally played, and when there's this feeling, it's a very thrilling thing to be part of music-making.

JOHN RONAYNE I found the good men, say Beecham, Klemperer, Karajan, Kempe, spent most of rehearsal balancing the orchestra, not by talking but by indications of hand, eye or body, and by force of character.

169

Members of the Royal
Philharmonic Orchestra
christen their new
pantechnicon with
champagne

So when the evening of the concert came, they had tuned the orchestra in rehearsal, and now had a fresh and eager instrument to play on. And I found also, specially when I was leading, that these men made you play better than you knew you could. You came off with this wonderful feeling, 'I didn't know I could play like that.' And not in solos, no, but in the ordinary tutti parts. Now on the contrary, someone like Sir Malcolm Sargent — specially him — obviously had some sort of hold on the orchestra, but to bad effect. He actually made you play worse. How many times I've heard players say, 'My god, I just can't play for that man.' He somehow took all the spunk out of the orchestra. He certainly had control, if you can call that control. He knew his scores, and prepared meticulously in rehearsal, but nothing different or enlightening ever happened in concert. Perhaps I'm being unfair to Sir Malcolm, but he struck me as a prime example of a well-known type of conductor.

ROBIN McGEE The average player, like me, can usually sum up a conductor in a few bars. You see if he's at ease, and if not you wonder why. Is he unsure of his ability and authority? Affectation is another turn-off. Orchestral players differ about who is really good, but we generally agree on the ones who are not good. I found it very tedious and wearying, having done a piece with a good man, to do the same music time after time with lesser talents. Sometimes I would even be stretched to inventing something to rehearse. Rather childish really, but I thought if we were going to be there for three hours we might as well work at something. So I might construct an error, or discover a problem. One gets, in the orchestra, to thinking in a blinkered way about these things, if one is cooped up in rehearsal with nothing new or revealing being done, specially if one is on tour with the prospect of playing the same piece rather poorly for the next three weeks. That becomes unbearable.

170

BILL LANG In the brass we need a good attack. Sometimes you have to ask for it, and I've never hesitated to do so. After all, it's the conductor's performance, and he's a fool if he thinks you are just trying to undermine him. 'I'm sorry, we have to have a definite beat to come in there together.' Any reasonable man will accept that. With Barbirolli, at the beginning, many a time I had to ask for a definite beat, and he was only to happy to give it. Well, they have such a lot to think about with the full score, you can understand them overlooking a little thing like that. But the good ones remember the next time, and that is where Monteux scored, he seemed to understand everything in the orchestra. I thought he was a genius. He knew the music backwards, and he barely conducted with two hands, generally with one, and he made tiny movements, never outside his body. These fellows who make violent sweeps, it's like crying wolf. With a small beat, you have to watch. When they whirl around the orchestra can be anywhere, and the worst is when they come down and don't stop. You don't know where the end of the beat is. Now, we've had Previn with the London Symphony for a long time, and some of the fellows grumble that his beat is a bit sloppy, but he's wonderfully quick and sensitive and he can read anything. I think we play very well with him, everybody pulling together. He does disappoint you at times, cutting corners, a bit casual, but still the orchestra plays well, far better than for a fellow that lays down the beat rigidly, and in the end it sounds like that, awful. Sargent did that. He looked marvellous and sounded terribly disappointing. Now Barbirolli, he'd been a cellist, and he was for the strings, all those sweeping gestures were for the bow, which was no help to the brass. But when you got used to him, you knew where to put the notes, and when you listened there was really something about it. It's a great mystery, conducting.

GARY KETTEL I'm sure Boulez mellowed a bit during the time I was in the band. A lot of the musicians hated him, you know, and hated his approach to music. And at first he was very, very precise, cold. I always got on well with him, because we had a little bit of repartee, and he kept me in check — shouted at me a couple of times, but I respected him for that. And he respected good players. In fact, he didn't expect good players ever to get anything wrong, and he'd be a bit annoyed if they did — puzzled also, 'Is there some trouble, are you all right?' That was the expectation, a high one. I liked the way he worked, because the only friction was with people who hated him anyway, provoking him on purpose. That wasn't necessary, because he's a very nice bloke. Some players will hate me for saying this, because they think he has no music in him at all. But a fault about conductors, made worse by the applause of the public, is that the bloke is conducting his own thing, not the music. For example, Mahler 6, done by Boulez and Solti. Now I thought Boulez did it amazingly. The tempi really keen and well judged. But Solti was just doing his own thing. Look at a Mahler score, every other bar is carefully marked. It's all there, you don't have to do anything else. Boulez was right on the spot — this bar got slower, that one moved on slightly, careful gradations of pace and

Pierre Boulez discusses a music score in a BBC TV studio

171

dynamics. Then people say, because of that exactness, he's cold. Now look at Solti, all indulgence and gesture, putting in his own pauses and accelerandi, and people faint with admiration, 'How artistic, how beautifully felt!' Solti's way can work for some music, but so often it's just unnecessary.

TONY PAY It's such an elusive thing, how conductors affect orchestras. Somebody like Stokowski, whom one might be tempted to write off as a silly old fool, staggered onto the rostrum at a venerable age, hardly able to lift a hand. Yet people are riveted by the sight of him, and scared stiff too. He drops a languid hand in a camp gesture, and a tough and cynical brass section lets go with a blazing fortissimo. 'Not together,' he snaps, and the next time it damn well will be together, because that's the way it has to be. And it wasn't a question of being convinced that Stokowski was a great musician. I thought many of the things he did were gross travesties, which perhaps worked in a superficial, glossy way. Maybe that was what he was after, for certain pieces are best presented in that way. I would listen to late Stokowski perform *Sheherazade*, for instance, because that's what it is, nothing more. But I wouldn't care to listen to a Mahler symphony from him, because Mahler can go several layers deeper.

Now, depending on how you looked at it, a Kempe rehearsal could be considered boring and frustrating. He might take a piece apart, and then he might not. Sometimes he would stop every few bars, generally with a rather puzzled expression, as if to say, 'How can you play it like this?' But what I admired in him was that he very rarely imposed something on the music. He tried to take the view implicit in what was written, the thing itself, and he put nothing on top of that – no 'glamour', no 'personality', not 'my' interpretation. When it came to the concert it was often immensely exciting and occasionally deeply moving, but it always had the sense of coming from within. He was never vulgar and had a way of making things you thought trivial, like Strauss and so on, very much not trivial. He balanced very carefully, and paid strict attention to dynamics. He would never sacrifice the whole for a particular part, and while, in particular passages, he might not be as striking as a less scrupulous man, I always felt the whole benefited.

Stravinsky had a very keen ear for a wrong note

BILL LANG But conducting *is* a bit of a mystery, and you're hard put to say sometimes just what effect the fellow does have. There's an old story, repeated many times, but with a lot of truth in it. A player goes to a pub after a concert. 'Good concert tonight, Joe?' 'Yes, not bad, not bad.' 'Who was conducting?' 'Do you know, I couldn't say. I never looked.'

Personality

Music should be transmitted and not interpreted, because interpretation reveals the personality of the interpreter rather than that of the author, and who can guarantee that such an executant will reflect the author's vision without distortion?
IGOR STRAVINSKY, *Chronicle of my Life* (1936)

RON BARRON It's sad that conductors nowadays are supposed to be able to do the full repertoire. I don't like that. For example, when Munch was here in Boston, I'm told that the pieces he knew were fine, for the others it just never worked. We get conductors from all over the world bringing particular pieces that they really understand, and then we get a man doing the same piece, for whatever reason, without really knowing it. It doesn't make sense. But any music director today is put in that spot. He's supposed to be omniscient, some sort of superman.

The old ways don't happen any more, the central European tradition of apprenticeships, learning conducting in small opera houses so that they really got it, in a restricted repertoire perhaps, but what they knew they certainly knew well. It's not easy now, with so many outside that tradition. Ozawa commented that he was very surprised to be asked to be music director in Boston – 'I don't have any roots in western music, I'm Japanese.' And I'd go along with that. He's a marvellous talent, incredible technique, easy to play for, most natural guy on the podium I've ever seen. But he must feel the pressure of an alien tradition, having to learn all that music that is not, as it were, in his bloodstream. It's true a lot of times that conductors are learning works on the orchestra. But it's hard on them. Public expectation – a new star is born! After a few seasons in a big orchestra nowadays, the average orchestral musician has such broad knowledge and general experience that, almost no matter who is up front, it's hard to impress him. I've seen it. So many conductors, so much music.

JOHN DE LANCIE I heard the Chicago Symphony on tour not long ago. They played three pieces, and one of the woodwind sections had a different solo player in each piece. But part of the personality of the orchestra comes from the character of the solo players. If you keep changing, the whole thing loses character – for me anyway. I deplore this submerging of personality, this growing similarity of orchestras. I recall the tremendous differences of forty years ago, and in those days you could hear immense differences between an English and a French orchestra, or a French and a Viennese. Huge differences, and in America also.

Well, an orchestra can have a very strong personal style, so strong that even the most powerful conductors can't change it in a short time. This was brought home to me rather hilariously in 1955. We were on tour, playing in Vienna, and one day, not long after the new opera house had opened, I was sitting in a café talking to a member of the Vienna Philharmonic. I told him I began my career under Reiner, and we got to discussing conductors. He said, 'You know, we did *Meistersinger* with Toscanini at the opera, and shortly after did it again with Reiner. Those were two men with unique styles: Reiner, very exact, marvellous baton technique, but nonchalant, like a great swordsman with that long stick of his; Toscanini, very straightforward, but so compelling, tense, nervous, then a great release of energy and emotion. Both tyrants, of course . . . but we played exactly the same for both of them.' I could hardly believe my ears — 'we played the same for both of them!' A testimony to the impact of 'guest' conductors, and men of that stature!

TOM STORER The London Symphony does have a way of playing, but it's not as if we were the Vienna Phil. playing the Vienna way. Who can make an impression with a Beethoven symphony on an orchestra that insists the last time it was done properly in Vienna was by Beethoven himself? We're not like that. We have a basic standard which duff conductors get because it's less trouble than arguing with them. In a successful concert the credit goes to the conductor, in a bad concert the blame goes to the orchestra. You must avoid that, so we give duff conductors a steady performance which may enhance their reputation and does ours no harm. And a conductor of some standing whom we don't know very well gets some approximation between what he wants and what we habitually give.

ALAN CIVIL I'm often amazed that the Vienna Philharmonic can have four concertmasters and several principals in each section, yet their playing usually comes out the same. In an English orchestra a deputy first clarinet may throw the whole sound out. Of course, in Vienna they play a small and careful repertoire again and again. We are expected to be far more wide-ranging and adventurous. The penalty of working the Viennese way, in our view, is boredom. It takes a very great conductor indeed to make endless repetitions of a standard classic bearable. No doubt about it, even in the Philharmonia, it was tedious to play Brahms 1 the number of times we did it on tour. It took a Klemperer to throw fresh light on Beethoven, and I found his Beethoven cycles marvellous. I mean, I don't want to play Beethoven with any other conductor. For an orchestra to play with conductors of quality for extended periods is the best thing, but not to the extent that American orchestras remain with one man. Conductors in America have tremendous power and can act very badly, and that power is usually bound up with the band of rich women who run the subscriptions. Szell had infinite power in Cleveland, and ruled pretty hard, though I found him a damn good conductor. Only Karajan has that kind of power in Europe now, and not all his players like him by any means. But he's created vast amounts of work and money for them, so they suffer him. He's a commercial asset, and everybody shares in the riches he brings in. Who can possibly follow him?

I would like to think that my disillusion about modern conductors came from a misplaced sense of nostalgia. But I'm afraid the standard *is* poor. There's a lack of the general music director, the man who can guide an orchestra through the repertoire. There are specialists, certainly. Boulez specializes in contemporary music. But if you ever have the misfortune to play Mozart or Haydn with him, it's appalling. You see, not using a baton is dangerous. In concert, Boulez goes twice as fast, a mad scramble, because he loses control of what his arm is doing. He uses the whole arm, which generates a terrific momentum as he tries to get all the beats in. But there is no necessity to organize music to such a degree. Boulez seems to feel that if he doesn't give the beats nobody can play, which is nonsense. Well, that's the mystery — how did Furtwangler get anyone to play then? Or Klemperer, who was such a wreck that he couldn't hold a baton? I remember Klemperer hobbling in on sticks yet managing to indicate the first beat of Beethoven 5 before he was even on his stool. Goodness knows where the downbeat came from, but we came in perfectly.

I came home the other night, put the radio on and heard a Bruckner overture beautifully played. I thought, the Berlin Phil? It was the BBC Welsh Orchestra. And I've heard awful nondescript records from the Berlin Phil., bad intonation, poor sound, fluffed notes. Professional orchestras are becoming indistinguishable one from another. I don't think I can tell English orchestras apart. And very few orchestras manage to keep up a good standard whatever the conductor. You'd think that the London Symphony could manage it, but I was with them in Israel, with Horenstein and Dorati. We were doing six concerts of the same programme, a subscription series for 18,000 people. Horenstein started. The first concert — Mahler 1 — was bad, and the others went down, down, down. Now poor old Horenstein wasn't a bad conductor, but he'd had a performance collapse and after that he just couldn't get a grip on the orchestra. Nor could the orchestra pull itself up despite him. Now, someone like Kempe would never allow that to happen. He had the gift of knowing how much he could take from the orchestra, but Horenstein never recovered from the first night. A week later Dorati came, full of life and beans, to find an orchestra that just couldn't respond — all suntanned from the beach, but musically dulled. Hopeless. Put Dorati in a fiery mood, specially as the Israelis couldn't believe this was the LSO.

LYNN HARRELL I think musicians warm to, and become inspired by, a man with a strong individual approach, yet who can hear what the orchestra is giving him and adapt that to his ends, though the result may be slightly different from what he had in mind. Then he relaxes the players, who don't have to make an impossible adjustment in too short a time. A guest conductor busy pulling everything apart just doesn't get the task done in the time available. The result can be a thoroughly unprepared performance. He can do better by careful attention to what an orchestra can offer easily. Right notes, good intonation, ensemble, spirit, these are the expectations from a good orchestra, and if the conductor can get them right the performance will be very satisfactory. Stylistic interpretation is difficult and comes last, and a conductor just passing through probably won't have time for it.

It's true that orchestras all sound much the same today, more so than they did thirty years ago. That's partly what is wrong with the whole musical scene. We've paid for greater technical accomplishment and polish with loss of individuality. But a forceful conductor can change things quite quickly. One of the last things I did with Cleveland was a concert under Bernstein – Mahler 2. Now the Cleveland Orchestra was such a precise, mellow, well-oiled machine. Wonderful players, smooth and glossy, not too exciting, and never, never rough. Bernstein came along, leaped off the podium a couple of times, flailed around, got thoroughly carried away, and achieved an electric result because of his showmanship. The cool Cleveland Orchestra was on fire. Force of personality can make that happen. It doesn't necessarily mean the man is a great conductor, because it is a demonstration of will-power rather than musicianship.

Too often conductors don't seem to want very much at all. Sometimes, I think, they feel they can't demand certain things, like different sounds for different composers, because that would be dictating to the players. But musicians really want to be asked to do something that challenges their ability and intelligence. Orchestral musicians are dying to try different tone-colours, different types of rhythmic motion, different kinds of sound, because that puts them in the driving seat, and gives them a real sense of recreating the composer's individual voice. But a lot depends on how the conductor conveys all this, because those jaded people in every orchestra, if you hit them with the wrong thing at the wrong time, they'll shut off immediately – you can't reach them. But a wise and intelligent conductor may intrigue them.

Appropriate Sound

The unhealthy greed for orchestral opulence of today has corrupted the judgment of the public

IGOR STRAVINSKY, *Chronicle of my Life*

PAUL FRIED In America, the greatest players seem to stay in the orchestras, rather than try their luck outside. So we have many players of real brilliance and power in our big orchestras. And no doubt about it, you do need a large sound for orchestral playing, because you have to cut through the full orchestra and be heard in a hall seating 2 to 3,000 people. I would say it's true also that conductors today want more and more power. Rarely do we have a man who gets a true *pianissimo*, uses that end of the dynamic scale. They like the loud part. They ask the player of an orchestral solo to play louder rather than tell the rest of the orchestra to be softer. When do you hear, 'Strings quieter please, listen to the oboe, if you can't hear him well you're playing too loud'? Too many conductors are keyboard players who have never played in the orchestra. You know, it's not the same. No matter how fine a pianist a conductor may be, his mental approach to music has been determined differently from orchestral players.

Alfio Micci

ALFIO MICCI It's hard for a conductor to balance an orchestra because, from where he stands, he can't really judge. To balance properly he'd have to go out into the auditorium and conduct from there. And strangely enough that's what Stokowski did, in Philadelphia. His assistant conducted most of the rehearsal while he sat in the hall, way back, listening and taking notes. Then when he conducted the final rehearsal he had a good idea of what was being heard and what lost. Our orchestras have grown very powerful. Poor soloists have to have a big, ferocious sound to get through. In fact, a string soloist must have a *gigantic* sound to compete with the Philharmonic, or Philadelphia, or Boston. Now, they are beginning to reduce the size of the orchestra in accompaniment, even for the big romantic concertos. We did a Brahms with Stern not long ago, Steinberg was conducting, and he reduced the size, and it was really sensitive, much better, because the soloist wasn't forcing all the time. It's hard to get a big orchestra to play softly, it really is, and if you play too softly you get inhibited. Stokowski again, when he wanted something very soft he told just the last three stands to play, and it was wonderful. Just the sort of thing he'd do because he knew sound marvellously. He was a great one to tinker with things, the music, the orchestra, seating plans, but he was so often right. Well, as I say, orchestras have gotten louder and I guess audiences in the States are used to the big, exciting, thunderous sound. And conductors like to get ovations, which they do after a noisy piece. But there's a proper style to playing different music, and you shouldn't play everything with big sound and big wide vibrato. The main thing is to listen, and I guess some are better at that than others.

PETER HADCOCK Ozawa is good at putting things together, great big pieces, the Strauss and Mahler showpieces that take a lot of cues. He does it well. He knows his scores, conducts from memory, and generally gets people to play well together. But he's not infallible. With him, if you're not sure where you are, just don't play, and he probably won't know, even quite important things. His weakness, and it showed following Steinberg, is his pacing. He seems to want a climax in every measure, and crescendos build up immediately. Steinberg kept the orchestra on a rein — 'Not so fast, not so loud' — until the true climax of the whole piece, and then he really let go. It would build up. Then Seiji comes and wants everything fast and loud. Unfortunately, as a player, you don't really know if you're playing at the right level. When we can hear, and the performance is going well, it's strange, everybody does listen and gets out of the way when he's supposed to. But we do tend, the more tired or more angry we get, to play louder.

177

Leon Goossens discusses
a score with conductor,
Colin Davis

Orchestras do sound much the same today. Characteristic voices –
Koussevitsky's Boston, Toscanini's NBC, or say Beecham's Royal Philharmonic – have disappeared, and in the good orchestras a general high
technical competence and similarity in sound is everywhere. No conductor that I've ever played for said anything to influence much the tone
quality of the orchestra. I've almost never had a conductor say anything
to me, that he wants a different kind of sound. A better sound, yes! That's
about as specific as they get. By and large never, 'I'd like a more French
sound, or a different kind of vibrato,' whereas in the old days I think they
might. Those old autocrats felt they must teach everybody everything,
including how to sound! But surely Russian music should have a different kind of tone from French, or Mozart be played in another manner
than Mahler. But I don't think we do. I don't notice many woodwind
players getting different tones in German and French music. I thought
the last conductor over here who probably got that was Szell. He told
everybody how to play every note, no matter how good one was, and he
was hated for it. But that orchestra sounded good, like the same guy
playing a hundred instruments, I thought.

178

ROGER SCOTT Long ago we played exquisite Mozart with Kertesz, van Beinum, Sargent. I hadn't played those works like that. If we played them in Philadelphia, we did it in a rather heavy-handed way. These were exquisite miniatures, full-blooded within a small frame, with cut-down sections. Now when Beecham did Mozart 35, he said, 'I want everybody playing, I like a bloody row,' and that's what he got. That's one approach. The other is to play the *Haffner* with two basses and four cellos and sweat blood, because it's excruciatingly difficult. We played the Bach *D major Suite* in Japan, and Ormandy was looking over, asking for more, and I muttered under my breath 'If you want more, let's have two more basses.' Luckily, he didn't hear me. He'd cut down the forces to get closer to the original, but he wasn't getting the Philadelphia sound that he was used to.

RON BARRON Refinement is a quality that has yet to sink in here, although the individual musicians would certainly be capable of it. Perhaps the art has been lost. One violinist, who has been in the orchestra almost sixty years, says there have never been such wonderful players, individually, top to bottom. He can't believe the virtuosity of the young. But in his opinion the orchestra isn't as good, because the ensemble and the sensitivity aren't what they once were. Of course, this is partly a business problem. With Koussevitsky, they really rehearsed. He was respected, he knew his players and they were pretty scared of him, and he really came down on anything wrong musically. Today, we just have too many concerts and not enough *good* rehearsals – they don't seem to define the problems, get at the impediments to good performance. It's not that we can't do it today, but nobody insists on it being just right.

ROLF SMEDVIG So few conductors have a concept of sound. Very few. One criticism I've heard of many American orchestras is that the style doesn't change, composer to composer, century to century – Bach played the same as late romantic music. Americans have always played Bach with large, full orchestras. Stokowski did it, then everybody was doing it. We very rarely cut down our forces to chamber orchestra size for anything. That's because the paying customers like the big sound. Imagine if we played Beethoven with the forces available to the composer. That would be something funny to our ears, because it's become ingrained that Beethoven is supposed to be played with big, full sound. And Bach too, for that matter.

HUGH MAGUIRE Perhaps one does miss the grandeur and spaciousness of some of the older orchestras. But this insistence on brilliance and power doesn't come so much from the musicians, it comes from the men backstage turning the knobs. Recorded sound, I think, affects the general trend of music-making. Musicians are being channelled into one area, as it were. There's one orthodoxy on how to play music, and that is fast, loud, brash and brilliant. Is it just a product of our times? In the old days I don't think anybody would consider that the performances of Toscanini,

Furtwangler, Bruno Walter and Beecham ever sounded the same. I certainly would not get confused among their recordings.

Schnabel once said that the making of records was the destruction of music, not its preservation. I think that is very wise and apt today. The jet-set, the opportunities to copy and conform, direct music in a certain way. And now all the London orchestras sound much the same to me. They didn't when Klemperer was about. I recall going to hear him conduct the *Eroica*, a symphony I'd played with many great conductors, and I was absolutely riveted, thrilled by what he did. But you know, orchestras and public might have quite different views on what makes a great conductor. I watched Karajan on TV and was so struck by the opening of Beethoven 9 — not so much what he was doing with the music, but his integrity, his overwhelming desire to get it across. That's great conducting, though not necessarily great musicianship. Yet among present day conductors, I would say Karajan is most unpopular. He is too strong, too powerful, too rich — too much outside the general run. I haven't worked with him, alas, for twenty-five years.

ALAN CIVIL I went to the BBC Symphony in 1966, more or less at the beginning of Boulez' time. We did about eighty percent modern and twenty percent classical. The awful tragedy, for the orchestra, was that eventually we were not able to play the standard classics. We could sight-read the most fearsome contemporary piece, but a Brahmns symphony — embarrassing! You lose the line if you don't continually play the classics, specially string players. Well, in so much modern music you don't play the instrument in the normal way, and I've found that tends to debase your basic sound. Certainly with the horn, after a lot of hand-stopping, flutter-tonguing, and all these comic effects, you just can't play something classical afterwards, the lip doesn't take it.

My experience is that most conductors don't ask for a particular kind of sound. Barbirolli would tell the strings exactly what he wanted, but when it comes to wind few seem to have any preference. A Russian conductor, used to the fellified sound of Russian horns, doesn't ask players here to use that vibrato. And I'm sure he wouldn't tell his own players to stop using it for certain pieces. It's as if they have blinkers on. Just look at the score, make sure the notes are together and in tune, and that's it. Now someone like Beecham was always after a distinctive blend, getting the relative sounds right — that's the secret of playing Delius. If one instrument offended, say a low second oboe note, Beecham would sort it out with the player until he got exactly the quality he wanted. Very clever. But now, generally speaking, it's so very difficult to tell any differences in orchestral sound.

RAY PREMRU I have a pet complaint — the level of volume demanded of us now. I can play loud, perhaps as loud as anybody, but I don't like to do it. There's a point on a brass instrument where, if you blow past it, the overtones and quality of sound actually go. I regret that our ears — musicians and public alike — have got accustomed, through hi fi and

180

Sir Adrian Boult

recordings, to hearing things in an unnatural way. In a recording, conductors listen to the play-back done very loud. Then in the concert they want to hear the music that way too, demanding from us, specially the brass, such a volume that the quality goes right off. Even a fortissimo should still be contained, have definition and quality. 'Play out,' they say, 'a bit more, a bit more.' One of the old school, like Boult, is so refreshing because he will reduce the dynamic level — 'No, no, pianissimo, strings, let the soloist through, less from everyone else.' That is the old idea of balance.

JOHN FLETCHER I wouldn't be surprised if narrower bores and smaller mouthpieces didn't come back. These things have always gone in cycles. Certainly the large-bore brass instruments are terribly loud. But to go back is difficult. The large instruments are versatile. You can get a very good blend in pianissimo, and also play loudly without that funny nanny-goat bleat that you have on badly played narrow-bore instruments. Of course, people only remember the bad side of the old instruments. What they had, well played, was a kind of vibrancy that translates to a charmless shout on the modern large instruments. This applies to horns, trumpets and trombones. On the tuba it's a gormless bellow which has nothing to do with music whatsoever. And I think orchestras have risen surreptitiously above a worthwhile, balanced level of noise. Fortissimos are too shouty and too common, not reserved for the great climax. The grading from mezzo-forte through forte is abolished, everything is fortissimo. And large-bore instruments can also be terribly lifeless. Similarly with strings, a player who makes a huge sound all the time has difficulty making personable music. I would welcome a movement back towards a more human scale in orchestral playing.

RON BARRON Symphony Hall in Boston is a wonderful hall, but it's bass-heavy, and we have a very strong bass section. They really get into the music and that gives us a problem. I had to have my ears examined a while ago, because I was sitting in front of the trumpets. As string players know very well, sitting in front of modern brass instruments is just not fair to the ear. That's why there's all this business with ear-plugs. It's a shame, it really is. I know the strings want the brass to be happy, to play out, but they don't want to die for it — or go deaf. It may be that orchestras are just getting too loud, I don't know. But again, it's conductors. Any young brass player wants to get a great, exciting sound. And Ozawa likes it. He's an energetic conductor, and he loves the excitement that brass can produce. He hires the driving players, not so refined and controlled. And I guess I have to kinda go along with that, most of the time. I like a person who really gets into it, wherever one sits in the orchestra. I guess that's traditionally part of the American way.

LYNN HARRELL I think there is some reaction against the power and loudness of the big symphony orchestra. Huge volume from large and highly developed instruments has lost its titillation. Loudness isn't exciting in itself any more. There's nothing worse than a very loud orchestra playing with no intensity. I mean, brass sections can now play *so loud* with no feeling of strength, of real power. There's a lack of physicality in the playing. The difference in loudness between piano and forte is not as crucial as the level of intensity. These Italian markings — piano, mezzo-forte, etc — have to do with the intrinsic physical excitement quotient of the tone, piano being relaxed and at ease, and fortissimo being with a lot of muscle, with clenched fists. With the older instruments — gut strings, narrow bores, smaller mouthpieces, etc. — it's easier to avoid the temptations of power, and to become more aware of the different physical intensities of the sound. And I think it's a very good sign that players are reconsidering these things. A trend towards less noise, a more intimate sound, is leading to a renewed sense of intensity rather than mere decibel output, and this is one thing that may lead orchestras back to more individuality.

The Man on the Box

> *The* musical *training of conductors — who before all else must be experts in aeroplane schedules, international tax laws, hair styling — is briefer with each season's increasingly rapid turnover in the* stupor mundi *market . . . The incidence of ego disease is naturally high to begin with, but under the sun of a pandering public it grows like a tropical weed.*
>
> IGOR STRAVINSKY, *Themes and Conclusions* (1966)

JOHN DE LANCIE Tyrannical conductors were pretty much the story forty years ago. Reiner was that way — Oh god, a holy terror. Stokowski also, in a different way, but the stories with that man over the years are

John de Lancie

pretty bloodcurdling. In those days the union was rather weak. Those old conductors would throw a man out without blinking. Players stood for tantrums and tyranny because there was a great insecurity. You can imagine, during the Depression, with millions out of work and many actually starving, if a man had a job playing twenty-eight weeks a year in a symphony orchestra, he hung on to it whatever happened. Tantrums and nonsense apart, I firmly believe that an orchestra works best under a benevolent dictatorship. You can't have a hundred chiefs. It's just that a conductor must understand the limits of propriety and decency, and in those days many didn't, being both foulmouthed and sadistic.

But this modern buddy-buddy approach, happy-go-lucky and not making any demands is not good either. This fashionable conducting, jetting around the world, couple of days here and there, what can they give or demand in that time? This is one reason, to my mind, why orchestras are losing personality, the whole thing becoming an homogenized product. You can't blame these men for wanting to take advantage of the extraordinary life offered to them. Fêted, pampered, praised, *and* very highly-paid — who can resist that? But it's not good for the orchestra, or for music necessarily.

GARY KETTEL The world of the ace conductor and the world of the pop star are not so far apart. If you shout at people enough, they'll believe it and pay their £15 a ticket, which allows some conductors to charge their outrageous fees. Look at Klemperer and Karajan at Salzburg, the people line the street and traffic is snarled up as far as Vienna. They might be good conductors but people have been brainwashed into this adulation. Some huge publicity machine supports these men.

ALAN CIVIL I definitely believe conducting standards are lower today than twenty-five years ago. To me, the big names of today aren't great conductors. They are more the product of publicity hand-outs. I was reading the other day about Sir Georg Solti's £4,000 a concert — I mean it's a bit of a nonsense, isn't it? To reach that figure when you think of the problems of the orchestral player.

It's the glamorization of conducting that does the damage I suppose, from records and specially from TV. You notice how TV always over-emphasizes the visual at the expense of the musical. A musician is not shown playing but shaking saliva from the instrument, or the camera is leering up the cellist's legs. And the conductor is the chief actor in these little visual dramas, preening himself, perhaps unconsciously, for the cameras. Terrible. The whole object of a conductor, in general, is to keep together a scattered body of ninety or so musicians. They need a focal point. Music — interpretation — comes from the actual playing of the notes, which is the work of the players, and occasionally a few men, very few, can so mould and impress the players that they perform their notes in a significantly different way. Those men are the great conductors. From the rest we want competent, clear direction. Give us a decent musical intelligence and a good beat and we'll get the job done. I'm all for giving conductors a chance, but very few of them seem to know the job. Now, they learn their works on orchestras, blatantly. There must be a first time for everyone, but that first time should be in a modest beginning, in an apprenticeship. It's a bit of cheek to present oneself to a good professional orchestra as a 'maestro'. I remember even Kertesz — a very nice man and developing into a fine conductor when he died — even Kertesz doing Bruckner 4 with the London Symphony, a work he'd done once before with a semi-professional band. He told the LSO that English orchestras didn't understand Bruckner, and didn't know how to play it. 'I know it's very boring for string players with this tremolo,' he said, 'but when you get to know, you'll understand it. Bear with me, gentlemen, and I'll teach you.' Second time he'd done it!

RICHARD ADENEY The old conductors were brilliant at producing tensions in the orchestra, frightening people. A man like Koussevitsky, he was a nasty bit of work, but a fine musician and a brilliant psychologist, knowing how to dominate and intimidate. He knew also, quite correctly, that if the orchestra really loathed him, yet was frightened of him, he would often get very good performances. I remember playing like an absolute angel for people I hated, through sheer tension and dislike. Very strange. But you had to be convinced of their musicality. Conductors don't have the power now to sack or intimidate. With our self-governing orchestras, if a man is really unpleasant, and unmusical into the bargain, we kick him out straightaway.

RODNEY FRIEND Well, conductors do come up too fast nowadays. But think of the amount of orchestral concerts going on, which have to have someone on the rostrum. Perhaps ten great conductors have died in the last twenty years, each doing approximately 100 concerts a year. That's 1,000 concerts a year waiting to be filled. Who's doing them? Conducting can be the easiest thing in music, or the most difficult. Easy because nobody hears the baton, and most difficult because a man can be destroyed in one go, if the orchestra so wishes. There is no easy territory in music.

HUGH MAGUIRE Older conductors remained individual because they remained apart. Each had his own orchestra, his own domain, and they weren't — they couldn't be — hopping around the world. They kept their work apart and felt no need to ape the others. Nowadays the younger men are more curious about each other, they are forever meeting and comparing. Go to the Festival Hall tonight, perhaps if Abbado is conducting, Barenboim, Previn, Dorati — whoever is in town — might be in the audience. Music-making has to some extent become one faction, fused along one prevalent line. Conductors are wanting the same sort of sound and playing because they are all great buddies, influencing each other. And there are no swines any more. When I first was leading, things weren't quite so agreeable. And the things older leaders have told me!

TOM STORER It's an anachronism, really, the great conductor in an egalitarian age. The education system breeds them no longer. Selfish autocrats get their faces pushed in in today's schools. But the fellow on the box must be an autocrat. He must have authority, and one hopes that authority comes from musicality and the respect of the players. Conductors nowadays are more circumspect, more timorous even, in how they treat the orchestra. They know that if an orchestra switches off a man, then the whole thing becomes a chore, and performances are going to suffer. For a little time a fresh and lively man can revive the tired appetites of the average orchestral player. But every conductor has limitations, chinks in the armour, and once a highly-bred orchestra starts to get restless it's time to stop. Have him back next year and the orchestra may love him again. The business of conducting seems to be in a state of transition. The old tyrants have been driven out by a changed society. The new men, pleasant enough, undemanding, are perhaps too much a reflection of ourselves. And luckily, we don't get the real incompetent duffers any more, the people who would buy a session or a concert. When I think of some I worked with in years gone by, who couldn't read a score, couldn't beat time, and certainly couldn't accompany! One old chump, we used to say, 'We'll jack him up so he can't get a grip with his feet and carry him along to the end.' We just put our heads down and played, leaving him frantically paddling about two bars behind. I was just thinking about him when Celibidache was taking some eccentrically slow tempi in Brahms, yet nobody thought of pushing *him* along. You don't bully conductors like him.

JOHN RONAYNE Orchestras, as well as conductors, change. In the time of Wagner, Nikisch, Richter, the conductor was an absolute dictator, and orchestras weren't very good at all. The orchestra has gradually improved to the stage now where the band can actually dictate to the conductor. Of the conductors today, I don't think any of them really interpret music. Perhaps orchestras are too competent, too experienced and too independent to allow them to do so. The orchestra just takes over. There needs to be something monomaniacal about a conductor, to do that job. But it's also one of the very few jobs you can get away with doing absolutely nothing. They say the baton is silent. To carry off such a job well needs an almost impossible combination of qualities. And the main thing is personality. A man can be a great musician and a great technician, but if he hasn't the gift of getting it over, if he can't *arrest* people, he'll be no good. Unfortunately, it is only too possible to make a very lucrative career on power to arrest only, without musicality or technique at all. The persuasive influence of advertising and promotion does the rest, and we have men with a hell of a lot of charm, flair and egotism, but very little of musical value to put over.

185

Concert, Recording and Other Music

*Tonight the musicians have come in dress suits and white ties. Their
faces show a most uncommon kind of excitement. Their hearts are
full of respect and admiration. They are playing admirably. No one
says a word.*

HECTOR BERLIOZ, *Evenings with the Orchestra*

RON BARRON

I HAD a fellow come up to me yesterday, in the Tanglewood grounds,
mailman from New Jersey. He was just thrilled to hear the orchestra and
to talk to me, because he'd seen me and the orchestra on TV. He said,
'People can't understand why I come up here. They say why don't I just
buy the record? You can't tell them, can you? Hearing it live is a different
thing.'

GARY KETTEL It's all part of performance if the horn starts to creep a
bit flat, but the player notices it and gets it right again. And a perfect live
performance is the most electrifying thing ever. It's an extraordinary feat,
almost unnatural, to hit it off straight. That's unnatural in a super-
human sense. A recording is unnatural in a mechanical sense.

HUGH MAGUIRE Is not music communication? I wouldn't say the
bigger the audience the better, but music has to be seen as well as heard.
The presence of an audience is an integral part of a performance. When
I went to the BBC Symphony I was very much struck by the difficulty of
making music in a vacuum, playing to a microphone for an unknown
audience. That's a great problem. Playing for radio is also different from
recording. There you are trying for a kind of perfection, but in radio you
are still concerned with immediate performance, and that without the
comeback of a live audience. That return is desperately important. On
radio you may suffer the same nerves and tensions as in the concert hall,
but you don't get the excitement that an audience generates.

BILL LANG I love a concert performance, many times you can get
touches of magic there. But recording can knock any beauty out of
music-making. Players become afraid to take a risk, they start playing in
straight-jackets. For instance, say on the trumpet you have an octave
slur in Brahms, doing an octave A, you keep two valves down, but there

opposite top
The BBC Midland Radio
Orchestra in session in the
Pebble Mill Studios

opposite below
Engineers and musicians
listen closely to the results
of a recording while
following the score

187

are harmonics in between which you have to avoid. Well, on record the player might play safe — pretend to slur, but really kind of soft-tongue. That doesn't sound so good. And it's the same with other instruments, they don't go for it, they get careful. Note-getting not music-making. This is where recording can destroy music. I'd rather hear a recording of an actual concert, warts and all.

ANTHONY CAMDEN In London, an orchestra is far more dependent on record companies than it should be. I mean, we probably do too many recordings in too short a time. We prepare as well as we can, as well as money allows. A company wants a certain piece of music and the union says it can only record twenty minutes in one session. Now the question that exercises the company is, what orchestra do we get to record this difficult bit of music in, say, two sessions? And they come to a London orchestra because we sight-read better. We'll get it done, but it's an incredible hassle. The work is on tape in two sessions, for the cheapest price, but we're not happy with it musically. We'd much prefer to make a record of something we've done in concert well and truly, with a conductor we know and trust. I don't listen to records myself, because I can't stand it, having taken part in the playing.

TONY PAY Recording engineers like now to have a control that I for one think they are neither adult enough nor skilful enough to use. Nor indeed should they have this sort of control anyway. But it has obvious advantages if you are trying to produce acceptable results from shoddy products, often with nothing but a marketable name to commend them. On multi-track machines the engineer can lop off the start of a ragged chord and take the first clear attack, or if a player is out of tune they can just fade down his knob. But to do this they must separate the players with their mikes, so they don't interfere, and then the individual players can't hear each other, possibly can't even see each other. Players are so isolated they've no idea what's going on. To put players in little boxes negates any true idea of music making, both relative intonation and ensemble become impossible.

Musicians have a responsibility to try to make recording as close to concert performance as possible. What we produce on record is often so much worse than what we do in the hall. Excitement and poetry go from records simply because we are so concerned to avoid mistakes. At a concert you think, 'Goodness, things are going well.' In the studio it's, 'Christ, things are OK so far, let's hope we get through this take all right.' If a demanding solo has to be done seven or eight times in succession, by the last time all flair and spontaneity are gone and you're physically and emotionally exhausted. A record becomes some sort of testament or document. Perhaps one should let the tiny errors go — 'If it shows me making mistakes, that's an accurate reflection of me, because I'm human and I do make mistakes.' There's the old story of a pianist listening to the final, edited tape of something he'd done, and saying, 'Isn't that wonderful?' And the editor replies, 'Yes, don't you wish you could play like that?'

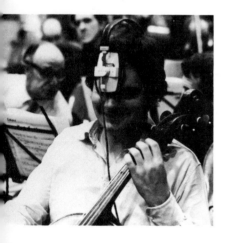

Recording sessions can
seem much more
complicated than taking
part in a concert

The impression an orchestra often gets from a record producer is 'produce the goods or else'. We're there on sufferance – watch out. I remember trying to solve a problem with a conductor and a producer, and the producer made it quite clear he didn't give a damn for my dilemma. If I'd been any good there wouldn't be any problem. And this unease is made worse by the knowledge that the record companies have the orchestras over a barrel. If you don't produce this time, they'll use another band next time. We are desperately trying to please, just in order to make an income, people who may have very minimal qualifications for making music live. But we all know there are wonderful records, and the only way we can judge past performance, or at least get an idea of it, is to listen on record. The making of records *is* important, more important than present practice seems to allow.

PETER HADCOCK I'd say that recording, more than anything, is either nerve-wracking or boring. It's not really a musical thing. A few conductors, like Colin Davis, want to give a performance, if possible, even in a recording. He likes to get us excited, and he lets things go wrong, unless it's a disaster, and then he stops. He hates stopping. But by and large we know first time through they are not going to keep much. Then we start jumping back and forth, bit here, a bit there. Down to the final second they're still worrying about a couple of passages.

We feel that a lot of things that we record are the wrong things. I don't think we have any weak players now, but for a while we had several bad first chair players, and it seemed like they were always picking pieces that featured them. You wonder why. It seems to me that the orchestra, when making records, just looks at it as a way for the management to make money, not as a way to enhance the reputation of the orchestra, or anything like that. I mean, the players try to do a good job, no one wants listeners to hear bad playing. But for instance, there's little interest in the play-backs. People with important solos reckon they'll be told if a take isn't good enough. The mood is one of plodding resignation, no fire, no electricity. Yet when Rubinstein came to do some concertos with Leinsdorf conducting, what a difference. Oh, crackling with life. He brought his own A & R man, his son-in-law, and there was no feeling of rush. All the time in the world. He didn't like the piano, so they fetched another and did it all over again. It really was a musical event, not just a manufacture, grinding out a bunch of right notes. Rubinstein has the power to say what he wants, and he does things in his own way. And I feel Davis does, to some extent. And I hope Seiji Ozawa is going to, but right now he's kind of stuck between financial pressures from the management and the recording companies. He's had some troubles with the A & R man, and I remember an occasion when the overture to *Semiramide* took something like three hours to get on tape. It was ridiculous, everybody playing worse and worse, going wrong out of sheer fatigue. Of course record companies like orchestras and conductors to get an adequate performance on tape in the quickest possible time. A Rubinstein, who says 'Scrap everything, start again,' is not popular.

(opposite)
The oboe player

191

Rodney Friend talks with piano soloist Artur Rubinstein

Mstislav Rostropovich

JOHN FLETCHER As far as I'm concerned concerts are the only things that matter. What are you doing? You're taking out a great musical work and having a go at making it live, now, in all its glory. Sometimes that succeeds, and then it's all worthwhile. Sometimes it doesn't work and then you say, 'Well, try again.' I'm very interested in records – I have an immense collection – but not so much from the musical point of view. They are a useful and necessary appendage to the act of concert giving. Making a record is a terribly phoney system. You may play appallingly, nothing going right, the conductor ghastly, yet the record may sound very good. It can also happen the other way. I can think of sessions that went superbly well, but the record has been very dull. The ingredients of music-making get chucked into a bran-tub and some wizard electronic chef produces a confection called a record. As with the printed word, too much importance is attached to records. If only people would regard them as disposable commodities, but they insist on treating them like judicial sentences. A whole industry of critics and broadcasters rests on records, making holy shrines out of something that just happened on a Monday morning. But of course, for people who live in remote parts of Cornwall or the Orkneys, where concerts hardly ever happen, the radio and records are lifelines to music. But what they get is the child of technology – a keg beer rather than a real draught, or something like the flashy lager dispensers in a fashionable bar.

Relief

Our players have reached the state of utmost technical perfection . . .
But if you are acquainted with performers and know their thoughts
and feelings, you will soon discover that the players, in spite of their
technical perfection, in spite of their successes, give the impression of
people walking on uncertain ground. It seems to be the curse of
public success and of technical perfection, that they leave one's soul
unsatisfied.

PAUL HINDEMITH, *A Composer's World* (1952)

Csaba Erdelyi

CSABA ERDELYI Actual playing in the orchestra doesn't make your playing deteriorate. But what does is the amount of time you have to spend in the orchestra without looking after your playing, without cleaning it up, without that private relationship with the instrument. It is always 'Be quick', serve the best survival of my section and myself in the orchestra. This stress accumulates day to day, and you have no time to find a personal balance with the instrument again. That is a dangerous trap for orchestral players here in England. It is like meeting your wife constantly but never talking. I do have the ambition to perform as a soloist, which for me is the most important, the most wholly satisfying thing.

MICHAEL NUTT The time I enjoy most is when the orchestra goes on a short local tour — maybe Arizona, New Mexico. After the concert I get out to the city limits, walk into a honky-tonk and ask to sit in with the band. 'Sure,' they say, because country fiddlers are few and far between. 'What d'ye do?' they ask. 'Oh, I'm a violinist with the LA Philharmonic.' Their chins drop — 'What have we got into, a goddamn classical vi-olin.' I tune up quietly and say, 'Let's start with *Orange Blossom Special*, or *Black Mountain Rag*.' I play a few bars and we're away like mad. The whole place lightens up, always — this classical fellow can play a bit. No respectable classical player is supposed to perform in a honky-tonk. In England, equally disreputably, I go to a pub and sit in with an Irish band. I love all that music. We've even got a good Irish band in LA — in O'Shaughnessy's, a great place.

BILL LANG There's not much interchange between orchestral players and the jazz and rock fellows. My kind of jazz would be dated now. I do play trumpet with some of the modern English jazz lads and feel a bit of a fool. I'm in there with an E flat trumpet playing what I thought was high. Derek Watkins could have gone probably a fifth higher, no bother, but they wanted a certain style. Derek said he couldn't get the right sound. He'd play a kind of scream, you see. They really go for it, nevertheless very safe and in tune. Very good, those lads.

RICHARD ADENEY Film sessions vary incredibly, sometimes very boring, other times exciting and amusing — nice music, lots to play, a good conductor who gets on with it. Music is usually put on the film last of all, done exactly to fit the action. The composer knows, using a stop-watch or frames per second, exactly how much music is needed, and places it to the instant. He writes music of so many beats per minute, so if it's played at the right speed it just fits. Sometimes we play listening to a metronome beat in head-phones — they call it a ticker-track. That's horrible, most disconcerting. But usually the conductor looks over the heads of the band to a large screen on which the film is running. He follows that and we follow him. And of course we sneak a look round in our rests for a rather fragmented view of the film — we see the robberies and the chases, but not the love scenes.

193

A recording session

PAUL FRIED I've given conducting some thought, except I'm left-handed, and as a flute player I realize I'd have to get to know more about strings. Years ago I started a little on the cello and it was really fun. One must broaden one's scope. Nowadays a soloist can often conduct and play as well. It's simple for a flautist, in a certain kind of music anyway, because the flute is a kind of natural baton. And in a small chamber group the flute is often the lead instrument, so you get used to taking the initiative. I think the flute is popular because you can play in the orchestra and also have a solo career, if you are good enough. And that's unusual.

ROLF SMEDVIG You can combine orchestral playing with brass quintet playing – absolutely so. Most players that are really serious will agree that you're going to get out of shape if you don't play demanding things. That can happen real quick. As assistant principal I don't get to play the orchestral solos too often, and if you don't have anything much to play, why practise hours a day? To have a solo, or a recital, or a quintet date coming up keeps you going. You get in good shape and your orchestral playing improves.

194

RAY PREMRU I used to play jazz, but I'd been away from it for some time. Then, about seven years ago, I got together a rehearsal band with an Irish composer and trombonist Bobby Lamb, who'd been with Woody Herman in the States. A lot of the session men were terribly keen, the fellows who do the boring commercials, so we got a large band, about 25-piece, with five French horns drawn from the orchestras, though the rest were jazzmen or studio players. At first we had to rehearse late, between 11 p.m. and 1, which was the only time we could all meet. We got some very good scores from within the band, from Steve Gray and Kenny Wheeler. Well, we thought this is fun, let's share it with somebody. So we put on some concerts, and I remember the reaction of the session boys – how wonderful to play for a live audience again!

LEONARD HINDELL I think every orchestral musician potentially is an artist, specially those playing in fine orchestras. But if we do not encourage that aspect in ourselves, then we will remain just functioning musicians. And I have this conflict, wanting to be not just Leonard Hindell of the Philharmonic, but a musician who can get up and play in his own right, and have the capacity to move people. That is lacking when you play in an orchestra, at least when you play second bassoon. You want personal recognition that you are a fine musician. You also want recognition that you are *contributing*, even if you are only 98th violin. You want to be known by name, that you *are* a violinist. In orchestras this recognition is often lacking.

ROBIN MCGEE I found playing in the LSO and in the London Sinfonietta complementary. I came to Brahms with the big orchestra refreshed, and then turned to, say, Berio with the small contemporary band as a challenge. But in a sense the LSO got in the way of everything else too much. In the symphony you were either dropping with fatigue or wondering where the next date was coming from. There should be a more pleasant balance. But playing music is a bit unbalanced anyway. You're either bored to death or frightened to death. In the big symphony there is always that difficulty with communication. How is the composer or conductor to manage that direct contact that every player craves? In a small group the conductor can relate to everyone easily enough. That's what we are dying for, we orchestral players. We want to be related to, to be seen as performers, as individuals, not just as a supernumerary bassoon, or whatever, so far away that the conductor can hardly see you through a telescope.

JOHN FLETCHER I end up a bit schizophrenic, in the orchestra one day and the brass ensemble the next. That is not always easy to do. Even in the orchestra some horrible technical passage will rear its ugly head, and because you haven't played hard stuff for a couple of weeks you get caught out. I find the switch both puzzling and refreshing. In the chamber ensemble one is constantly stopping down, pruning the sound to a very concentrated core, and breathing in a completely different way. Back in

195

the orchestra, I find it hard to produce the sheer volume of sound, breathing has got very restricted, and that's worrying. I suppose a run round the block and some fortissimo notes before setting off in the morning would help. Then again, coming from the orchestra, where I've been socking out minims, suddenly to go to chamber music, I can sound very rough, a bit uncouth until I get back to a more finely-judged playing. The two worlds are absolute opposites, and I have never heard a tuba player really successfully bridge them. If you're a born chamber player, you can't make enough noise for an orchestra, enough weight of tone. And an orchestral player stepping into a chamber group sounds rather crude and overbearing.

I very badly want, if possible, to keep both kinds of music going for ever. You see, the sound of just brass would drive you mad after a while. The Philip Jones Ensemble, the big group, did a four-week tour of the East, producing a variety of noises, but all of us were getting more and more dissatisfied. I got back to England and went straight to an LSO rehearsal — Christmas carols with Julie Andrews — and I sat back glowing with pleasure at the sound of strings. A wonderful sound, a string section, if you are a brass player and have been deprived of it for a while.

TONY PAY The variety and freedom we have in England is very satisfying. The symphony orchestra is not exclusive. I can't think of any outstanding English orchestral player who doesn't work outside the orchestra. I asked a Czech clarinet player if he still played in the Czech Nonette. 'No,' he said, 'I can't play in the Nonette and the Philharmonic at the same time.' Well, I thought, that's a bit of a sadness, because one side of a musical life informs the other. Playing in contemporary groups has clarified for me certain ways I had of looking at the traditional repertoire. Some would say that before our era the phrase, not the note, was the basic building block, though naturally phrases were made up of notes. Our concept of something being completely specified by its position, dynamic and duration — as in twentieth-century music — was alien to earlier musicians. On the other hand, to reduce the problem of clarinet playing to an ability to play any note at any dynamic at any time, over the instrument, simplifies technical requirement, and if you can do that you're a pretty good clarinet player! You may not be a good musician, but at least you have the grounding. If you can bring to earlier music the technical discipline of the twentieth-century, then at least you have a greater possibility of doing what you want musically. But there's a danger too. I remember going back to Kempe and the RPO after a Sinfonietta tour with Stockhausen. Kempe said, 'You've been playing too much Stockhausen, I can tell. For the first few days there is a difference, then you are yourself again.' Neither our playing nor our ears can escape twentieth-century influence. After *The Rite of Spring*, certain works in the older repertoire were never the same again.

Dissent

Each orchestral member is a poor disappointed devil. Collectively they are like a suppressed crowd of rebels, and, as an official body, they are bumptious and vain. Routine gives their playing the varnish of perfection and assurance. For the rest, they loathe their work, their job and, most of all, music.

FERRUCCIO BUSONI, *Briefe an seine Frau* (1937)

ELEANOR GOULD

Eleanor Gould

EVERYTHING was easy for me in school, even though I had started at three I was bored to tears. I was always the biggest in the class, despite being the youngest. I just didn't quite fit in. My parents split up, (my father disappeared soon after I was born) and I was very much on my own, into books and music. As I got older I decided that music was what I wanted to do. So I took some violin lessons, first in class, which was bad because they don't teach you appropriate hand positions. Then I decided I wanted to try violin seriously, so I auditioned at Manhattan School of Music. The director laughed, 'Go take private lessons for six months, then we'll see.' A big chuckle because he thought I'd never play properly, with the violin properly in the palm of my hand and the bow clenched, sawing away at a Bach concerto, but damn well in tune. Anyhow, I took private lessons, and spent two months on nothing but a C major scale in two octaves, in front of the mirror, to get my hand positions corrected. I was a teenager and nobody thought I'd stick with it. But I decided I wanted it, I guess it was the first real challenge I'd had. Then my teacher suggested that I try the viola, since I have long arms, and as soon as I picked up the viola it felt like me, because it sounded like my voice, and I was still pretty gungho about the voice – I'm a mezzo or contralto, whatever you like to call it. The viola was as close as I could get to singing with an instrument. It felt part of me, and I stuck with it.

I ended up going to Mannes, working in the garment industry part time. I studied with William Kroll, and was just overwhelmed by his marvellous musicianship and his ability to communicate. But he's difficult, very negative. If he said 'Very nice' and patted you on the back, you knew you'd done badly and he wasn't going to waste his breath, but if he picked on you for every little thing, you were doing pretty well and were worth bothering with. I'd come home in tears when he said 'Very nice', and my mother could never understand it. Mannes had strong academic courses, gave a well-rounded education. I don't believe in just learning the instrument. I want to know what the world, and music, are all about.

197

Most music schools lack proper instruction in the history of music, in knowledge of styles and ornamentation, in types of playing. I took a degree course, first at Mannes, then at the University of Illinois. At Mannes I'd been a nobody. There were top-notch performers there, and I was just a beginner, also very shy and introverted. Mr Kroll used to call me the scared rabbit. But before I went to Illinois, I'd been gaining background as an orchestral player.

The coach at the National Orchestral Association in New York said it was a good idea to take auditions, even though we weren't quite ready for a job, just get the experience. So I went for an audition, just like that. Mr Kroll, when he heard, said, 'You're going to play in an orchestra? I'm not going to waste time with you,' and he disowned me. I figured if he wasn't going to teach me, I'd better go. I was offered the job in Halifax, and I took it. There were two openings, principal and assistant principal viola. Of course, they were hoping to find someone else as principal as I had no experience, and I agreed to play principal until a better qualified person turned up. They would make up my salary. Well, there was nobody else, and I was principal! I spent hours studying scores, going over every note, because I was very, very scared. I was still a teenager, though I looked older. I did OK on that job, but they never gave me the principal's pay, so after four or five months trying to get the money, and after discussing it with the union, I left for another job in Atlanta. Immediately, Halifax offered the money, but I just said 'Good-bye' in mid-January. I finished the year in Atlanta, at the back of the section, taking it easy.

With that experience I was a little more confident about my playing, and went to Illinois as a big chief – a professional. The dean and the viola teacher, John Garvey, came to the bus station and personally took me through registration. Although Kroll is known primarily for chamber music, he is a very strong technician, with fantastic left-hand technique. Garvey helped me more with expression, with coming out and being a performer. I decided then to try to avoid orchestral work. I thought perhaps Mr Kroll was right, that most orchestral players hate music, specially string players who sit in sections, because they are very squelched. You study and practise for years to develop your tone, get a big, round sound, then you sit in a section and use a tenth of it. You subjugate your musical ideas to the conductor, your bowing and fingering to the section leader. You're so downtrodden, you can't possibly feel fulfilled.

I don't know how the expectation gets so way out with musicians who go into orchestras. Is it the schools, or the people themselves, that foster the illusion of every good musician being able to make it as a soloist or a chamber music player? The one American orchestra I've heard that really had a feeling of community and ensemble was the LA Philharmonic. I hung around with them a while ago in New York, and I was very impressed. I saw how they worked together and I thought, 'Boy, this is a whole different thing, I wouldn't mind playing in that kind of orchestra.' Everywhere else I've been people have been grumbling all the time. You come out of an orchestral rehearsal, 'Ugh, the conductor was lousy, the music was lousy — stupid fingerings, idiotic bowings.' Every bloody thing is wrong. They're so negative, I don't like to live that way. The LA Philharmonic seemed to work well together and play well, and had more spirit than I'd seen in other groups here. The New York Phil. players hate what they're doing. Periodically I'm invited to audition for the New York Philharmonic but I chose to continue enjoying music. Many of the players seem to hate what they are doing. They are all frustrated soloists. I know some of them from our student days. They just despise what they're doing, every minute of it. So many orchestral players seem to lead sour, frustrated lives. I remember being horrified in Halifax, because I was just a kid at the time. My mother warned me to watch out for the men, but I thought that was just her hang-up. But she was absolutely right. It was wretched, and especially on tour. And the drinking. Before we'd get to the hotel on tour, the bus would pull into the provincial liquor commission, and everybody would buy a supply of booze. Except me, because I was under age. Eventually the bus driver must have guessed and asked me what I wanted. I started getting something like blackberry brandy, just to be part of the crowd. One orchestra will drink Scotch, another bourbon, and they sure do drink a lot, and they run around a lot.

Now, I love music. I came into it because I cared about it. I don't want that destroyed. And that's why I got out of orchestral playing, as a full-time job. I felt I was starting to get the same way as the others. I was trained at Mannes that when you have a rehearsal at nine you're there at twenty of, in your seat, with your instrument tuned and the music open on the stand. At the stroke of nine the baton goes down and you play. Well, the more jobs I do, the more I see people wandering in haphazardly, not bothering to tune, chatting, putting magazines on the music-stand. When I was in the Cincinnati Orchestra I would come in early, go to the ladies' dressing room and start to warm up. Two of the older, tougher women in the orchestra told me, 'We don't want to hear playing when we're not paid for it. Get out.' I was ejected from the room and started to warm up in the hallway under the stairs. By the end of the season I realized that I also had stopped warming up — 'Why should I be the oddball, I just annoy people.' I didn't warm up, then I saw my playing was beginning to slip. And I was still learning, still at a very early stage. I enjoyed playing under Max Rudolph, the music director, a fine musician and a good person who cares. So I left Cincinnati and decided that was it, as far as full-time orchestral playing went.

I'd been recommended to Cincinnati by the assistant conductor at Pittsburgh. They phoned me, asked if I'd like to audition. 'Don't bother,' I said, 'I don't want an orchestral job.' 'Come at your convenience, you name the day, we'll send a cheque to cover all expenses.' My teacher said not to be a fool, 'If they're paying, go have yourself a nice weekend.' OK, I went. Well, it was printed on the back of the cheque that my endorsement, if I passed the audition, was an acceptance of a contract. I didn't think a thing about it. I didn't want them, and I didn't think they'd want me. I hadn't been doing much orchestral work just then. They put me up in the Artist's Suite at the Sheraton-Gibson Hotel. I hadn't prepared anything in particular. I played a couple of pieces, did some sight-reading, then went to sit outside. They came out and waved a contract at me, 'You have to sign, you've agreed.' What was I going to do? Cincinnati seemed the end of the world.

I loved it there, the place. It seemed rather European, and the people respected music and musicians, which is not true of other places in the States, I'm sorry to say. But I got worn down by the orchestral company. I couldn't find anybody in that orchestra who wanted to play chamber music, and had to get together with a bunch of amateurs for Sunday night sessions. Now, the people I know who care about music just love playing chamber music and will get a group together at the drop of a hat. Not in Cincinnati. I asked to be alone on the 6th stand, because my sight is poor and that way I could have the music under my nose. Only then I didn't get to play Haydn – we had a Haydn series that year – because only three stands were used. I complained to Mr Rudolph, who replied. 'No one in this orchestra has ever complained before about *not* playing.' He encouraged me to go back to school and get a doctorate, so I went off to Boston University, but was very, very disgusted there. In the student orchestra, where I had to play, we spent three rehearsals a week for three months on Sibelius Second Symphony – I was going raving mad. The conductor was something else. You could follow his beat or play in time, not both. I just wasn't learning anything, and I hadn't come to Boston for a bit of paper, I wanted an education. The first class with the viola teacher, I started warming up with a chromatic scale. His chin dropped, 'Ah, you'll have to show me how to do that, I never could do it.' The guy is in the Boston Symphony. Soon after I walked out. I just couldn't go to lessons with somebody like that.

The attitude toward women is still very bad in American orchestras. I'll tell you, some orchestras wouldn't even listen to me. For instance, I called up Detroit, after I'd played in Cincinnati. The personnel manager said, 'Oh, a woman? How old are you? . . . Well, being a woman and so young, don't bother to audition.' It's taken a long time to get women into the major orchestras. In the years when I was thinking of an orchestral career, it was pretty damn hard. If there was a woman, she was just a token, like they take in token blacks now. Cincinnati, not being one of the Big Five, was a little different, having about fourteen women, mainly strings, harp of course, but also a trombone and a trumpet player. But in the last five years or so, the big orchestras have been forced, by the union and by legislation, to let the barriers down. A friend of mine, a fine cellist, was refused an audition by a major orchestra, on the basis of sex. She sued, through the union, and the orchestra was forced to accept her. They've got a damn good cellist. Now, my policy has always been if they don't want me, I'm not going to force myself. But she was married to a member of the faculty at an area university, she wanted to play, and didn't see why she should have to leave town. It used to be, for a woman, that you had to go to some small, provincial orchestra, or forget about orchestral playing.

Well, I found out what those small, provincial orchestras were like.

200

At one stage I was persuaded to go down to Shreveport, Louisiana, a professional orchestra — supposedly — and allowed to write my own contract. I put in an escape clause, and I exercised it after one year. It was a deadly place to live, and the orchestra . . . I remember we did *Carmina Burana*, which has a 7/4 movement. The conductor was waving away, and the players were looking at each other, nobody together. 'What's the matter, why can't you do 7/4? Look, one, two, three, four, five, six, sev -en.' That's how he was beating it. Some of the places I've been — the conductors! The big orchestras — New York, Philadelphia, Boston — they don't get the really bad ones. But then, you see, those orchestras generally don't pay any attention to the conductors anyway! The problem with the lesser orchestras is that the musicians are really hanging on the conductor, and that's where he has the most influence. The New York Phil. is going to sound like itself whoever is conducting. To get a decent performance from a second-rate orchestra is a real challenge.

I joined a resident quartet, at Northern Michigan University, and I thought, at last, exactly what I wanted. But it's very isolated on Lake Superior. The quartet rehearsed three times a week but gave only one full recital and one half recital in the whole year. The first violin hated to perform. Sure, we had a full-time teaching schedule as well, but we could have managed a recital once a month, my goodness. I was rather bored. The next season I taught at Berea College, Kentucky, played in the Lexington Philharmonic and worked on my BMA. Then my mother died. I went back to New York to sort out her apartment, decided it was home and I was going to stay right there. I've been in New York ever since, freelancing, drifting in and out of Cincinnati to keep my doctorate alive, playing chamber music whenever I can. New York offers me the chance to combine some orchestral playing and chamber music, with solos, and singing, which I still do. I can get my feet going in all directions.

I've a girl friend who is a really fine violinist in the Metropolitan Opera orchestra. She's gone through the ranks of several orchestras and now she's in the Met. Where does she go from there? They get the top money, better than the Philharmonic, because they work more, those long operas but in my opinion, sitting in an opera-pit — the very worst kind of squelching. How can anybody do that *every day?*

Every step, every breath you take, someone has it noted. It's a nightmare. You reach the point where you have to decide if the money is worth it. That's why I got out of regular orchestral playing for a living, because I felt I was going away from the type of musician I wanted to be. I thought I'd rather just eat a little more simply, have fewer possessions, and then play the kind of music I wanted. But I don't have a family and heavy financial responsibilities, and I want to keep out of that rut. You get used to that stupid pay-check and find it so hard to walk out. My singing teacher, Charlotte Povia, has been telling me for three years, 'Just get out and do nothing but sing.' I thought I don't have the guts — if I don't work today how am I going to eat tomorrow? But, you know, it's been a year, I haven't starved and I'm much happier being with singers as they take a much more positive attitude toward life.

Alan Hacker

ALAN HACKER I studied at the Royal Academy two years only, first with Jack Brymer, because he was the star player. I was introduced to him through relatives, and he was very good to me, but already I was going in another direction. However, it is good to come in contact early with a player you revere. Then he left the Academy and Reginald Kell, Beecham's clarinetist from pre-war days, came back from America, and I really got on a lot better with Kell. He was very much in the Leon Goossens tradition – he felt he'd learnt from Goossens – and perhaps it was this that drew me to him. The one saving grace of a music school, then as now, is if you have a dedicated teacher, and in Kell I had that. But in truth the Academy itself gave me nothing. I was 4th clarinet in 3rd orchestra, then 4th clarinet in 2nd orchestra. I shared parts with the composer Harry Birtwistle. I once played the long clarinet solo at the start of Sibelius 1 – my moment of glory. But that hardly constitutes an orchestral training, and as a result of my non-education at the Academy, even though I'm a university lecturer now, I've got a real chip on my shoulder over those wasted years.

I started playing in the London Junior Orchestra, and also accompanied various choral societies. I was about seventeen. I remember doing the Weber *Concertino* the same afternoon I took 'O' Level French. In some ways I began a semi-professional life much too early. Perhaps it was to do with the class I come from, or with Battersea, the London suburb of my birth, but very early I felt obliged, if not exactly to do well, at least to put my nose to the grindstone. This was partly encouraged by a sort of epilepsy, a *petit mal*, I suffered when I was about eleven. I had odd things done to me, lumbar punctures and holes drilled in the back of my head. I had to take drugs regularly, and I felt in a way that my mind was slowing up. And this *was* happening, because the drugs were relaxants. But it all helped to create this drive to work, to play the instrument, be a professional, something almost puritanical. I rather admire the fellow who can go off to the pub and stay there for hours. It's not in me to do that. I wish I could. At the end of the second year at the Academy, aged nineteen, I joined the London Philharmonic. I was not conscious of any ambition to be in an orchestra, but I had this . . . *gravity* just to play and do the best I could professionally. I joined as second clarinet.

I found the organization of the LPO, the London self-governing system, very bad. It sounds so democratic – indeed it is – but I don't think musical performance works in that way. Performance must be directed, certainly in the case of the large symphonic pieces of the late-nineteenth century, and it is the opinion and musical judgment of the conductor that matters. An orchestra appoints a director – it was Steinberg when I joined the LPO – and for a couple of years everything is fine, then the longer he's there the less the band like him, partly because he is beginning to impose his own imprint. The result is an unhappy stalemate. If the conductor doesn't like the 1st horn, and 1st horn is chairman of the board that appointed him – what then? And it's bad to play in an orchestra where a back desk fiddle player has an eye – or ear – on you, because he happens to be on the board, and he may be on the board for his own ego, being musically a rather neglected member of the band. That doesn't lead to joyous music-making. I was, I suppose, a bit of a black sheep, playing apart from current clarinet style, and this disturbed a lot of people. Not the older members, because aspects of my playing were more traditional than the current style, but generally a different type of sound in an orchestra is disturbing to many players. They want a certain kind of anonymity, someone who plays like an orchestral player.

I was playing in a classical concert at York a while ago, and it was so exciting because we were all trying to find an appropriate style and voice for the composer and the period. No one in the band was playing like an orchestral player. When I joined the LPO I was told how long it takes to become an orchestral player, all the craft there is to learn. To an extent, that's true. But with sensitivity, you should be able to play any type of music, in any position, in any band. So much orchestral training is a lot of bull-shit. You either play with sensitivity, or you don't. I'm sorry to sound controversial, but I did think that the majority in the orchestra were very cowed, over-cautious both musically and in their job, because they feared for their position. With no contract, there was no security. People were rather nervous, and the tension of nerves and insecurity didn't help the music. In a sense, the essence of self-government was not to rock the boat. I recall a flute player who questioned the terms of our employment, to do with tax and insurance. He took the matter right up to the minister, and was told privately that his claim was just, but for his trouble he was chucked out of the orchestra. His wife was pregnant at the time, and she became a little unbalanced. Cases like that make me feel quite hard about these orchestras. There is this nasty side to orchestral *life*, springing from the institutional nature of the orchestra, but I certainly don't feel sour and bitter about my old orchestral *colleagues*. When I see and play with my old pals it's very nice, a great feeling of fraternity. Playing music, any ensemble music, is like going into battle each time, though you've done the piece fifty times before. Imagine playing an exposed part — say the oboe in the slow movement of the Brahms fiddle concerto — what a great release of emotional tension after that! And this spending of emotion in a concert gives everyone a very strong sense of community.

I was still with the LPO when I was stricken by the illness which put me in this wheelchair. Luckily for me, the orchestra had just started a sick fund, so while I was at Stoke Mandeville Hospital I was paid about £20 a week, a good sum eleven or twelve years ago. When I came out the orchestra faced a tour of Germany, and the board asked if I could manage it. I had a car with hand controls and Chris Seaman, the LPO timpanist and now a conductor, had agreed to go with me. So I said I could do it. Then the board wrote to say that they didn't think I was capable. They were prepared to give me sick pay — well, I wasn't bloody well sick any more, was I? Certainly a wheelchair is a nuisance, but I'd been rehabilitating myself, and I needed to play, not sit at home with sick pay. So I resigned from the orchestra. Then I had some pretty hard times. I'm doubly incontinent, and I was trying to get organized with a urinal

system. That may seem musically irrelevant, but it isn't if you are dis-
abled, for it's in your mind the whole time. And I found I was allergic
to the glue and rubber I was using, so I had these awful times playing in a
ballet orchestra – *Swan Lake*, ironically – and I'd be in the gents with the
second clarinet, trying to get my waterworks back on while they were
starting Act II. Somehow I had to get my wheelchair through the band to
the first clarinet position. It was very hard. But that was what I needed,
to get back into life again. And I'm sure I did the right thing, leaving the
LPO in a rather grand way, on a matter of principle.

André Previn in rehearsal

There's something about actually playing in an orchestra day after day. Let me give an example. The beginning of Tchaikovsky's *Romeo and Juliet* is scored, rather unusually, for 1st clarinet, 1st bassoon, and 2nd clarinet, 2nd bassoon. Second clarinet — my position for eight or nine years — is playing at the bottom of the A clarinet, because I suppose, Tchaikovsky wanted the dark, reedy tone of the A's longer tube. Anyway, someone suggested swapping the parts around — it's the kind of joke musicians play on a conductor — and we did that on many occasions. And in all my time with the LPO not one conductor spotted the fact that we'd switched parts. Again, the wind in the LPO used to substitute a rather rude little figure in a passage towards the end of Tchaikovsky 5, even on recordings, and no one seems to have spotted it, other than the players. Well, I mentioned these things not so much as a condemnation of the players — I was one of them myself. Obviously we were bored, and we had a fairly cynical view of the competence of conductors who could pass these things. I'm trying to make a point about the nature of the large symphony orchestra, about the attitudes it generates, and the musical result of those attitudes. Too often the players are either just not interested, or they are complacent. English orchestras, in the wind section, felt second to none, and critics would reinforce this. If, say, the Dresden Orchestra came fifteen years ago, the reviewers would write, 'Ravishing strings, but of course they can't equal our wind players.' Well, I don't think that's true any more, and in any case complacency is death to music. Whenever you play, the music must have an element of unselfconscious freshness about it, but that is so terribly hard to achieve in a symphony orchestra, specially those that work as hard as the London orchestras work. If orchestras are to become creative again, they must change their ways of working.

Perhaps if symphony orchestras are not careful, they will die. Vast, wasteful, burdensome beasts, musical dinosaurs, great bulk and little brain. There is an 'organization', the London Orchestral Board, the fund-giving custodian, responsible in some sense for the employment of all these orchestral players. But that's the wrong way round. Career structure and administration are coming before the making of music. These orchestras are kept going, at great expense, because they are *there* — like Mount Everest. 'We have this monster, we must feed it.' Maybe this is the worst possible way to look at the orchestral set-up, but that's healthy and right, to help it to improve. I refuse to think that I'm merely being cynical and destructive, because I love the orchestra and its music. Orchestras will no doubt continue to get grants, but whether they will remain a vital force in future music is another matter.

Orchestral players understandably prefer the late-classical and romantic repertoire, because that *is* their repertoire. There is music after Richard Strauss, but the instruments the orchestra plays are essentially nineteenth-century instruments. Many date from an earlier age, but they have been altered to produce more sound, more brilliance, more facility. Now, when a composer writes he has in mind a particular sound that stems from particular instruments. The music of the nineteenth century suits the orchestra best because the composers had just those instruments in mind. The modern large orchestra was born of that era and is, in effect, stuck in that era. And that means there is a problem, now being recognized, for the symphony orchestra to play other music, specially baroque and early classical. Many people will no longer tolerate the grossness of the big symphony orchestra playing, for example, Bach's *St Matthew Passion*. Tomorrow I'll be recording *Eine Kleine Nachtmusik*, that staple divertimento of the symphony orchestra, on single strings, as Mozart wrote it. There is a penalty for playing old music. If we want to go on making it fresh and alive and sounding like new music, we naturally find out more and more about it. And we find that a lot of music, including some of the very greatest, is just not suitable for the symphony orchestra as it is now constituted.

The modern orchestra is powerful and noisy, but the sound is blander and far less exciting than in Mozart's time. This, I feel, is serious. And I'm quite sure that this is why a lot of young people today are not roused when they hear the Mozart *G minor symphony*. We have faith in the supreme musical talent of Mozart, yet something is wrong if the kid in the street doesn't stop when he hears the opening of that symphony. I think part of the trouble is that the kid is not actually hearing the sound Mozart wanted him to hear, and which Mozart heard in his own head. Well, someone sympathetic listening to this diatribe will say that the symphony orchestra is in business — and they'll have to use that word — to play a wide selection of music, and it would be silly to have dozens of instruments of different periods lying at the feet of every player. Of course it would. But I think the point is that we need more knowledge of different periods, and more adaptability, from orchestral players, and far greater honesty in performing practice. Then I think 'classical' music would sound more vital and perhaps begin to regain some of the ground so entirely lost to pop music.

And that brings us full circle to proper teaching, and to a proper professional expectation — to want to do music right, rather than just wanting to hold down a job. It's not a question of antiquarian or pedantic interest, it's a question of *rightness*, to respect the composer and his music. For example, in the middle of the slow movement of the Mozart E flat symphony there's a dark but aggressive section in this rather serene piece. Then the horns play, right in the middle of the texture, an F sharp in unison. Now an F sharp on the horn of Mozart's time would have produced a very distorted sound, specially two horns together. And that's the way Mozart scored it, he knew what he was doing, for natural horns, so at that point there should be a rather curdled noise that is extremely dramatic. You'd never get that in a modern orchestra. Add these small points together and I feel you arrive at a very different kind of classical orchestral performance. I think the reason why the man in the street doesn't much like Mozart — other composers too — is that he feels in his bones there is actually something wrong with the way the music is being played. He turns aside. Isn't it the task of the orchestra to help him back?

(opposite)
A recording session
conducted by André Previn

206

Speculations

Aristotle averreth music to be the only disposer of the mind to virtue and goodness, whereof he reckoneth it among those four principal exercises wherein he would have children instructed.

HENRY PEACHAM, *The Compleat Gentleman* (1622)

If the ruler's love of music were very great, then the kingdom would come near to being well governed.

MENCIUS, *Works*

JOHN DE LANCIE

SUPPORT of orchestras is such a difficult problem to try to work out. Suppose we just leave the whole thing to supply and demand? Obviously our musicians will have to take a lot less pay, by about fifty percent at least. The only alternative I know of is government subsidy, and why not? In America we give a lot of lip-service to free enterprise, but we are so far along the road to a socialized government that we might as well call it that. Everything else is subsidized. You grow potatoes or tobacco, or you *don't* grow them, and you get paid anyhow. Imagine a country with a $500 billion a year budget, or something like that, yet the government can only manage to scrape up $30 million a year for all cultural activities. That's just a joke, isn't it?

LEONARD HINDELL A lot of people think joining the Philharmonic is just like becoming a member of a private club. A comfortable, benevolent institution, with little relevance beyond its walls. Well, there is something rather hidden and mysterious about the life of an orchestra. The public sees soap-opera or superstars. Our intrigues, our politics, our disputes, our contracts, our strikes, our earnings are all bandied about — a TV soap-drama. Everybody knows all about Bernstein or Rubinstein. But who knows the man or woman sitting in the 4th cello chair? That person lives in a community, the orchestra, itself part of a larger community, the public. And the two communities must come closer together. It's true that many players resist innovations, new programmes, new ideas, new initiatives. They feel they are trained musicians in a major orchestra, and this is not the place to experiment either with new music or new directions. I feel we want, with each contract, the normal desires of working people — more money, more time off, more benefits. But I think we must do something for these advances, something more for society, for the life of the community. Not compromise artistic standards, but reach out, try to make the orchestra a more widely-based institution.

(opposite)
The cor anglais player

209

ROGER SCOTT We don't have the small, specialist chamber orchestras here. In Philadelphia we have the Philadelphia Orchestra. The big symphony orchestras have no competition. We play baroque music and the purists among us shudder, because the forces are far too large, and the style is not correct. It's a dilemma. If we don't give our audience a reasonable amount of what they want, we lose subscriptions and cut our own throats. Young firebrands say, 'We should play pure music, and we should do contemporary pieces.' But can we risk the audience dropping away? We walk a tightrope in programme planning. I was just reading in a local paper: 'Dull programme at Robin Hood Dell.' What can we do, in the summer season, with just one rehearsal?

In the States, culture has not been part of our heritage, across a broad base. Only recently, since the end of the War, has a professional musician been acceptable. When I started, in Pittsburgh and even in Philadelphia, people would ask my wife, 'So your husband plays in an orchestra, but what does he do for a living?' How do you answer that? Now, I played a summer in Israel, in 1960. A young bass player, a gentile, told me, 'When I go to the market, the butcher says to me, "Oh, you're a member of the Israel Philharmonic?" and reaches under the counter for a better cut of meat.' I think we are a bit more respectable now in the States. Our fund-raising drives bring home to the public just who these musicians are. Just humans with a part in the community.

It is frightening, the money needed to support a big symphony orchestra. We have an annual fund drive. This year we had a marathon for a week which raised, what? — about $220,000. Everyone, players, management, board members, was on the phone, taking pledges and so on. Our local classical music radio station gave us a lot of exposure. But that is only a small part of the financial picture. We get a little from the National Council for the Arts, but they go for artsy craftsy ventures, and some of us professionals resent this, because the public gets little benefit. We used to get money from the city, and still do for our summer season at the Dell. Our recording guarantee was peeled back this year. No question, we'll need state support in the future, if we are to continue, and I know the management is worried about that. When government gets in, it wants — and rightfully I suppose — a say in how the money is spent. We are up to astronomical figures in salary.

Fortunately, people in the States do give money for a great many cultural ventures. But all the arts need this patronage. And now people in the street say, 'Why should I give money to upkeep the Philadelphia Orchestra when those fellows are making far more than I do?' When I joined the orchestra I think we got $3,000 a year. I said to a friend, 'If I ever make $5,000 a year I'll be happy.' We've risen astronomically above that, and our people are still not happy. Can we earn more and work less, and expect the audience to support us? I really don't know what direction . . . Well, in the old days, when the orchestra was only going part time, someone like Cyrus Curtis would say at the board meeting, 'Gentlemen, what's the deficit?' and write a cheque to cover it. That's gone. Now we depend on $10 here, $5 there. We want any contribution whatsoever. In this marathon we offered a coffee-mug, a Beethoven mug: 'Have coffee with Beethoven.' $5 a mug, ridiculous, for a thing worth 40c. We sold so many we had to re-stock. All that is not only welcome, it's necessary. All the orchestras are having to do it. It provides funds, and it gets people interested in the orchestra, which to me is more important. They buy a mug, then they might just go to a concert, which is really what all our efforts, musical and practical, are trying to achieve.

We used to play in Convention Hall, which is a barn — 12,000 people. The city gave a grant. The music was not very satisfying — horrible sound system. But it cost the audience just two stamps, one to mail in the application, another for the self-addressed reply. And in the old Robin Hood Dell, which was all open air, we'd get between 5,000 and 15,000 a concert. Those audiences cut across a vast section of the population. I feel we should be reaching different people. I'm upset that we don't go to the schools and play as much as our contract allows. The management doesn't do it, but it's part of our social obligation. If I were in big business, and the orchestra approached me for funds, I'd want to say, 'What are you doing for the community? Are you just playing for subscribers, or are you, as Pittsburgh used to do, going into the steel-mills? Are you going to the schools, or, as St Louis does, bussing the kids to the hall?' It doesn't matter how you do it, you have to play your part, in all society, and build audiences for the future. Who knows where it will rub off? We've had a couple of black players come in from Philadelphia. I'm sure they got started somewhere along the line at a concert of the Philadelphia Orchestra. That's how I got started.

ROLF SMEDVIG All musicians dream of having their art accepted by the whole of society. But it's not going to be. Let's face it, in the States a symphony orchestra is a very new thing. A hundred years ago a brass band was a big deal in most American cities, and what a horrible sound that is, horrible. And I speak as a brass player! To make a large, intelligent audience takes years and years of listening, of choice in music and programmes. We don't have that tradition. It would be unheard of to put on a concert in Symphony Hall, $8 a ticket, and then play Bach with single strings — maybe fourteen players. Audiences should have a chance to hear that, but not by the Boston Symphony. Our audiences are very unsophisticated, they don't know an authentic performance from a stone wall. In Europe I think the audiences are more trained, more knowledgeable. But not in, say, Detroit — are you kidding? And Boston — I've got to say it though I don't like to admit it — not in Boston either. Our audiences just want the big, spectacular pieces.

We do what they want. Our patronage comes from prosperous people, and to go to Symphony Hall is a social event. For a wider audience we need wider exposure. Nine out of ten people have never heard classical music. On the radio they hear nothing but pop, rock, dance music, band music perpetually. Radio stations in Europe, or so I found, would play a rock piece, a jazz piece, then maybe a Mozart symphony. Here, the young just listen to a bunch of crap, all the time. They don't know what else there

André Previn conducts

is. 'Orchestral music? Who wants that boring stuff, to sit there and be quiet?' I mean, it's too much like thinking, too difficult.

LYNN HARRELL Can the big symphony orchestra go on? My first thought is to clasp my hands and pray. Orchestras in the States are like toys in rich men's store cupboards. The players are just employees and it's not surprising that they think like employees, just as far ahead as the next pay-cheque. They resent having to listen to the dumb businessmen on the boards making decisions that have very little to do with artistry or even music. They know they should be out grabbing converts for their music, but they play in a way that doesn't interest the kids, and in a format the kids find ridiculous. Only the banker in a TV Western wears those kind of pants. I'm amazed that the preparation for the future is so little, and so poorly done.

In most large American cities a very large proportion of the population is black. What does the orchestra do for the blacks? I find it sad in America, the lack of give and take between jazz and classical idioms and musicians. Black jazz musicians can teach us a lot. In the thirties, jazz brass sections were improvising semi-quaver off-beats at a fast tempo, absolutely together. In the orchestra, the conductor needs a huge, slow downbeat to try to get the start of a Bruckner symphony together, and often the players can't get it. You can't get rhythmic subtlety and freedom in classical players unless it's part of their musical life. The thinking is different. Jazz is still, after many generations, in touch with its roots – music for dance, for physical function. In our music, we have the names of the dance – minuet, gigue, allemande, bourrée, etc., but the

212

function, the dance in the music, is lost. We've become more and more cerebral, to our detriment, and most jazz musicians, and the ordinary listener too, sense this and regret it. If these people could hear a Mozart symphony played with the rhythmic subtlety and sense of a good jazz group, then very likely they'd take to Mozart. If only that feeling could be instilled in the training of classical players. And that feeling can be made audible, it really can. Compare a Rossini overture by Szell, or Karajan, no matter how exactly played, with the same piece by Toscanini, the difference is between just smiling and wanting to jump for joy. Toscanini just had, I don't know how, so much more feeling for the rhythmic movement required in that kind of music. And when he got it with the NBC Symphony you could just laugh with joy.

RON BARRON The future has to start with the kids, and with an understanding of such things as folk-music. You've got to have some roots before you go any place. Western European art music has never meant much to the ordinary man here. But my impression in Europe, in say Holland or Germany, is that the ordinary guy can pay a little bit of money and hear a concert, and that's no more extraordinary than going to the football game. A friend in The Hague told me that it's in the city charter, there has to be an orchestra. You just don't run the city without your art museum and your orchestra. Now, the people may not go, but they accept it as an enduring, natural institution. Hardly anything gets that kind of public consensus in America.

JOHN FLETCHER Institutions have to adapt to society. We live in a socialized way, every move under the scrutiny of the general public, with very many bright people wanting a say in things, and the institutions of music have gone democratic. When Beecham was running the RPO and Walter Legge the Philharmonia, the whole orchestral scene was just right for them. We're talking about, first, an extraordinary conductor who stamped his personality on a very fine orchestra entirely devoted to him — a wonderful state of affairs. And in the second case we had an extremely capable and ruthless man who knew where to find the greatest conductors, the greatest players, *and* had a say in EMI recordings. Two sets of unrepeatable circumstances. Legge ditched the old Philharmonia and Beecham died. The era fizzled out, and everything went democratic. And I notice that people who trumpet on about that era have come up with no alternative, but make suggestions that I'd rather die than see carried out. If Walter Legge would reappear and wield the same power without the impediment of little men, I'd gladly try his system. But there's no place for the Legges now. We do not fear great men. They are cut down to size in the corner of the room, on the TV screen, and made into domestic pets. I'm not nearly so pessimistic about the conductors and orchestras of today as some of my colleagues. I think both have adapted to changing conditions pretty well. People commend the old times. It's like saying how wonderful the War was! It's a pity that the present always gets ripped the most. The musical world is now crowded with pretty good people. I think there's a lot of good conducting and a lot of very good playing going on *now*. We're very lucky to live now, in London.

In essence the symphony orchestra is a nineteenth-century creation, and plays that music best. It is the gallery for the nineteenth- and early twentieth-century masterpieces. And what the sophisticates forget is that the public loves the big orchestra and its works, new listeners are constantly being shovelled in at the bottom end, the more the better. It's our duty to give these audiences what they delight in. If the orchestra dies, at least here in England, it will be because the public no longer wants it. We just don't get enough in subsidy to keep the thing artificially alive.

I would venture to suggest that the full symphony orchestra is the biggest, most complex and the most varied of man's artistic creations. And I do think, with some notable exceptions, that most of the greatest music has been written for it. Then of course one immediately thinks of Bach's small-scale works. But the big orchestra *is* an astonishing creation, terribly inefficient, terribly expensive. Long may it last. But I do nonetheless worry that orchestras are out of touch with new, or even well-tried modern music. People blame the orchestras, but we are in a quandary. We have neither the money nor the right kind of organization to do that music in the best possible way. Small specialist groups like the Fires of London and the London Sinfonietta can expand or contract as the music demands, and they do that music marvellously, undoubtedly the two best groups of their kind in the world. It's to groups like this that modern music must look, not to the big orchestras. Then the composers' guild points out that works for the big orchestra are being written, and it's our job to help form public taste, even to push it, yet we still play 700 hours of Brahms and one-and-a-half hours of Osbert Cucumber. Unhappily, one can only say that 700 to one-and-a-half is about the right proportion in terms of what the public enjoys. But crowds for unusual music can be brought in, as the LSO has shown with Previn. Orchestras have played far too safe, with very nervous programme building. We don't want to go mad, get in the history book but empty the hall, but we must somehow overcome the innate conservatism of all big orchestras against what we call squeaky gate music. The concerts are often not very well done, and the audience depressingly few. A fifth of a house is no good to anybody, when you walk in it's like sticking a pin in a balloon. We get awfully depressed on the platform to see those few, forlorn people we call rent-a-crowd, always the same faces. We must get more used to modern music, and we must do it better, and the public – why not? – must stir itself.

ANTHONY CAMDEN It's so hard to do all that we want to do because of this perpetual struggle with finances. In the London Symphony, on our tiny grant, we could blow the whole lot on three concerts if we wanted to. We try to build up conductors whom the audience will come to hear, no matter what the programme. That is a great thing about André Previn. He stands so well with the public that they'll come to his concerts for almost anything. He's done Messiaen's *Turangilila Symphony*, in the

Festival Hall, to an eighty percent capacity audience. And we did a work by the composer of *Star Wars* five years before the film. That's because of Previn. Now, with Celibidache, whom some regard as a very great conductor, but who doesn't make records, doesn't go on TV, has no PR follow up, then we have to work damn hard to put on Hindemith's *Mathis der Maler* and get a decent audience. We know that most people like the standard repertoire, but we also realize we have a duty to the continuance of music today. Next year, for our seventy-fifth anniversary, we've commissioned six full-scale orchestral works from Tippett, Walton and Berio among others. We'll be doing a lot of modern music in that season, and justifiably so after seventy-five years.

But I don't see the symphony orchestra going on as when I was young, or when my father was in the orchestra. Who knew anything about orchestral players then, those remote, formal figures on the distant stage? We feel now that the audience must somehow be brought in, encouraged to mingle, look, understand what's going on in the orchestra. If they understand what a wind section is, about the problems of string intonation, about balance, about the different sound of a horn section in England and America, then people are going to feel much closer to the orchestra and to the music we play.

TOM STORER Everyone says to the orchestra 'Change your ways, adapt.' What so few explain is how we are to do it. Take first the question of modern music. It's extraordinarily difficult to follow out the composer's 'aleatoric' instructions in a large symphony orchestra. I mean if a lot of these serious-minded gents actually knew what happened when we are solemnly told to bang this or hit that in some vast, complex maze of a pattern, they might go home and have another think. If you are sufficiently bored or ill-used, you'll do anything or nothing. But composers seem perfectly satisfied either way. Some devastating travesties of experimental music have been pronounced the best possible performance by the composer. So do they know what's happening? And we don't like to use our instruments in the way we are sometimes directed. We've been trained to play a legato line, to use the instrument melodically, and don't take kindly to some of the strange percussive effects asked for now. We've gone up a creek and I'm sure I don't know the way out.

Then take the case of the older music. I'm very interested in baroque and early classical periods. But I don't think the large symphony orchestra can adapt itself to these fields. Too many specialists, in England anyway, and the small chamber orchestras do it too well. We can put on Mozart, with cut-down sections, that's OK now and again. But the rest of the band want employment, and we don't always do Mozart as nicely as, say, the English Chamber Orchestra. But it's very good that we should do it, very salutary for players who spend their lives tearing the pants off Tchaikovsky. We should be made to play Mozart, or perhaps allowed to play it, that's a better way to put it. But I wonder if there might grow up an orchestra of players who can adapt to the style and instruments of almost any period? After all, most wind players in England now have a baroque oboe, or a boxwood clarinet at home. And I certainly think a change is bound to come in brass instruments in the not too distant future. In brass departments the symphony orchestra has outstripped its own strength. Strings and wind haven't changed much. Strings have become more strident to fill the vast spaces of modern halls, and wind instruments have more keys to facilitate passage work. But brass have had the dubious benefits of science. A modern trombone section is positively lethal. Any string section that sits in front of that lot ought to be entitled to industrial injury. They can, and do, actually damage the ears. If I'm in front, I have to stop playing when they open up. Now you can't kid me that any sort of orchestral balance can be struck on that basis. No doubt, the sound of a symphony orchestra in full cry in Strauss is marvellous, but it should be confined to Strauss and his like, because that's really where our modern sound came from. You *can* play Beethoven on the grand orchestra, just as you can play Bach on the grand piano. The notes are there and it's sufficiently great music to stand the transmutation. But it's not in the spirit of the music. Bach can be done on the Moog synthesizer, and he must have been a hell of a good composer to survive that.

ROBIN MCGEE What will happen? As far as I can see, orchestral members are only concerned with *now*, or at the most the next couple of years. They drift along — concerts, recordings, sessions — immediacy. Earning a living, paying the mortgage, bills. Democratic orchestras have some of the disadvantages of democratic government. One lot gets in and does this, another lot follows and undoes it. Very little is planned, mapped out, taking the long view.

How strange that something like the *Rite of Spring* hardly warrants an extra rehearsal now. That's the level of competence we've arrived at. Orchestras know it — stock in trade. But where are the new pieces like that coming from? The present repertoire will last the lifetime of most now in orchestras. But the next generation of players, are they just going to go on playing the same stuff? I was asking a young composer of film music why he didn't write for the orchestra. He said he'd like to, but he would have to be commissioned, and if he wrote like Brahms or Wagner it wouldn't be any good, and if he didn't the audience wouldn't come. If somebody doesn't form a vital link between what's being played and what's being written, eventually the whole thing is going to stop. Perhaps we might just hand over music to electronics, composition for the recording studio. Of course, in the pop field writing for recording is the rule, thirty-two-track knob-twiddling — not for concert at all. But that makes yet a further distance between player and listener. Technology can produce music, but to cut out the presence, the physical appreciation, lessens the force of any music. Music is not just for the ear.

Lutoslawski has some interesting theories about this essential interchange between the audience and the band, about those tensions on the platform that are communicated to the audience unrealized. These tensions in a big orchestra are terribly wearing on the players. One wonders if composers include technical problems just to create this kind of tense excitement. I can't imagine if the extremes, in Mahler for example, are calculated. I don't know how you write music. Do you think about this sort of thing? Isn't it supposed just to flow out? Often, as a player in modern music, one feels that we are merely subjects of experimentation. Recently a composer wrote a piece for the London Sinfonietta, and he found it was too short. So we just put in a whole lot of repeats — 'Those seven bars, and twenty-four over here, and that should be just about right.' The viola player said to me, 'We are witnessing one of the great moments of creativity, one of the deepest secrets of the composer's art.'

I find playing brand-new stuff, even though it may not be very good in the end, both a challenge and a reward. Composers are, after all, trying to give players a new freedom, not the old vocabulary but another way of saying things. And to me that is more interesting than doing yet *another* rehearsal of Beethoven 7 with, whatever you like to bet, an inferior conductor, three hours of it. Well, at the moment we can do both in England, and a lot else besides. But I wonder about my two sons, if they go into music. Their world will be as different from mine, as mine is from the world my pianist-father knew.

Before a television recording

217

EPILOGUE

CECIL JAMES

WHEN I go to a concert, as one of the audience, I'm always slightly disappointed. I don't get the same, I won't say musical effect, but electric feeling, that you get in the orchestra. So I enjoy my concert-going sitting on the platform. Thrilling, a wonderful feeling. Well, consider the orchestra — that's one of man's greatest creations. Add up all the sweat and strain of composers, all the man and woman hours of practising, all the skill and effort of the instrument makers, and bring all that together. Quite a thought, really. But composers are no longer writing much for the symphony orchestra. Mainly, it's a practical matter. If you write for vast forces, umpteen percussion, quadruple everything, *and* it empties the hall, it's just not on. So they write for smaller groups and smaller audiences. There aren't any great symphonists at the moment, are there? I suppose eventually the thing will

Practice . . .

die on its feet, take a different form. But the establishment of the modern orchestra is pretty recent, and why should it be in just *that* form — so many desks of strings, two each of flutes, oboes, clarinets, bassoons, brass of various kinds, timps, percussion and harps? I think the trend is swinging towards smaller groups, people who specialize a bit. That's lovely to hear, but I still like the red meat of a symphony orchestra, unleashed. It's the most thrilling sound. But in my latter years I've had a lot of pleasure in smaller groups, with baroque orchestras, playing bass continuo with one bassoon, cello, organ or harpsichord. I used to think — typical orchestral player! — that Bach was a bit long-winded before I started doing this. But I wouldn't like to do it all the time, any more than I'd like to do wind quintets, and in my time I've done a terrific amount of wind quintet playing. My first love is still the symphony orchestra. Maybe that's a peasant's approach, I don't know.

Despite the financial difficulties, there is a strange fascination in music, in any art. I was playing in Salzburg once, with the Dennis Brain Wind Quintet. It was a hot morning and we were sauntering up to look at the castle, licking ice-creams. Some tourists stopped us, they couldn't believe we were the same fellows who had looked so serious and formal on the platform the night before. Lined us up and photographed us. Musicians licking ice-creams, just like ordinary humans. Music *is* something apart. Players keep pouring out of the schools, more than ever, no matter how hazardous the profession. If you are keen on music and your instrument, it's a lifetime preoccupation, whatever the hardships and frustrations. Most musicians grumble away and say they won't let their children take it up. But it's surprising how many children follow their parents into music. And it can be a way to make a pretty good living. I think musicians are well paid. In fact, sometimes it's embarrassing to take the money, you've enjoyed playing so much. Of course, you never quite refuse it! And now, after forty years and more of blowing the bassoon, I still get a tremendous lot of fun, though sometimes my ears are twisted abominably, tutoring youth orchestras — steering lively young kids on the bassoon. I never thought I'd get to that stage, but I have.

List of Musicians

List of Orchestras

First Violins
Hugh Maguire
Rodney Friend
Marie Wilson MBE
John Ronayne
Alfio Micci

Second Violins
Gillian Eastwood
Michael Nutt

Violas
Csaba Erdelyi
Eleanor Gould

Cellos
Raymond Clark
Lynn Harrell
Tom Storer

Basses
Roger Scott
Robin McGee

Flutes
Richard Adeney
Paul Fried

Oboes
John de Lancie
Anthony Camden

Clarinets
Antony Pay
Alan Hacker
Peter Hadcock

Bassoons
Cecil James
Leonard Hindell

Horn
Alan Civil

Trumpets
William Lang
Rolf Smedvig

Trombones
Ronald Barron
Raymond Premru

Tuba
John Fletcher

Timpani & Percussion
Gary Kettel

Harp
Sidonie Goossens

The voices in this book speak from experience gained in the following symphony orchestras:

United States and Canada
Atlanta Symphony Orchestra
Boston Symphony Orchestra
Buffalo Philharmonic
Cincinnati Symphony Orchestra
Cleveland Orchestra
Halifax Symphony Orchestra
Los Angeles Philharmonic
Montreal Symphony Orchestra
New York Philharmonic
Philadelphia Orchestra
Pittsburgh Symphony Orchestra
Rochester Philharmonic

Europe
Bavarian Radio Orchestra, Munich
BBC Symphony Orchestra
Bournemouth Symphony Orchestra
City of Birmingham Symphony Orchestra
Hallé Orchestra
London Philharmonic Orchestra
London Symphony Orchestra
Philharmonic Orchestra
Queen's Hall Orchestra
Radio Eirann Symphony Orchestra, Dublin
Royal Liverpool Philharmonic
Royal Philharmonic Orchestra

Illustration Acknowledgments

Figures in bold type indicate colour plates

The following abbreviations have been used:

LSO: London Symphony Orchestra
NYP: New York Philharmonic
RPO: Royal Philharmonic Orchestra
RTHPL: Radio Times Hulton Picture Library
EMI: EMI Limited

Index

SAXONVILLE